INTERNATIONAL POLITICAL ECONOMY SERIES

General Editor: Timothy M. Shaw, Professor of Political Science and International Development Studies, and Director of the Centre for Foreign Policy Studies, Dalhousie University, Nova Scotia, Canada

Recent titles include:

Paul J. Nelson
THE WORLD BANK AND NON-GOVERNMENTAL ORGANIZATIONS:
The Limits of Apolitical Development

Ann Seidman and Robert B. Seidman
STATE AND LAW IN THE DEVELOPMENT PROCESS: Problem-Solving and
Institutional Change in the Third World

Tor Skålnes
THE POLITICS OF ECONOMIC REFORM IN ZIMBABWE: Continuity and
Change in Development

Howard Stein (*editor*)
ASIAN INDUSTRIALIZATION AND AFRICA: Studies in Policy Alternatives
to Structural Adjustment

Deborah Stienstra
WOMEN'S MOVEMENTS AND INTERNATIONAL ORGANIZATIONS

Larry A. Swatuk and Timothy M. Shaw (*editors*)
THE SOUTH AT THE END OF THE TWENTIETH CENTURY: Rethinking the
Political Economy of Foreign Policy in Africa, Asia, the Caribbean and Latin
America

Sandra Whitworth
FEMINISM AND INTERNATIONAL RELATIONS

International Political Economy Series
Series Standing Order ISBN 0–333–71110–6
(*outside North America only*)

You can receive future titles in this series as they are published by placing a standing order.
Please contact your bookseller or, in case of difficulty, write to us at the address below with
your name and address, the title of the series and the ISBN quoted above.

Customer Services Department, Macmillan Distribution Ltd
Houndmills, Basingstoke, Hampshire RG21 6XS, England

Economic Adjustment in New Democracies

Lessons from Southern Europe

Diane Ethier
Associate Professor of Political Science
Université de Montréal
Québec, Canada

Translated by Roy Cartlidge

First published in Great Britain 1997 by
MACMILLAN PRESS LTD
Houndmills, Basingstoke, Hampshire RG21 6XS and London
Companies and representatives throughout the world

A catalogue record for this book is available from the British Library.

ISBN 0–333–69556–9

First published in the United States of America 1997 by
ST. MARTIN'S PRESS, INC.,
Scholarly and Reference Division,
175 Fifth Avenue, New York, N.Y. 10010

ISBN 0–312–17368–7

Library of Congress Cataloging-in-Publication Data
Ethier, Diane.
Economic adjustments in new democracies : lessons from Southern
Europe / Diane Ethier.
p.   cm. — (International political economy series)
Includes bibliographical references and index.
ISBN 0–312–17368–7 (cloth)
1. Europe, Southern—Economic conditions.   2. Europe, Southern–
–Economic policy.   I. Title.   II. Series.
HC244.5.E78 1997
330.946—dc21

96–52879
CIP

This book is printed on paper suitable for recycling and made from fully managed and sustained forest sources.

10   9   8   7   6   5   4   3   2   1
06   05   04   03   02   01   00   99   98   97

Printed in Great Britain by
The Ipswich Book Company Ltd
Ipswich, Suffolk

Contents

List of Tables and Figures

List of Acronyms

AD:	*Aliança democratico*
AFM:	Armed Forces Movement
AP:	*Alianza Popular*
BBV:	*Banco de Bilbao et Viscaya*
BCA:	*Banco de Credito agricola*
BCI:	*Banco de Credito industrial*
BCL:	*Banco de Credito local*
BEE:	*Banco exterior de España*
BHE:	*Banco hypotecario de España*
BP:	balance of payments
BT:	balance of trade
CAB:	current account balance
CAP:	Common Agricultural Policy
CC.OO:	*Commissiones obreras*
CDS:	(Spanish) *Centro democratico y social*
CDS:	(Portuguese) *Centro democratico e social*
CEOE:	*Confederacion española de las organizaciones empresariales*
CET:	common external tariff
CGTP-IN:	*Confederacion general de los Trabalhadores Portuguese-Intersyndical*
CID:	customs import duty
CiU:	*Convergencia i Unio*
CNT:	*Confederacion nacional de los Trabajadores*
CP:	*Coalicion Popular*
CPF:	Confederation of Portuguese Farmers
CPI:	Confederation of Portuguese Industries
CPM:	Confederation of Portuguese Merchants
CPU:	collective production units
CSF:	community's support frameworks
DC:	democratic consolidation
DCG:	durable consumer goods
DFI:	direct foreign investment
DGPE:	*Direccion general del Patrimonio Español*
DT:	democratic transition
EA:	Economic Adjustment

EAGGF:	European Agricultural Guidance and Guarantee Fund
EAR:	(Communist) Party of the Hellenic Left
EC:	European Community
ECC:	European Communities Commission
ECG:	Essential Consumer Goods
ECSC:	European Coal and Steel Community
EDU:	European Democratic Union
EEC:	European Economic Community
EFRD:	European Fund for Regional Development
EFTA:	European Free Trade Association
EIB:	European Investment Bank
EK:	Enosis Kentrou
EL:	economic liberalism
ELT:	*Estatuto de los Trabajadores*
EMI:	European Monetary Institute
EMS:	European Monetary System
EMU:	Economic and Monetary Union
ERE:	National Radical Union
ESCPs:	Economic and Social Cohesion Policies
ESF:	European Social Fund
EU:	European Union
EURATOM:	European Atomic Energy Community
FF:	French francs
FPE:	*Fondo de promocion del Empleo*
GAL:	*Grupos anti-terrorista de Liberacion*
GDP:	gross domestic product
GSP:	Generalized System of Preferences
ICO:	*Instituto de Credito official*
IFA:	Interconfederal Framework Agreement
IG:	interest group
IGE:	intermediate goods and equipment
IMF:	International Monetary Fund
IMPs:	Integrated Mediterranean Programs
INH:	*Instituto nacional de hidrocarburos*
INI:	*Instituto nacional de Industria*
IS:	*Izquierda socialista*
IU:	*Izquierda Unida*
KKE:	Pro-Soviet Communist Party of Greece
Mecus:	millions of ecus
MFA:	Multi-Fibre Arrangement
MG:	manufactured goods

MNF:	Multinational firm
NAE:	National Agreement on Employment
NAFTA:	North American Free Trade Agreement
NATO:	North Atlantic Treaty Organization
ND:	New Democracy
NEM:	National Institute of Employment
NIC:	newly industrialized country
OECD:	Organization for European Cooperation and Development
PASOK:	Panhellenic Socialist Movement
PCE:	*Partido comunista español*
PCP:	Portuguese Communist Party
PCPE:	*Partido comunista de los Pueblos de España*
PCSC:	Permanent Council of Social Concertation
PEDIP:	*Programa especifico da desenvolvimento da industria portuguesa*
PNV:	*Partido nacionalista vasco*
PP:	*Partido Popular*
PPM:	*Partido popular monarquico*
PR:	proportional representation
PSDP:	Portuguese Social-Democratic Party
PSOE:	*Partido socialista obrero español*
PSP:	Portuguese Socialist Party
RCP:	Revised Convergence Program
R&D:	research and development
RM:	raw materials
SCMs:	structural change measures
SDP:	German Social Democratic Party
SEA:	Single European Act
SFs:	structural funds
SMs:	stabilization measures
SMEs:	small and medium enterprises
SSS:	social security system
TC:	transition cost
TEU:	Treaty on European Union
VAT:	value-added tax
UCD:	*Union del Centro democratico*
UGT:	*Union general de los Trabajadores*
USAID:	United States Agency of International Development
USO:	*Union de los sindicatos obreros*

Acknowledgements

I wish to thank the Social Sciences and Humanities Research Council (SSHRC) of Canada and the *Fonds pour la Formation de Chercheurs et l'Aide à la Recherche* (FCAR) of Quebec for the grants awarded since 1992, without which this work would never have been completed. I would also like to thank the graduate students who, in the capacity of research assistants, collaborated in compiling the references, tables and figures: Michel Lopez, Vincent Marimbu and Edith Gouin. Discussions with several of the major authors cited in this work proved to be particularly fruitful. In this regard, I owe a special debt of gratitude to Lawrence Whitehead, who invited me to one of the sessions of his international research team on the relationship between economic liberalism and political democratization, and to Joan Nelson and Nancy Bermeo, who provided me with preliminary versions of certain works referred to in this text. Finally, I wish to thank Roy Cartlidge, whose translation contributed not a little to the clarity of the final text.

Introduction: Democracy and Successful Adjustment

RECENT RESEARCH AND MAIN FINDINGS

In the period following 1975, all the countries that had opted for inward-looking capitalist or socialist development strategies found themselves, as a result of the limitations of these strategies and the growing liberalization of markets, confronted with an economic and financial crisis. The progressive worsening of this crisis, in the context of the petroleum shocks of 1973 and 1979 and the recessions of 1974–75 and 1980–83, brought these countries face to face with the increasingly urgent need to instigate a process of economic adjustment. This process, which was defined notably by the authorities of the International Monetary Fund (IMF) and the signatories to the Washington Consensus (Williamson, 1993), involved the adoption and application of a consistent set of short-term (one to five years) stabilization measures (SMs) and long-term (over ten years)[1] structural change measures (SCMs) aimed, on the one hand, at correcting macro-economic imbalances (inflation, balance of payments deficit, government budget deficit) and, on the other, at increasing the openness, liberalization and competitiveness of the national economy. This transition towards a new outward-looking development system, a condition judged to be indispensable for a sustained recovery of growth in the context of globalization, entailed major long-term economic costs, particularly for the social groups that benefited from the former inward-looking development strategy (civil servants, enterprises focused on the local market, recipients of state assistance programs, and so on) (Nelson, 1990b, 3–4).

The fact that these economic changes coincided with the third wave of political democratization in modern history (Huntington, 1991), which resulted in a series of transitions from authoritarianism to democracy in roughly 35 capitalist and communist countries in Southern Europe, Latin America, East Asia, Central Europe and Africa,[2] has led a number of specialists to question the interrelations between these two processes. With the exception of a few studies (in particular, Whitehead, 1993), most of the research devoted to this subject since 1990 has not sought to determine whether the economic crisis and the imperative of the neo-liberal shift constituted one of the causes of the democratic transitions. They attempted rather to answer the following question: Is it possible for the fragile new democracies to achieve liberal reforms without compromising their survival and their stability?

This question was inspired in large measure by the theses of modernization theory that have had such a great influence on the discourse of democratic development in recent decades. According to these theses, the stability of a democracy is primarily guaranteed by its consolidation, that is, the deepening of its legitimacy and institutionalization, as a growing number of citizens ascribe to democratic values and comply with democratic rules of resolving conflicts based on negotiation and compromise rather than confrontation. Among the various factors that favour consolidation – time, performance, and memories of the former authoritarian regime, and so on – two are particularly decisive: institutional reforms that widen the representation and participation of various interests within the political system, and the government's ability to promote economic development and a more equitable distribution of earnings and wealth.

These theses, such as the economic successes of certain liberal authoritarian regimes (South Korea before 1987, Taiwan before 1986, Chile, 1973–88, Mexico, 1982–93, China since 1978), the economic counter-performance of certain new democracies (NDs) that are resistant to liberal reforms (Argentina 1984–89, Brazil, 1984–94), and the movement towards authoritarianism of a number of NDs involved in the neo-liberal trend (Peru 1980–90), led many scholars to believe that only authoritarian regimes were able to achieve economic adjustment without compromising their political stability. This conviction was founded on the following argument:

Economic adjustment, which strongly limits the state's flexibility with regard to redistributive action, restricts the legitimacy of all political systems, thereby posing a threat to their stability. In authoritarian regimes, however, this threat is countered by the presence of a repressive power, which eliminates the possibility of public contestation; in consolidated western democracies, this risk is attenuated by the existence of more egalitarian economic and social conditions and by the presence of institutions which favour social concertation. Having the possibility of participating, through the intermediary of parties and pressure groups, in the negotiation of stabilization and structural change measures, interest groups either obtain compensation for the costs of adjustment, or agree to reduce their expectations and to submit to reforms that are unfavourable to them, since they keep open the possibility of renegotiating, at a later point, the content and the effects of these reforms to their advantage. In other words, a consolidated democracy facilitates adjustment, either because it allows for a more equitable distribution of the costs and benefits of SMs and SCMs, or because it compensates for the economic sacrifices and political gains, that is, increased participation in the political decision making process.

In the NDs, on the other hand, the problems of legitimacy raised by the liberal reform are exacerbated by structural socio-economic inequalities and the absence of institutions likely to reduce or to solve the conflicts related to the cost of implementing these reforms. Because they were confronted with a serious economic and financial crisis and the imperative of continuing adjustment during or immediately after their establishment, the NDs had no time to pursue the process of institutionalization. Once more subjected to the relative control of bureaucrats and the military, and having to cope with the persistent problems of clientelism characterized by elitist or competitive political parties and civil societies that are weakly organized or dominated by a few corporatist organizations, they are incapable of circumscribing and tempering the expression of conflicts of interest. The conclusion of this analysis is very pessimistic, as it implies that the NDs are faced with a dilemma in which every possible outcome is negative: either to strengthen their legitimacy through the pursuit of expansionist economic policies, even at the cost of worsening their economic and financial crisis and compromising their political stability for a longer period; or to implement the economic adjustment in spite of all opposition, which presupposes restrictions on democratic rights and freedoms and therefore the evolution towards a *democradura* or a new brand of authoritarian political regime.

The empirical and comparative analysis of economic adjustment outcomes and determinants, in several democratic and authoritarian regimes in Latin America, Eastern Europe, Africa and Asia (Remmer, 1990; Nelson, 1990a, 1994b; Przeworski, 1990; Köves and Marer, 1991; Haggard and Kaufman, 1992; Bresser Pereira et al., 1993; Haggard and Webb, 1994a; Smith et al., 1994; Williamson, 1994; Armijo, 1995; Diamond and Plattner, 1995a, for example), have however partially invalidated these initial pessimistic hypotheses. Indeed, these studies reveal that democracies are no less likely than authoritarian regimes to carry out economic adjustment, since the number of cases of success and failure (rejection, postponement, partial or/and temporary application) of the SMs and the SCMs of this process are comparable in both types of political systems (Nelson, 1990a; Remmer, 1990; Haggard and Kaufman, 1992). They show that the success of economic reforms is definitely conditioned by a set of economic, political, historical, institutional and international factors that are largely independent of the nature of the political regime (Diamond and Plattner, 1995b, xi). Among these it is the internal political factors that are judged to be the most decisive. According to the most recent overview of the subject (Williamson and Haggard, 1994, 525–97), three of these play a decisive role in every scenario:

(1) the government's determination to carry out the reforms; (2) the support of a team of technocrats and economists able to develop a coherent program and an effective strategy for implementing the adjustment measures; and (3) the possibility for the government to apply the reforms systematically and over an extended time period.

There exists a wide consensus among the authors on the fact that the government's commitment to adopt and launch a coherent set of measures for achieving stabilization and structural change depends primarily on a convergence of views among its members regarding the effectiveness of these reforms or of their ability to resolve the economic crisis. In the light of the assessment of the case studies, it appears that neither the objective size of the economic problems, nor the composition of the government, nor the ideological orientation of the party/parties in power, nor the electoral cycles, nor the constraints of the external conditional aid, play any decisive role in this regard. Governments are not necessarily more united and determined the more severe the economic and financial crisis becomes, nor are they necessarily more united and favourable to adjustment when they are directed by a single majority party rather than by a coalition of political forces; conservative governments are more likely to support adjustment than liberal, social-democratic, populist or socialist governments; cohesion and resolution among the members of the executive are not always higher at the beginning of the electoral mandate; the impact of the conditional aid disbursed by the financial institutions varies in accordance with the degree of dependence of the beneficiary state. It follows from these observations that the only factor likely to encourage government members to adopt an adjustment program in every possible case is its optimistic evaluation of the economic effectiveness of SMs and SCMs and the conviction that the implementation of the latter will not promote major political conflicts.

As for the government's ability to implement reforms, this is mainly conditioned by the nature of the relations existing between the executive, the major institutions of the political system (bureaucracy, army, parties, subaltern administrations) and the organizations of civil society. According to various authors (including Haggard and Webb, 1994a), there are two types of relations judged to be most favourable for the implementation of reforms: an autonomous executive that exerts a power of control over political institutions and interest groups, or an executive that is able to establish relations of cooperation and concertation between these two categories of actors. According to this typology, highly centralized authoritarian regimes, non-consolidated democracies characterized by a majority government and weak and divided political institutions and pressure groups, and consolidated democracies characterized by representative political organizations and pressure groups that are influential but open to compromise, would be more able to carry out the reforms, whereas corporatist authoritarian regimes, populist democracies, and representative and competitive democracies, within which the executive is submitted to the dictates of specific interest groups or faced with opposition from powerful yet divided parties and pressure groups, would have great difficulty meeting this challenge.

This analysis is more optimistic than the hypothesis derived from modernization theory, since it implies that only certain types of non-consolidated democracies are less likely to succeed in the adjustment process. The most recent studies on the subject (Nelson, 1994a, 1994b) are still relatively encouraging, since they show, on the basis of certain cases (for example, those of Mexico (since 1993), Argentina (since 1989), Poland and Hungary (since 1990)), that liberal economic reform and the democratization of the political system are two compatible, dialectical processes. This new research in fact reveals that the adjustment process in these countries has progressed in parallel with the transition from authoritarianism to democracy (in Mexico) or of the consolidation of the new democratic regimes (in Argentina, Poland and Hungary). According to their argument, the economic reforms would have encouraged these democratic changes in various ways. In particular, the deregulation and privatization of several spheres of the state sector would have led to a weakening of political control over certain particular interest groups opposed to the liberal model (bureaucrats, trade unions, public monopolies, and so on), thereby strengthening the role of the parties and of the parliament, and increasing representation of, and concertation among, the various interest groups. In return, these transformations would have facilitated public acceptance of the adjustment measures. Some authors (Przeworski, 1990, 1995; Armijo et al., 1995) maintain that on the whole, the consolidation of democracy is a prerequisite for the success of economic reforms within democracies, while others consider that this transformation of the political system can be achieved during the adjustment process even though prior consolidation of the democracy is preferable (Nelson, 1994a, 1994b; Haggard and Kaufman, 1995).

However, most scholars consider that the organizational and institutional characteristics of the state are not the sole major determining factors of the political risks of adjustment or of the government's ability to apply the reforms. The attenuation of transition costs is considered an equally important factor, particularly in the democracies, since it permits a means of containing public dissatisfaction with the reforms. The methods for attaining this objective are nonetheless a matter of controversy. The most liberal theorists such as Sachs (1994), Aslund (1995) and Balcerowicz (1995) believe that the best way to reduce transition costs is to proceed rapidly with the stabilization and restructuring of the economy. In their view, such shock therapy has two advantages: by reducing the length of the period necessitating financial sacrifices, it limits the risk of mobilization, due to the fact that it has short-term economic benefits associated with it (such as lowering inflation and boosting investments and exports), and it permits public opinion to be rallied more rapidly. For their part, more social-democratically inclined authors (Haggard and Kaufman, 1992; Bresser Pereira et al., 1993; Nelson, 1994a, 1994b, 1995; Desai, 1995; Graham, 1995) consider that reforms can best be achieved when they are applied gradually and are accompanied by government measures aimed at helping the most affected groups and sectors. According to these authors, it is impossible to implement structural changes in a short space of time. Given that such measures are necessarily spread out over several years, and that they involve far more severe long-term costs than stabilization measures, the state can only limit the risk of contestation by slowing the pace of the reforms and by attenuating their negative effects. The defenders of this approach are aware that the expense of the compensation measures is a function of the financial situation of each state, a situation which may, however, be modified by external aid in some cases. They consider that the nature of the compensation measures nonetheless appears to be a question that is as important as their extent. Their attitude in this regard is that improving and extending the universal social policies (education, unemployment insurance, retirement plans, and so on) to those who are victims of the adjustment are more effective and more equitable than ad hoc assistance (pre-retirement or redundancy bonuses, temporary employment, and so on) awarded to certain more influential lobbies.

THE CONTRIBUTIONS OF SOUTHERN EUROPEAN CASE STUDIES

It is my view that in spite of its very important findings, this theory remains incomplete since it does not permit a precise evaluation of the impact of the economic ideology of the decision makers, of democratic consolidation, of the regional integration processes and of the non-conditional aids on the adoption and application of the adjustment measures.

This analysis of the factors favourable to the determination and cohesion of the government does not, in fact, take into account each leader's degree of commitment to the values of economic liberalism. While it is true that the traditional ideological orientation – conservative, social-democrat, populist, and so on – of the party/parties in power has no decisive influence on the leaders' attitudes towards adjustment, it is also true that each ruling party's position on economic liberalism, a position which largely transcends the left–right split in the political spectrum, has a decisive influence on the opinions of the members of the government with regard to the effectiveness of the adjustment measures.

Furthermore, the thesis proposing that the consolidation of the political regime in democracies is a favourable, even central, condition for the negotiation and acceptance of adjustment measures, remains largely speculative, particularly since none of the case studies carried out until now deals with an already consolidated democracy. The difficulties that numerous western democracies (France, Italy, Denmark, United States, Canada, and so on) are currently experiencing in the implementation of adjustment measures show, moreover, that this question needs to be pursued in greater depth. Finally, none of the existing research allows us to verify to what degree the prospect or attainment of membership in a regional economic bloc contributes towards the success of the adjustment, since the authors neither pay attention to the prospect of integration into the European Union (EU) (in the case of the Eastern European countries) nor to the creation of Mercosur (in the case of the countries of the southern cone of Latin America), nor to membership in the North American Free Trade Agreement (NAFTA) (in the case of Mexico).[3] There are several factors that suggest that these processes may have a complex influence on adjustment scenarios: membership in a regional integration agreement imposes a certain numbers of liberalization measures on the state in question, both before and after membership is achieved; it creates new conditions of competition which significantly increase the need for adjustment measures; it can have beneficial economic effects (boosting investments, exports and growth) and may be accompanied by generous non-conditional aid (for example economic and social cohesion programs within the EU, and the recent bailing-out of the Mexican peso), which are likely to produce an attenuation of the transition costs and, consequently, greater acceptance of the adjustment measures; it is plausible to believe that membership by the new democracies in a regional bloc made up of already consolidated democracies would encourage the consolidation of their own political regimes.

The aim of this work is to evaluate, through a comparative analysis of the economic policies implemented in Greece, Spain and Portugal during the period 1975–95, both the possibility of generalizing the propositions developed by the body of literature referred to earlier and also the specific impact of the new variables listed above. The case of Southern Europe, which, surprisingly, has been ignored by these authors until now,[4] is in fact of major interest in this regard, since it involves three countries that, on the one hand, were able to start the consolidation of their new democratic regimes before the imposition of the neo-liberal shift following the 1980–83 recession

(Pridham, 1990a; Morlino and Montero, 1991; Higley and Gunther, 1992; Gunther et al., 1995) and on the other, benefited from a very special regional environment, due to their membership in the European Community (EC). The three states entered into negotiations with the EC with a view to securing membership upon the completion of democratic transition (1975–78); these negotiations led to the admission of Greece in 1981, and of Spain and Portugal in 1986. During these talks, and in spite of the existence of a relatively serious economic crisis in the three countries, the EC did not attempt to apply any formal pressure to oblige them to adopt the adjustment measures. On the other hand, the three candidate states had to improve their social policies in order to bring them in line with those of the member states of the EC, which contributed towards the further consolidation of their democratic regimes. The Community also awarded these states various non-conditional financial aid packages aimed at helping them to adapt to the shock of membership. Besides the provisions related to the application of the value-added tax (VAT) and the liberalization of exchanges of goods, capital, service and persons, the membership treaties and the Single European Act (SEA), which were put into effect concurrently between 1986 and 1993, did not impose any stabilization and structural change programs on Greece, Spain and Portugal. On the other hand, the SEA allowed them to benefit from a considerable increase in non-conditional aid in the form of economic and social cohesion after 1988. The Treaty on European Union (TEU), adopted in 1993, proved to be more constraining from the point of view of adjustment, insofar as it made entry into the future Economic and Monetary Union (EMU) conditional in respect of the convergence norms, which involved the adoption of more liberal and restrictive economic policies. Nevertheless, these constraints were accompanied by increased support to economic and social cohesion.

The work is divided into two major parts. Part One is devoted to an assessment of the impact of the economic crisis and the imperative of the neo-liberal shift on democratic transitions in Greece, Spain and Portugal (Chapter 1); this is followed by a survey of the economic policies of the three countries since the end of the democratic transitions until the present, with a distinction made between reforms adopted and reforms effectively applied by successive democratic governments (Chapters 2, 3 and 4); finally, there is a comparison of the results of economic adjustment in all three countries, taking into account the following criteria: (a) the adoption, by the governments, of a coherent set of stabilization and structural change measures; (b) the effective, long-term application of these measures; and (c) the attainment of the macro-economic objectives targeted by both types of measures (Chapter 5). Part Two is an analysis of the degree to which the results obtained by each of the three countries with regard to economic reforms can be explained by the theories proposed by the second body of literature and the additional variables presented above. Chapter 6 examines the non-decisive and decisive factors that determine the government's commitment to undertaking liberal reforms. Chapter 7 scrutinizes the conditions that improve the government's ability to implement reforms without compromising political stability and social peace.

Part One

Economic Policies of Southern European Democracies

1 The Economic Context of Democratic Transitions

The transition from authoritarianism to democracy (1974–78) in Greece, Spain and Portugal occurred in the context of an economic crisis characterized by slower growth rates, mounting inflation, worsening balance of payments records, increased state budget deficits, and higher unemployment (see Table 1). Although aggravated by the oil crisis of 1973 and the recession of 1974–75, this crisis was fundamentally the result of the limitations of the new and more liberal import substituting models experienced during the period 1960 to 1975 (Hudson and Lewis, 1985, 1–54).

These models were aimed at speeding the growth of the existing essential consumer goods (ECG) industries through the development of intermediate goods and equipment industries (IGE)[1] and at a partial opening-up of the economic system to the outside.[2] In exchange for access to foreign sources of capital, which permitted them to invest massively in the development of IGE industries, the Southern European governments relaxed their legislation with respect to direct investment by American and European companies. During the sixties, in fact, these companies had wanted to delocalize their production in order to benefit from the comparative advantages of the newer industrial countries (cheaper manpower, more liberal tax systems, and so on), increase their economies of scale, improve the competitiveness of their products in western markets and take advantage of the new opportunities offered by the ongoing process of industrialization in those countries (OCDE, 1988). In Southern Europe, as in Latin America, the rationale behind the introduction of these multinational firms (MNFs) was twofold: to permit development of certain branches of the ECG industry (such as agro-food) for the export markets, and the creation of mixed enterprises with the state in certain branches of the IGE sector (for example, the petrochemical sector) aimed at supplying western and local consumer goods industries. The social transformations that attended this industrialization strategy – modernization of social structures (urbanization, transfer of labour from the primary sector to the secondary and service sectors, widening of the middle income bracket) and the development of the Welfare State[3] – created a new demand for durable consumer goods (DCG),[4] thus encouraging the MNFs to invest in this third sector at a later date.

13

On the whole, this new import substituting model (called 'open import substitution' in comparison to 'classical import substitution') gave rise to a trisectorial productive structure: an IGE sector controlled by the state and the MNFs that was partially turned towards exports; an ECG sector dominated by local, small and medium enterprises that was progressively oriented towards foreign markets; a DCG sector monopolized by the MNFs that was completely focused on the national market (Jacquemot and Raffinot, 1985). This opening and transformation of the production system, combined with the new constraints of the external indebtedness of the governments, obliged the latter to adopt a selective import (IGE in particular) and export (IGE and ECG) liberalization policy. These changes brought about an increase in the volume of international trade and a modification of its composition and geographical distribution. The transformation of the trading structure primarily resulted in an increase in imports of combustibles and IGE and a rise in the relative share of exports of manufactured goods (IGE and ECG), which constituted the largest part of exports and the end of the period. Furthermore, the share of external trade between the EC[5] and the sub-European countries continued to expand, to the detriment of trade with the United States.[6]

Open import substitution brought about strong growth in production and international trade during the sixties. Nevertheless, the economies of Southern Europe continued to be characterized by poor performance in the agricultural sector, which was dominated by small and medium family farms, and in industry, which was dependent on *labour-* rather than *capital*-intensive production activities. IGE and DCG industries remained underdeveloped, particularly in Greece and Portugal. It was these structural problems that led to a levelling-off in internal consumption and the subsequent slowdown in investments and production at the beginning of the seventies. They were also responsible for the deterioration in the balance of trade (BT), the increase in exports, consisting primarily of low added-value agricultural and manufactured goods that were unable to compensate for increased imports of high added-value IGE (see Table 1). The BT deficits, moreover, limited these countries' ability to pay back their external debts, resulting in ever higher levels of indebtedness.

These problems were perpetuated by the inability of the Southern European countries to strengthen their chances of membership in the EC during the period 1965 to 1975. Only a process of this sort, in fact, could have reduced the cost of imports, increased export opportunities and provided the increased resources and incentives necessary for the modernization of the productive structures. This process was, however, compromised by the authoritarian nature of the political regimes in power. In fact, in 1962, the EC adopted the Birkelback report which reserved the status of member for states that guaranteed 'on their territories, true democratic practices and respect for fundamental rights and liberties' (Whitehead, 1986). This position explains Brussels' rejection of Spain's application for membership or association in 1962 (Solbes Mira, 1990, 481). It was not until 1970, after eight years of laborious negotiations, that Madrid managed to reach a limited Preferential Trade Agreement with the European Economic Community (EEC).[7] The political conditions set by the Birkelback report also motivated the freeze of the Partnership Agreement signed between the EEC and Greece in 1961, during the dictatorship of the colonels (1967–74).[8] The case of Portugal constituted something of an exception to the rule. In fact, its membership in the European Free Trade Association (EFTA) allowed it to sign two free-trade agreements with the EEC and the European Coal and Steel Community (ECSC) in 1972, due to the imminent entry into Europe of the Six, of two of its principal EFTA partners: the United Kingdom and Denmark.[9]

The agreements reached with Spain and Portugal did not lead to any attenuation of the problems of the Iberian economies during the first half of the seventies, since their application was very gradual and coincided with the first oil crisis and the subsequent recession of 1974–75. In fact, the development of a climate of stagflation in the industrialized countries in the period following 1973 exacerbated the economic instability of Greece, Spain and Portugal. The increased import bill and the slowdown in exports resulted in higher BT deficits; the return of immigrant workers and the consequent decrease in income transfers reduced the Invisible Balance surplus. Higher inflation contributed to the decline in investment and growth. Lower government revenues, combined with a higher level of indebtedness, brought about the appearance of budget deficits (see Table 1).

The deepening economic crisis contributed to a breakdown of consensus within the authoritarian regimes and to the emergence, within them, of a reformist movement that favoured transition towards democracy. It also strengthened the pro-democracy opposition movements in civil societies (Maravall, 1993, 83). The economic crisis was neither the sole nor the principal cause of the crisis in the dictatorships and of democratic transitions in Southern Europe,[10] but it is undeniable that some of the political actors in the three countries supported democratization of the political regime primarily because it constituted the key to membership in the EC: the only realistic means of solving the economic crisis.[11] This said, the attitudes of the various pro-democracy political forces toward the economic crisis and the project for inclusion within the EC vary considerably from one country to another.

In Spain, all the political forces, with the exception of the extreme right, wanted to guarantee the survival and consolidation of democracy through measures aimed at turning around the economic situation and eventually gaining membership in the EC. This explains why the parties on the right who negotiated the democratic transition – the *Union del Centro democratico* (UCD), the *Partido socialista obrero español* (PSOE), the *Partido comunista español* (PCE) – supported the request for membership in the EC submitted in July 1977 by the UCD government of Adolfo Suarez and signed the *Pactos de la Moncloa*, on October 25, 1977. These pacts defined the major features of the measures of stabilization and structural change that would have to be adopted by the future democratic governments in order to eliminate the most serious economic imbalances, to ensure a long-term recovery, and to adapt the Spanish economy to the new conditions required for entry into the Common Market. As pointed out by Fuentes Quintana (1990, 25), all the forces favourable to democracy in Spain were aware that the latter could not be consolidated, if it did not demonstrate its economic effectiveness. These considerations convinced the major political parties to make the concessions needed to implement an economic program whose costs and benefits were not equivalent for each of their clienteles.

The *Pactos de la Moncloa* contained four series of SMs:

1. the application of an anti-inflationary monetary policy;
2. the implementation of a budgetary policy aimed, through a reduction of consumer spending and redirecting part of this towards productive investments, in order to reduce the public deficit and to stimulate growth;
3. the liberalization of the exchange rate of the peseta;
4. the introduction of an income policy based on supply rather than on demand:

    (a) adjusting salary increases to the planned inflation rate rather than to the historical inflation rate;
    (b) reducing social contributions by companies;
    (c) liberalizing and opening up the financial system;
    (d) liberalizing the exchange of goods and services.

They also included five categories of SCMs:

1. reform of the budgetary policy aimed at improving the health of the public finances;
2. harmonizing the tax system with that of the member states of the EC;
3. liberalizing the financial system;
4. liberalizing the labour relations system: flexibility in hiring and firing policies and reducing employers' social contributions by 50%;

5. improving the effectiveness of the control and financing of public
    corporations   (Fuentes Quintana, 1990, 30).

In Greece and in Portugal, the pro-democratic forces were far more divided
over the question of the economic crisis and membership in the EC, with
the result that an agreement similar to the *Pactos de la Moncloa* was
impossible. In Greece, the right, assembled within the New Democracy
(ND) of Constantin Caramanlis, supported a liberal, Europeanist capitalist
plan. This explains why, in June 1975, several months after its accession to
power in December 1974, the ND government submitted Greece's request
for membership in the EC. The forces of the centre, represented primarily
by the Panhellenic Socialist Movement (PASOK), were hoping for the
preservation of the protectionist, nationalistic development model and were
opposed to integration within the Europe of the Nine. The communists, who
were grouped together in the pro-Soviet Communist Party of Greece (KKE),
supported a Soviet-type communist plan, and were also opposed to entry into
the EC (Verney, 1990, 203–4; Spourdalakis, 1992a). In Portugal, the centre-
right parties and the Socialist Party (PSP) of Mario Soares supported the
adoption of a more liberal capitalist model and membership in the EC. It was,
moreover, the first PSP constitutional government that was to submit
Portugal's application for membership in the EC, in 1977. On the other hand,
the Communist Party (PCP) of Alvaro Cunhal, with the support of radical
elements in the Armed Forces Movements (AFM) and groups of the extreme
left, defended the establishment of a socialist society, and opposed entry into
the EC in the name of safeguarding national independence. Overall, several
economic plans were promoted by the various political parties and
organizations; some of these supported economic liberalism, while others
advocated the pursuit of the previous introverted nationalist strategy or the
establishment of a socialist model.

The widely divergent attitudes of the political elites towards the economic
issues of the post-authoritarian period are of prime importance in explaining
the orientations and the results of the economic policies implemented by the
democratic governments in the period 1975/78–94 (see Part Two). The post-
authoritarian period was in fact characterized in all three countries by a series
of profound economic changes which were to render the adoption of
stabilization and structural change measures increasingly more urgent. The
transition to democracy was accompanied, in the case of Spain, and
immediately followed, in the case of Greece and Portugal, by the start of
negotiations for membership in the EC, as the applications submitted for this
purpose by Athens, Madrid and Lisbon at the end of, or during, the transitions,
received a rapid, favourable response from Brussels.[12] In the course of these

negotiations, which were to last four years in the case of Greece (1976–79) and six years in the case of Portugal and Spain (1978/79–84), the three countries were confronted, to differing degrees, with the necessity of carrying out a certain number of reforms in order to offset the adverse effects of widened membership, both on the countries of the EC and on their own economies. Moreover, the fact that these negotiations were followed or accompanied by a worsening of the economic crisis, precipitated by the second oil crisis and the recession of 1980–83, strengthened demands for a process of adjustment. Finally, the constraints of membership in the EC[13] were underscored by the completion of the European Single Market between 1986 and 1993,[14] and the construction of the European Economic and Monetary Union[15] as of 1992. The records of the policies adopted in Greece, Spain and Portugal during the period 1975/78–95, nonetheless show that the reaction to these constraints was very different from one country to the next. In Spain, the adjustment process was begun during the democratic transition and continued without interruption, both under the centre-right governments of the UCD (1977–82) and under the centre-left governments of the PSOE (1982–96). In Portugal, the adjustment process was much slower. Actually begun seven years after the establishment of democracy by the PSP–social-democratic party (PSDP) coalition (1983–85), it was subsequently deepened and continuously systematized by successive PSDP governments (1985–95). In Greece, no overall systematic, long-term adjustment program was implemented by the ND and PASOK governments that alternately came to power during the post-authoritarian period.

2 Spain: An Early and Durable Process of Adjustment

THE BEGINNINGS OF REFORMS BY UCD GOVERNMENTS: 1977–82

The *Pactos de la Moncloa* had established the framework (joint action between government, political parties and unions) and the orientation (heterodox liberal) of the economic policy to be developed by the new democratic regime. These pacts, which were negotiated under the first democratic government formed by the UCD and led by Adolfo Suarez, were naturally to serve as a guide for the economic initiatives of this government (1977–79) and for the second UCD government led by Calvo Sotelo (1979–81). Depending to a large measure on joint social action, the two administrations began applying the stabilization and structural reform policies set out in the *Pactos de la Moncloa*, while at the same time pursuing, in several respects, an expansionist, demand-side economic policy. During the period 1977–82, the negotiation of the membership treaties,[1] officially begun in February 1979, was to have a limited impact on the adjustment process, since it was centred on examining the problems inherent in the entry of the Iberian countries, and slowed down by various conflicts between the member states.[2]

Through the intermediary of the Bank of Spain, monetary policy was liberalized (abolition of foreign exchange control, adoption of a floating exchange rate, devaluation of the peseta, increase in interest rates) in order to promote investments, boost exports, increase currency reserves and reduce the demand for credit and the level of inflation (Ariztegui, 1990, 317–27). The reform of the fiscal policy, which was aimed at increasing government revenues in an attempt to reduce the budget deficit, gave rise to an increase in income tax and heritage tax in 1977. In addition, the second UCD government proceeded with studies aimed at setting up a succession tax and a value-added tax (VAT), aimed at bringing it in line with the EC's requirements. In 1982, in fact, the EC made continued negotiation of the membership treaties conditional on Spain's introducing a VAT system simultaneously with its entry into the community (Solbes Mira, 1990, 487). The need to adjust salary increases to the real rate of inflation resulted, in 1978, in the adoption of a decree fixing such increases at between 14% and

16%. In 1980 and 1981, these levels were determined by interconfederal framework agreements (IFAs) negotiated between the *Confederacion española de las organizaciones empresariales* (CEOE), the principal employers' organization, the *Union general de los Trabajadores* (UGT), the socialist labour union, and the *Union de los sindicatos obreros* (USO), the independent union organization;[3] the *Commissiones obreras* (CC.OO), a union with communist allegiances, did not participate in the negotiation of the IFAs but agreed to apply them. In 1982, the government, the CEOE, the UGT and the CC.OO negotiated the National Agreement on Employment (NAE), which established various measures intended to reduce the growth of salary costs: limiting salary increases to between 9% and 11%; reducing employers' contributions to social security (compensated by increased contributions by the state); widening the new rules of the labour relation board (see below) to permit the hiring of temporary and/or part-time workers. The drive towards liberalizing the exchange of goods and services gave rise to negotiations being undertaken in regard to Spain's membership in the EC in 1978.

The liberalization of labour relations was begun in 1977 with the adoption of decrees aimed at marking the right to strike, which was recognized in the constitution of 1978. The latter decrees authorized the government to suspend the right to strike in the public sector when such action threatened the provision of essential public services, and defined the conditions for a legal strike vote. These were invalidated, however, by the constitutional court in 1981. Subsequently, the liberalization process primarily consisted in the adoption of four pieces of legislation: Royal Decree number 17 of March 1977, the law on trade unions of April 1977, the *Estatuto de los Trabajadores* (ELT) of March 1980, and the basic law on employment of October 1980. The first legislation regulated the right to strike and softened the very restrictive firing conditions of the Francoist regime; the second guaranteed the freedom of union association. Its clauses were revised and complemented by the constitution of 1978, which recognized the right to unionization, while forbidding closed shops, and guaranteed the right to strike and the right to negotiate collective agreements. The ELT established the framework for exercising the rights recognized by the constitution. It responded to the wishes of the unions by granting a large place to social partners in the conduct of labour relations, by improving employees' working conditions[4] and by recognizing the validity of Francoist laws 'when they are not in contradiction with the statute'. The statute did liberalize various Francoist regulations, however. In particular, it legalized non-permanent and undetermined length labour contracts and softened the conditions for authorizing individual and collective layoffs[5] (McElrath, 1989). The basic law on employment modified the rules with regard to unemployment insurance benefits. These legislations were complemented by the IFA of 1979 between the CEOE and the UGT, which established a new labour relations framework.

In addition, the second UCD government undertook the restructuring of the industrial sector. In spite of the trisectorialization of the productive system caused by open import substitution, the Spanish manufacturing sector actually remained largely dominated by small enterprises (90% of companies employed less than 100 workers and accounted for 50% of industrial production) and the traditional labour-intensive industries (one-third of jobs and 25% of the added value of the sector being provided by three branches: food, clothing and textiles, furniture and wood products). The Spanish enterprises were geographically dispersed, were very unspecialized and obsolete from the technological point of view, and were no longer able to compete effectively with ECG from the newly industrialized countries (NICs) on the Spanish and international market. The enterprises in the public sector represented another source of problems. Through the holdings of the central government,[6] the Bank of Spain's portfolio companies and the regional and local public administrations, the state exerted direct or indirect majority or minority control over more than 900 companies, which for the most part operated in the infrastructure (water, energy, transportation and communications), IGE (coal, iron and steel, chemical, petrochemical) and service (construction, banks, tourism, and so on) sectors. This state control had encouraged a concentration of capital and production units in these sectors, but the size of the companies remained far smaller than those of the same kind in the western countries. Highly dependent on foreign technology, most of these were also in debt or running a deficit. In several branches (metallurgy, iron and steel, textiles, shipbuilding, aluminum, fertilizers, railroad equipment) public and semi-public companies were no longer managing to sell their products on foreign markets because of production over-capacity at the world and European levels. Overall, the economic and financial situation of the public and private industrial sectors had deteriorated seriously since the middle of the seventies, resulting in the loss of over one million jobs and forcing the governments to nationalize or subsidize companies in difficulty at the cost of an increase in their level of indebtedness and their budgetary deficit.

The second crisis of 1979–83 convinced the government of Calvo Sotelo of the urgent need for action in this respect. In 1979, the government undertook negotiations on industrial restructuring with a number of enterprises. In 1980, it issued various decrees with regard to the restructuring of certain branches and ratified Law 76, which provided for the award of certain tax initiatives for companies which agreed to a merger. In 1981, a royal decree extended the restructuring process to 11 branches of industrial branches undergoing difficulty: integrated iron and steel, special steel, carbon steel, common steel, semi-transformed copper products, shipbuilding, textiles, shoes, motor vehicle parts, electronics components and household appliances. Five companies were also subjected to the restructuring: General Electric, Westinghouse, Talbot Automobiles, Asturiana de Zinc and Standard Group. The UCD reforms, however, rapidly came up against union protest movements in various regions and with technical problems (such as underestimating the cost of implementation and supervisory difficulties). Due to these constraints, most of the investments carried out by the state served more to mop up the losses of the companies than to resolve their structural problems (Salmon, 1991).

In agriculture, the action of the UCD governments primarily consisted in grouping together the minifundios of the centre and the north of the country. It should be remembered that within the framework of the industrialization process of the sixties and seventies, the contribution of agriculture to the GDP, employment and exports had declined markedly.[7] Nevertheless, this decline had not been accompanied, as in many other countries, by an improvement in productivity, the share of agriculture in total added value, which was one-fifth in 1960, having fallen to one-fifteenth in 1980 (Balboa and Delgado, 1990, 122). The poor output of Spanish agriculture was a consequence of the absence of technological modernization, excessive diversity or dispersion of production activities and dual property structures characterized by the existence of large latifundia in the South and the multiplicity of minifundios in the centre and the North of the country. In 1977, small operations of 1 to 5 hectares still represented 57% of total operations and accounted for less than 50% of total agricultural production. (Hudson and Lewis, 1985, 25). In order to improve productivity in this sector, the UCD governments proceeded, between 1977 and 1982, to concentrate 14 million operations of an average of 0.35 hectares within 2 million operations of 2.64 hectares; this allowed for the reallocation of 5.2 million hectares of land, affecting almost one million farmers (Salmon, 1991). This reform was in part motivated by the prospect of membership in the EC. The member states, particularly France, a significant part of whose agricultural production was very similar to that of Spain, had been demanding since 1980 that Madrid proceed with a restructuring/ specialization of its agriculture in order to attenuate its comparative advantages with regard to European agricultural markets.

Because of their limits, their contradictory effects[8] and the impact of the recession at the beginning of the eighties, the UCD measures were unable to prevent a worsening of the economic crisis. First of all, the stabilization policies did not produce the desired effect. According to Linde (1990, 37), the period 1979–82 was characterized by a very light drop in the inflation rate from 15.7% to 14.4%, a considerable deterioration of the trade balance, which dropped from +US$1125.7 million to –US$4101.8 million, and an increase in public administration funding needs from 217.6 to 1155.3 million pesetas. Second, the structural changes were insufficient, with the result that the major problems identified by the *Pactos de la Moncloa*, including the social security and public corporations deficit, and the uncompetitiveness of industry, still persisted.

THE DEEPENING OF REFORMS BY PSOE GOVERNMENTS: 1982–96

As soon as it came to power, the PSOE showed its determination to deepen and accelerate the economic adjustment process (Maravall, 1993, 94). The government of Felipe Gonzalez, which assumed office in December 1982, adopted during 1983 a stabilization program for the period 1983–86. This program had four objectives:

1. to cut the inflation rate in half by applying a restrictive monetary policy and by limiting salary increases;
2. to reabsorb the BT deficit by devaluing the peseta by 8%, and improving the competitiveness of companies and provide support to exports;
3. to decrease the state budget deficit through spending controls and a 20% increase in income tax;
4. to re-establish growth through a policy of investment promotion.

In conjunction with this program, the government announced a vast structural reform plan that included the restructuring of declining industries, the reorientation of the energy policy, the flexibilization and restructuring of the labour market, the modernization of agriculture, the liberalization of the financial sector, the reform of the public and the social security sectors and the education system (Segura, 1990, 63–4).

The PSOE's first mandate (1982–85) was characterized by the application of most of the SMs that had been announced: the interest rate was raised, the peseta was devalued by 8%, income taxes were increased, and regulations with regard to foreign investment were relaxed. Nevertheless, the limits on salary increases were smaller than had been foreseen, and public expenses continued to grow, particularly in the social domain. The SCMs announced in 1983 were also undertaken, as well as the continuation and finalization, in 1985, of the negotiation of the EC membership treaties. The period 1983 to 1986 in fact constituted the crucial phase of the discussions between Madrid and Brussels, the questions related to the liberalization of movements of capital, the introduction of VAT, and environmental protection, having been resolved in 1982 and 1983, and those related to industry and agriculture finalized in 1984 and 1985. During this period, the socialist government had to pursue its reforms of the agriculture sector, in compliance with the 1980 agreement, and it also had to undertake the restructuring of industries which were experiencing problems with overproduction in the EC, in order to guarantee the finalization of the negotiations (see Table 2).

In the course of its second and third terms of power (1986–89; 1990–93), the PSOE further pursued the SCMs in every sector of the economy, at the same time as applying the provisions of the membership treaties and the SEA (see Table 2).[9] These reforms, concurrently with the maintenance of a restrictive monetary policy, permitted a stabilization of the currency, a reduction in the rate of inflation, a decrease in the BT and the current account balance (CAB) deficit and a lessening of the relative weight of the central government's budget deficit (see Chapter 5), justifying the entry of the peseta into the European Monetary System (EMS) in 1989. The adoption of the TEU by the EC Council in 1991, however, forced the socialist government to deepen its austerity policy in order to attain the convergence norms fixed by the TEU for the completion of the first phase of the EMU (see Chapter 1, note 15). In 1992 a decree promulgated the Plan for Economic Convergence. The main macro-economic objectives of this plan were: faster economic growth (from 2.4% in 1991 to 3.5% in 1996); a reduced trade deficit (from 2.9% of GDP in 1991 to 2.3% in 1996); and a drastic cut in the annual public sector annual rate of borrowing (from 4.4% to 1% of GDP). To realize these objectives, the government opted for two paths of SCMs: economic deregulation (dissolution of monopolies in telecommunications, road, sea and air transport; the reinforcement of transparency in the operations of the banking, finance and insurance sectors; a reduction of public agencies and institutions; a freeze in the size of the public sector; a greater efficiency in the health sector) and radical labour market reforms (see below) (*European Industrial Relations Review*, 1992, 12–15; ICEX 1992). The PSOE's economic policies have been the subject of various studies.[10] It would require a detailed summary of these studies, however, to arrive at an overall portrait of the reforms adopted between 1982 and 1994 that takes into account the specific impact of the agreements reached with the EC.

The reform of the industrial sector[11]

The UCD had been unable to advance the restructuring of the industrial sector to any significant degree. With greater support from the unions and subjected to stronger external constraints during the final phase of the membership negotiations and the post-membership transition period, the first three PSOE governments were to be far more active in this issue. The publication of the white paper on reindustrialization in 1983 was followed by the adoption of decree law 8/1983, which was converted into law in July 1984, and by the proclamation of the law with respect to restructuring and reindustrialization of December 1984. This law covered the 11 branches of industry targeted by the royal decree of 1981, in which, moreover, the EC had an excess. The adoption and the implementation of the law in 1984 was largely in response to the demands of the Community, which wanted Spain, before its membership and during the subsequent transition period (1986–93), to reduce its production capacity in the industrial branches in which it had excesses. These constraints were more precise in the case of iron and steel industry: protocol number 10, appended to the membership treaties, imposed on Spain a reduction of hot laminated steel production to 18 000 tons per year and an apportioning of its steel exports towards the EC during the period 1986–89.[12]

The content and the terms of the restructuring measures varied from one branch of industry to another. In the branches where an atomized property structure prevailed, the state gave financial aid to all the companies. In the textile industry, assistance was directed toward modernizing design and marketing techniques. In the special steel and home electrical appliance sectors, which were experiencing a price war, the state implemented measures for coordinating and rationalizing production costs, aimed at increasing economies of scale and specialization. In branches monopolized by a few industries (integrated iron and steel, shipbuilding), the restructuring measures were primarily applied by the *Instituto nacional de Industria* (INI). It was in these branches that restructuring caused the most social problems, since in certain regions the entire community depended on one single company. In order to produce rapid results, the restructuring process demanded radical measures that the socialist government did not hesitate to apply. It created the *Centro de Desrarrollo tecnologico e industrial* in order to accelerate technological modernization; it contributed toward the financial restructuring of several companies (the cancellation or restructuring of debt, the issue of new lines of credit or loans, and so on); it reduced companies' production through tax measures (tax abatement, extending or splitting the payment of income tax or arrears in social security) and cutting down labour costs (liberalization of hiring conditions through the legalization of undetermined length work contracts, liberalization of firing conditions, financial contribution to pre-retirement, and so on); it maintained customs protection on certain products; and it encouraged the merging of companies and social dialogue between bosses and unions (McElrath, 1989).

In the public sector proper, restructuring took various forms:

(a) the liquidation of non-viable companies (including Diajes Ita, Aplesa, Potasas de Navarra);

(b) the reduction of production capacity in excess companies, through the complete or partial closure of certain factories (including the aluminum plants of Valladolid and Avilés, the Sagunto blast furnaces, the Enfersa fertilizer company at Puntes de Garcia Rodrigues);

(c) the restructuring of an entire industrial sector (such as that of Resol in 1987);

(d) the internal restructuring of a branch of a state holding (for example, branches of the INI's electronics and armaments);

(e) the merger of enterprises (such as the Alugasa and Endasa aluminum operations);

(f) the sale or the ceding of certain companies to other public holding companies (for example, the sale of INI's food companies to Tabacalera in 1988);

(g) the specialization or diversification of production;

(h) technological modernization;

(i) upgrading the effectiveness of product quality management methods;

(j) the privatization of companies. This was carried out through the large-scale opening of branches and sectors completely controlled by the state with the participation of the private sector; the sale of lands, of real estate holdings and private interest industries; the issue of shares in the stock market, and so on. Salmon (1991, 36) points out in this regard that between 1984 and 1989, the privatization policy did not have any significant effect on the size of the public sector, since it only affected unimportant firms running a deficit in the food and textile sector; the only exceptions to this rule were the sale of S.F. to ASE Brown Boveri, in 1985, and that of SEAT to Volkswagen in 1986 (see Table 3). The transactions carried out in 1989 and 1990 (including the partial privatization of the Repsol group (hydrocarbons) and the sale of MTM (engineering) to GEC-Alsthom) (see Table 3) were, however, more important, as they indicated an openness on the part of the PSOE to a more systematic disengagement of the state from the production sector.

The restructuring of the public sector was also seen in the reduction of direct control and financial assistance on the part of the state; the abandonment of the traditional nationalist perspective in favour of promoting the multinationalization of companies; the elimination of various forms of protection of the national market, the disappearance of public monopolies and the exposure of the entire economy to more intensive competition. For example, new laws opened up the public tobacco transportation and telecommunications market to competition in 1987, breaking the monopoly of Campsa, Tabacalera and Telefonica.

Table 4 indicates that the application of restructuring measures in the industrial sector continued throughout the period 1982 to 1991, the length of the reforms in each of the branches varying between three and ten years. In total, 791 companies were affected, 683 of which were in the textile sector, 27 in small shipyards, and 17 in electronics components. 79000 jobs, or 28% of the total employment of the industrial sector, were eliminated. The branches in which there was the most considerable concentration of lost jobs, in absolute and relative value, were integrated iron and steel, special steel, shipbuilding and home electrical appliances. Of the layoffs, 25% were absorbed by early retirement. The other laid-off workers had the choice between generous compensation and unemployment insurance benefits or a share in the *Fondo de promocion de Empleo* (FPE) for three years. In this case, the FPE paid them 80% of their salaries, offered them professional training courses and offered employers incentive grants for hiring these workers.

Major resources were devoted to the reform of industry. For the period from 1984 to 1986 alone, the cost of state assistance was estimated at 1 billion pesetas (Salmon, 1991, 118). Between 1989 and 1989, a total of 650 billion pesetas was invested in the modernization and rationalization of production costs. Overall, the largest share of state financial assistance was devoted to the financial reconstruction of companies and to compensation for lost jobs. Furthermore, Spain benefited from pre-membership assistance from the EC to help restructure its declining industries. After membership, it gained access to various statutory EC assistance programs, most of which related to industry.[13]

The restructuring of industry was accompanied, when the membership treaties came into force on January 1, 1986, by a progressive liberalization of exchanges of manufactured goods, which extended over the period 1986 to 1993. In accordance with the transitional measures included in the treaties, customs import duty (CID) was abolished in eight successive steps.[14] Taxes with an equivalent effect to the CID were eliminated as of January 1, 1986. Contingency measures were also suppressed as of 1986, except in certain sensitive sectors in which the EC and Spain benefited from delays of between two and three years.[15] The common external tariff (CET) was applied to imports from non-member countries, which meant a 50% reduction in duties collected. Spain was also obliged to accord advantages to third countries that the EC had consented to them under the Generalized System of Preferences (GSP) and the Multi-Fibre Arrangement (MFA). The membership treaties also imposed on Spain the standardization of its legislation on patents, commercial monopolies and the registering of imports with those of the EC; harmonizing its production and marketing structures with those of Europe of the Twelve, and finalizing the restructuring of its iron and steel industry between 1986 and 1991 (Flaesch-Mougin, 1986, 32–41; Ethier, 1991).

The reform of agriculture[16]

In 1983, the PSOE government adopted the agrarian reform bill, aimed at achieving compliance with the EC's pre-membership requirements (see above) and preparing agriculture for the shock of membership. The purpose of this law was to increase the quantity and competitiveness of agricultural products through the modernization of production structures, in order to respond to the needs of the internal market and to increase exports to the EC. The modernization process included the expropriation of uncultivated or under-used lands in large estates, particularly in Andalusia, and the continued restructuring of minifundios in the centre and North of the country undertaken by the UCD governments. In actual fact, the redistribution of land holdings in the south was very limited due to the reform of the common agricultural policy (CAP) implemented between 1984 and 1987 under the SEA, to which Spain was subject upon admission into the EC. In particular, this reform encouraged the reduction of cultivated lands and a decrease in agricultural labour. The agrarian reform bill also did not permit a deepening of the process of consolidating the minifundios undertaken by the UCD governments between 1977 and 1982. The peasants showed themselves hostile to any new concentration of land, with the result that enlarging farming operations was only possible in cases in which the latter were abandoned by the heirs or the descendants of the owners (Salmon, 1991, 58).

Although the transformation of property structures proved to be difficult, several other agrarian reform measures nonetheless permitted an improvement in the productivity of operations and the quality of agricultural products: irrigation work, exploitation of underground water reserves, professional training for the work force, restructuring of production activities (development of new strains or transfer of certain of these to more fertile soils).

The agricultural sector was also transformed by membership in the EC and the application of the CAP.[17] Before entry into the EC, the state intervened through various mechanisms at every stage of agricultural production: establishing planting zones, determining input and prices, controlling imports and local retail distribution. The membership bill limited the central government's intervention power by encouraging transfer of a major part of jurisdiction over agricultural and regional development to the Autonomous Communities.[18] It imposed the progressive disappearance, between 1986 and 1993, of tariff barriers on exchanges of agricultural products; the adjustment of the price of imports from non-member countries to the CET; the elimination of non-tariff barriers; the end of state controls on production processes. From that point on, prices were determined by those in charge of the CAP and certain national cereal (SENPA, FORPRA) and tobacco (Tabacalera) organizations. Preferential assistance that was not compatible with that of the EC had to be eliminated. On the other hand, Spain was able to benefit from assistance provided to agriculture by the member states through the CAP: support for agricultural prices, levies on agricultural imports from third countries, and export subsidies. Since its entry into the EC, 95% of Spain's agricultural production has been covered by price support measures of the 'guarantee' section of the European Agricultural Guidance and Guarantee Fund (EAGGF). Furthermore, Spain receives assistance from the 'guidance' section of the EAGGF to help it modernize its agricultural structures and provide professional training to farmers.

The liberalization of the financial sector

The liberalization of the financial sector was begun in 1983, but the most decisive measures were only adopted after 1986, with the application of the provisions of the EC membership treaties, of the SEA and the TEU, which provided for the abolition of obstacles to the free circulation of capital between Spain and the other states (Baeza, 1990, 364). The law decrees of June 27 and September 25, 1986 completely liberalized foreign investments in Spain and Spanish investments abroad.[19] The fact that this liberalization came about in an economic climate characterized by high interest rates and the disappearance of trade barriers provoked a major influx of foreign investments (see Table 5). In order to avoid renewed inflation and a re-evaluation of the peseta, particularly at the moment of the latter's entry into the EMS,[20] the government adopted various measures in 1988 and 1989 to limit borrowing in pesetas by firms residing on the national territory (Baeza, 1990, 365). In 1991, however, the government adopted certain decrees aimed at increasing the liberalization of foreign investments, loans, and technological transfer (Andersen, 1993).

The liberalization of the flow of capital was attended by an opening and a deregulation of the banking sector. This process was instigated by the Adolfo Suarez government's Royal Decree 1388/1978, which granted the four foreign banks established in Spain[21] the right to carry out the same operations as a national bank. PSOE decree 1144/1988 contributed significantly to this trend by authorizing the creation of private banks, by sanctioning the establishment of financial institutions in Spain in the form of subsidiaries, branches or representative bureaus, and by granting all banks – private and public, foreign and national – the same operating possibilities (Baeza, 1990, 391). Furthermore, in March 1987, the government of Felipe Gonzalez ratified a series of deregulation measures (abolition of state control on interest rates of transferable and short-term deposits; the elimination of commissions on banking services, and so on) which reduced by over 50% the share of deposits that banks were obliged to invest in state financing activities, thereby freeing up a mass of capital for the private sector. In 1988, the budget law converted the *Instituto de Credito official* (ICO) and the banks under its control – *Banco de Credito agricola* (BCA), *Banco de Credito industrial* (BCI), *Banco de Credito local* (BCL), *Banco exterior de España* (BEE), *Banco hypotecario de España* (BHE) into a public company. This change of status permitted the state to reduce its financial assistance, forcing the ICO to finance itself on the private capital market and to become more competitive. At the end of the eighties, the government also encouraged the internationalization of the private commercial banks. This process primarily involved the six largest private Spanish banks: *Banco de Bilbao et Viscaya* (BBV), *Banco español de Credito* (Banesto), *Banco central, Banco de Santander, Banco hispano-americano*. This process resulted, in particular, in the formation of alliances between Banesto and the Portuguese bank *Totta e Açores*, BBV and the *Banque nationale de Paris*, Santander and the Royal Bank of Scotland. In parallel with this internationalization process, the Spanish banks diversified their activities, creating investment divisions in stocks and securities; they became the principal intermediaries between investors and borrowers, the primary parties responsible for payment systems, and the primary suppliers of liquid assets in the economy (Salmon, 1991).

The reform of labour regulations[22]

The socialist governments continued and deepened the reform of the labour laws undertaken by the UCD. The content of the legislations adopted during the period prior to 1982 indicates that the PSOE tried to reconcile the demands of management and the unions while solving various contradictory problems such as reducing labour costs and lessening unemployment. These legislations improved employees' working conditions from various standpoints: they preserved the rights and liberties recognized by the unions through the *Pactos de la Moncloa* and the constitution of 1978 (freedom of association, right to strike, right to consultation, and so on) while tightening up the conditions for exercising these rights. They widened the autonomy of employers with regard to hiring and work organization, which at the same time contributed towards decreased job security, reduced labour costs, improved competitiveness of companies, and the introduction of measures (early retirement, shared work, and so on) aimed at reducing unemployment.

A first series of actions consisted of amending the ELT adopted in 1980. In 1983, a law was passed lowering the maximum number of regular hours worked per week to 40 and increased the number of vacation days per year from 23 to 30. Law 32 of August 1984 and the complementary decrees ratified in the same year relaxed the eligibility conditions for the professional training courses and increased the duration of these courses to three years; they authorized work-sharing between employees on the verge of retirement and unemployed workers;[23] and they reduced employers' contributions to social security. Since the unions had refused any new relaxation of hiring conditions,[24] the law of 1984 liberalized the labour relations system by easing the constraints related to the hiring of non-permanent workers. In July 1985, a royal decree imposed the conferring of full retirement on laid-off workers of 46 and over. In 1986, a new royal decree reduced the total annual number of overtime hours from 100 to 80, while abolishing overtime limits on a weekly and monthly basis. The most important modification to the ELT was the law of 8/1988, which imposed fines of up to 15 000 pesetas on employers who did not respect the rules of the ELT concerning the hiring of workers (non-discrimination, minimum age, length of part-time contracts, and so on).

The constitutional law of August 1985 on trade union freedom imposed certain constraints on the exercise of union freedom. In virtue of this law, unions which levied payments on non-union workers, in order to cover the costs of negotiating collective agreements, had to pay fines; in order to be recognized as a legitimate interlocutor by employers, every union has to have at least 1500 representatives elected on companies' workers committees at the national level. If no restriction to the right to strike is adopted, the unions' claim to promote workers' participation in the management of the companies becomes a dead letter, in compliance with the EC's wishes. On the other hand, the powers of government joint action bodies created by the UCD (such as the National Institute on Employment and the Professional Health and Security Institute), were reinforced. In order to comply with the terms of the membership treaties and of the SEA, the Spanish authorities also incorporated into that legislation, in 1982, the EC directives with regard to the unrestricted movement and the quality of treatment of workers from the member countries.[25]

However, it was in 1992, in the framework of the Plan for Economic Convergence that the most radical reforms of the labour legislations were announced, depite the strong opposition of the unions. The main recommendations of the Plan aimed to enhance the flexibility of the labour market (elimination of functional and geographical barriers to labour mobility, elimination of l00 remaining Francoist labour ordinances that limit the hiring and firing liberty of the enterprises) and to improve the vocational training of manpower (creation of 60 000 new training places per year for unemployed workers; establishment of a social fund intended to fund permanent jobs).

The reform of social security and fiscal systems

The various socialist governments introduced a large number of modifications to the social security system (SSS) between 1982 and 1992.[26] These changes were aimed at harmonizing Spain's legislation with that of the EC countries that were the most advanced in the social domain, in order to promote the free circulation of labour, while avoiding a massive migration of companies and jobs towards the South. Neither the membership treaties, nor the SEA, nor the TEU imposed any specific reforms on Spain with regard to social security, as this remained, with the failure of social Europe,[27] under strictly national jurisdiction. It was rather the indirect constraints related to the liberalization of markets that led the Spanish authorities to act in this area. The willingness of European leaders and Spanish elites to consolidate the new democracy, the necessity to compensate the economic compromises of unions and leftist political forces by social gains, and the socialist convictions of the government, constituted other important determinants of these social reforms (Duquette and Ethier, 1996).

According to Jimenez Fernandez (1991, 55–9), 'the primary efforts deployed by Spanish social security were directed at setting up an integrated social protection network'. For instance, the *Ley general de sanidad* of April 1984 universalized the access to health insurance. Between 1986 and 1991, the number of beneficiaries increased from 32.5 to 39 million, that is, 99% of the population (Gonzalez and Fernandez, 1993). The 1984 *Ley de prestaciones de desempleo* increased from 26.4%, in 1984, to 43%, in 1990, the percentage of unemployed persons covered by the unemployment insurance (UI), a proportion equivalent to the average protection offered by the EC member states. The main objective of this reform was to give access to UI to some categories of unemployed persons who could not before have benefited from subsidies given that they had not contributed to the regime: breadwinners; 45-year-old unemployed workers not qualified for other social aid programs; 55-year-old unemployed workers qualified for the retirement pension; and persons wishing to return on the labour market after a period of emigration, a professional disease or accident or a prison sentence. Until 1992, the amount of UI benefit payments was higher than in other EC member states (80% of the salary rather than 65%) while the duration of these payments was shorter (3 to 24 months) (Aguilar et al., 1992, 136). However, the 1992 Plan for Economic Convergence has reduced the amount of benefit payments to 70% of the salary while lengthening by 6 months, on average, the period of insured employment (*European Industrial Review*, 1992, 13). Grappling with the highest unemployment rate in Europe and having less financial resources than most of its partners, Spain has chosen to focus its employment policy on professional training and jobs creation rather than on UI. A very large spectrum of new measures intended to comply with these two objectives were adopted during the eighties. It includes, notably, social assistance benefits and anticipated access to retirement pension for 46-year-old workers, numerous training programs and grants and the financing of temporary and part-time jobs (Eurostat, 1990). With regard to retirement and disability pensions, the main innovations were their extension to non-contributors and the increase of annuities by 30%. Hence, the retirement annuity in Spain is higher than everywhere else in the EC; it is equivalent to 100% of the average wage earned during the last eight years of employment whereas in most EC countries, the annuity does not exceed 65% of the average salary earned during employment (Aguilar et al., 1992). By the means of these reforms, the government wanted to provide all beneficiaries with a secure income, at least equivalent to the minimum wage. In order to improve the living conditions of old and disabled citizens, the PSOE has also enlarged the range of free health services to which they have access; it has increased the number while humanizing the functioning of old people's homes. Pension benefits and social assistance allowances were increased for the neediest cases. Funding for these reforms came primarily from wage contributions (two-thirds of the SSS budget and 28.3% of the salary in 1994) of which five-sixths are paid by employers and one-sixth by employees. The other third of the SSS budget is provided by the state. On the whole, the betterment of the SSS has obliged the central government to increase by 27% its social transfers during the eighties.[28]

The socialist governments also completely reworked the Spanish tax system. In conformity with the requirements of the membership treaties, they replaced the range of indirect taxes with a single VAT in 1986. In order to respect the provisions of the SEA, they adapted corporate income tax to EC standards in 1991 (Mocoroa, 1991). In 1992, they harmonized individual income tax and specific taxes while adapting the rate scale and the procedure for collecting the VAT to the directives resulting from the SEA (Andersen, 1993). Overall, these changes lightened the tax burden on companies and increased it on individuals, which promoted the growth of tax receipts by the state and contributed toward a decrease in the budget deficit.

3 Portugal: A Late but Accelerated Process of Adjustment[1]

THE CONFLICTING ECONOMIC POLICIES OF THE FIRST
DEMOCRATIC GOVERNMENTS: 1974–83

> In Portugal, the tasks of establishing political democracy and reforming
> the economy beyond capitalism were attempted at the same time. This was
> to produce considerable political instability and to aggravate the economic
> situation. (Maravall, 1993, 85)

The transition from authoritarianism to democracy in Portugal began with
the *coup d'état* of the AFM[2] on April 25, 1974, and ended in April 1976 with
the adoption of a new constitution and the election of a first legislative
assembly. During the transition process, the country experienced six minority
provisional governments, directed by the AFM. The first seven years of the
new democratic regime saw three successive legislatures (1976–79; 1979–80;
1980–83) and six governments: a minority socialist government (1976–77);
three coalition governments composed of the socialists (PSP) and the social
and democratic centre conservatives (CDS) (1978–79); two governments
directed by *Aliança democratico* (AD), a coalition formed of the forces of
the moderate right-wing social-democratic party (PSDP) and the CDS
(1979–80; 1980–83) (see Table 6).

As has already been emphasized, the transition toward democracy was not
attended by any economic compromise among the major political forces in
Portugal. On the contrary, it was characterized by a confrontation of different
ideologies and economic development programs. This situation explains the
contradictory and conflictory nature of the economic policies implemented
by the provisional constitutional governments during the transition process
and during the first years of the new democratic regime. The period 1974–83
can in effect be roughly divided into two sub-periods: the transition towards
democracy proper (1974–76), characterized by the political domination of
the forces of the left and the promotion of a nationalist, socialist and
expansionist economy; the first seven years of the democratic regime

35

(1976–83), characterized by the political predominance of the forces of the centre and right, and of unfruitful attempts at economic adjustment.

The six provisional governments of the period 1974–76, formed by radical elements in the AFM and supported by the PCP and the many groups of the extreme left, in fact promoted an anti-capitalist, socialist and nationalist economic program. However, no one questioned the application of the free-trade agreement of 1972 (see Chapter 1, note 9). The first government of Palma Carlos (April–July 1974) froze US$2 billion in private capital and closed the stock exchange, which triggered the exodus of the major Portuguese financial groups. The four subsequent governments of General Gonçalves (July 1974–September 1975) greatly increased public spending in order to carry out a series of nationalizations. They nationalized the 32 national banks, several major companies in various sectors (water distribution, railroads, merchant marine, commercial aviation, refineries, iron and steel, tobacco, fertilizers, cement, beer) and a host of small companies. These nation-alizations affected 27% of Portuguese companies, most of which belonged in the category of large modern enterprises (Makler, 1979, 156–7; 1983, 261).[3] At the beginning of its mandate (September 1975 July 1976), the sixth provisional government of Admiral Pinheiro de Azevedo continued the expansionist policy of its predecessors by raising salaries by 25% and increasing state assistance to industries in difficulty (shipbuilding, iron and steel, chemical industries) in order to avoid layoffs. The nationalist and expansionist approach of the transitory governments, combined with its socialist measures (expropriation of the Alentejo and of the Algarve latifundia and the establishment of agricultural production cooperatives managed by the PCP) deepened the Portuguese economic crisis. These measures resulted in a major public deficit, worsened the balance of payments (BP) deficit, increased the state's foreign debt, and brought about a major increase in inflation, a decline in investments and an exodus of capital and private companies. The annual average growth rate of the GDP which had been 7.6% between 1970 and 1974, fell to 2.7% between 1974 and 1977. This deterioration of the economic climate, concurrently with the return of 600000 émigrés from Angola and Mozambique following the end of the colonial war in Africa, led to higher levels of unemployment. It also contributed to increased dissent over the economic orientations of the future democratic constitution among the members of the constituent assembly elected in April 1975. The existence of this double political and economic crisis and the urgency for Portugal to obtain new loans from the EC,[4] the United States and the International Monetary Fund (IMF) incited the government of Pinheiro de Azevedo to opt for a more liberal economic policy, half-way through his mandate. This change of direction was evidenced by a commitment to freeze nationalization projects and to adopt a national economic restructuring plan characterized by greater fiscal discipline, control of workers' demands and the application of measures favourable to foreign investments.

The new democratic constitution ratified in April 1976[5] reflected, in many respects, the point of view of the radical forces of the left who had led the transition process. It contained several provisions of a socialist nature, including Article 89, which stipulated that 'the development of the revolutionary process imposes the collective appropriation of the means of production and the confinement of the private sector to a residual role at the economic level', and Article 105 which stipulated 'a progressive and effective socialization of the economy' and announced 'the creation of a socialist society'. The first minority constitutional government of the PSP, directed by the moderate and modernist partisans of Mario Soares, nonetheless adopted a liberal-leaning economic policy. When he came into office in 1976, he promulgated decree law 44, which established the mechanisms for privatizing state companies; stopped the land collectivization process and proposed peaceful coexistence between the public and the private sectors. The escudo was devalued and subsidies to companies reduced; the annual salary growth rate was limited to 15%; and a more restrictive monetary policy was put into force. Concurrently with these measures, the government of Mario Soares in 1976 negotiated an additional protocol to the 1972 free-trade agreement with the EC;[6] in March 1977, he submitted Portugal's membership request to the EC. The same year, the IMF granted a new loan to Lisbon on condition that the authorities reinforced the austerity measures. The Soares government's submission to this demand led to its defeat and the formation of the PSP–CDS coalition government, again led by Mario Soares, in January 1978. The tightening of the stabilization measures, with the support of the IMF, allowed for a re-establishment of a balance in external trade but it fed dissention within the cabinet and the parliament, bringing about the overthrow and the recomposition of the government on two occasions during the period 1978–79. Nevertheless, negotiations aimed at membership in the EC were initiated in October 1978, following the issue of a favourable recommendation by the Council and the Commission.

The relative majority obtained by the forces of the right (CDS) and the centre-right (PSDP), during the regular elections of 1979 and those anticipated in 1980, led to the formation of two AD coalition governments in 1979–80 and 1980–83. Considering the earlier conflicts generated by the economic stabilization policy, these governments moderated the adjustment measures. The attentist and laxist attitude of the two AD administrations emphasized the economic imbalances, resulting in higher inflation and a worsening of the BP deficit. The second AD government nonetheless succeeded, through an agreement with the PSP, to have the National Assembly ratify, in 1982, an amendment to the constitution which consolidated democratic institutions[7] and eliminated the provisions relating to the socialization of the means of production. While slowing down the adjustment process, both AD governments were nonetheless to make progress in the membership negotiations in the EC.[8]

THE ACHIEVEMENT OF REFORMS UNDER SOCIALIST AND SOCIAL-DEMOCRATIC GOVERNMENTS: 1983–95

Several factors, including the deterioration of the economic situation, the revision of the constitution in 1982, the approaching failure of EC membership negotiations, and public discontent with government management,[9] created, as of 1983, conditions more favourable to the stabilization of the political situation and the deepening of the economic adjustment process. The period 1983–95 was in fact characterized by four legislatures (1983–85; 1985–87; 1987–91; 1991–95): the first was dominated by a PSP–PSDP coalition government; the second by a PSDP minority government; and the last two by a majority PSDP government. Relaunched with some difficulty by the PSP–PSDP government, the adjustment process was widened and speeded up without interruption by the three PSDP governments in the period following 1985 (see Table 6).

During the first 100 days of its administration, the new PSP–PSDP government, which emerged from the elections of 1983, succeeded in passing, without opposition, a law re-establishing private initiative in the banking and insurance sectors; a modification of the labour legislation authorizing collective layoffs 'in the event of extreme urgency'; a re-examination of the agrarian reform;[10] and the creation of a High Authority charged with warning the competent jurisdictions of all instances of corruption in the army and the national, regional and local public service sector, and of denouncing such instances of corruption. It also announced a stabilization program developed jointly with the IMF, aimed at obtaining a new loan of US$749 million and a guarantee of US$120 million and US$622 million in loans from the World Bank and private banks. This program was intended to reduce the DCG's deficit from US$3.2 billion (13% of GDP) to US$1.2 billion (9% of GDP), through a decrease in imports of DCG and a 12% devaluation of the escudo aimed at boosting the growth of exports. For 1984, it imposed a US$15 billion ceiling on the public external debt and a decrease in the central government's GDP/budget deficit ratio, from 10% to 7.5%. These objectives were conditional on a reduction in public spending, on an increase in taxes and indirect taxes, on the creation of an emergency tax on property revenue and labour, and on an increase in the price of basic consumer goods. In order to curb inflation, the program included an increase in interest rates (OCDE, 1984). The application of these measures, however, proved to be problematic. The unions, the Catholic Church and the PCP mobilized their members against the stabilization program, holding it responsible for rising unemployment, a worsening of poverty-related problems and delays experienced in the payment of wages.[11] The effects of the government policies were thus less beneficial than anticipated. External trade figures were improving without resolving the problem of the BT deficit; the value of foreign investments[12] was increasing in step with the inflation rate, which jumped by six points compared with 1983, to attain 31%. The persistence of economic difficulties, in a context marked by the finalization of membership negotiations in the EC, and Portugal's commitment to bringing about a turnaround in public finances and a vast agricultural, industrial and public sector modernization program, provoked a crisis in the government. Accusing the PSP of having blocked the implementation of the economic adjustment program adopted in 1983 because of its concessions to the unions and the PCP, the representatives of the PSDP resigned *en masse* from the government on June 12, 1985, forcing the holding of the elections slated for October 1985.

As soon as it came into office, the new PSDP minority government, led by the new leader Anibal Cavaco Silva, took over the preceding government's economic program, and began the implementation of its structural reforms in order to maximize the benefits of membership in the EC. At the time of the official signing of the membership treaties, on June 11, 1985, Cavaco Silva in fact declared:

> We should adapt the financial, economic and administrative structures so as to reap the advantages of membership. Even better, we should guarantee that membership in the EEC will intensify the process of modernizing the Portuguese economy in a decisive manner, in order to ensure the competitiveness of industry and tourism, and increase the productivity of the agricultural sector.   (Rudel, 1986, 182) (translated by R.C.)

It did not take long before the beneficial effects of pursuing adjustment and membership made themselves felt. In 1986, the year the treaties come into force, liberalization of the trade of goods, services and capital,[13] combined with the positive impact of the stabilization measures, brought about renewed production, a 25% salary increase, a 19.6% lowering in the inflation rate to 11.7%, improved purchasing power, a 14% drop in the BT deficit, and an increase in the CAB surplus of US$1800 million (Rudel, 1986, 182). The increased state tax receipts resulting from the implementation of VAT and these higher salaries and profits allowed the central government to make an advance payment of US$1700 million on its external debt. It also financed the 45% increase in pension payments: a measure aimed, on the one hand, at bringing Portugal's pension plan in line with that of the other member states of the EC, and on the other, at increasing the purchasing power of seniors. In the area of labour relations, the social-democratic government obtained from the National Assembly the authorization to legislate by decree in order to facilitate layoffs on economic grounds. The support of the majority of representatives was not easy to obtain, however, due to the persistence of an 11% unemployment rate and the high percentage of precarious jobs.[14]

In 1986, Portugal also received 1360 million French francs (FF) from the EC to assist it in developing new technologies and modernizing/rationalizing fishing, agriculture, viticulture, communications and industry, particularly the branches of shipbuilding, textiles and shoes. The structural problems of the Portuguese economy were, in fact, comparable to those of Spain: an agricultural sector characterized by a predominance of small family operations, which were either unproductive or totally neglected, in the islands (the Azores), the North and the centre of the country; unproductive collective production units (CPUs) or major private holdings that often specialized in products that were in competition with those of other countries in the EC: vineyards, olive groves in the East (Alentejo) and the South (Algarve) of the country; an industry dominated by traditional small or medium enterprises (SMEs) in the ECG sector (textiles, shoes, clothes); or ensnared in the problems of obsolescence, overproduction or indebtedness in the largely state-run IGE sector (shipbuilding , iron and steel, petrochemicals, and so on).

The positive effects of membership and the liberal economic policy of the Cavaco Silva government were to favour the ratification of the SEA in 1986 and – a situation that was without precedent since the Marigold Revolution – the PSDP obtained an absolute majority of seats in parliament in the advance elections of 1987. As soon as it came into power, on July 1987, the new Cavaco Silva government announced that it wished to proceed with a new review of the constitution to enable it to implement its entire economic adjustment program. The social-democratic leaders nonetheless stated that this program would not involve the privatization of public services (transportation, mail, Air Portugal) and that the transfer of other government enterprises to the private sector would be done gradually. For the period 1987–91, the government announced a large-scale privatization of radio and television, a revision of the basic law on agrarian reform, a liberalization of labour legislation, in particular with regard to hiring and firing, and the disengagement of the state from social security.

None of these measures were carried out in 1987. Nevertheless, the continuation of the stabilization measures and the maintenance of a high level of growth brought the inflation rate down to 9.3% and the unemployment rate to 6.6%. A new advance contribution of US$600 million further reduced the external debt. The guaranteed minimum wage was increased, bringing the purchasing power of Portuguese citizens to its highest level since 1972.

1988 was marked by continued growth, a further reduction in economic imbalances, and by the start of the structural reforms announced in 1987. This situation was facilitated by contributions and increased assistance from the EC aimed at achieving the European Single Market. The major transport modernization projects were begun: construction of a high-speed train (TGV) between Oporto and Lisbon and a new international airport in the suburb of Lisbon; modernization of the airports of Oporto, Faro and Açores, repairs to 3000 km of roads, and the construction of a new Lisbon–Estoril motorway. The 1988–93 phase of the PEDIP project was launched, aimed at promoting modernization, restructuring and consolidating SMEs in the traditional industrial branches. The new programs for the economic development of backward regions were begun in Alentejo, Beirra, Tras-os-Montes, Madeira and the Azores.[15] In the fishing sector, the government financed the construction of 52 new boats, reduced the volume of catches and subsidized the development of aquaculture activities.[16] The adoption of the revision of the basic law on agrarian reform sanctioned the near-disappearance of cooperatives and CPUs, and legalized the retrocession heirs of land expropriated after the revolution of 1974 to the former owners and their heirs. Several former owners, exiled abroad, preferred, however, to sell their land and their operations to new private interests, often of German or Dutch origin. The adoption of the law on the delimitation of the private and public sectors, authorizing state companies to sell 49% of their social capital to private interests, marked the beginning of the privatization process. In 1988, this process saw the partial privatization of the daily *A Capital*, the periodical *Annuaire commercial*, the Aliança Seguradora and Tranquilidade insurance companies, the Union and *Totta e Açores* banks, and of UNICER breweries. However, since the government was unable to get parliament to adopt its constitutional reform project, upon which the deepening of the adjustment process depended, especially with regard to privatization, denationalization operations were limited. An agreement was nevertheless reached between the PSDP and the PSP on certain goals of the constitutional review: eliminating legal obstacles to the privatization of public companies; issuing 20% of the shares of privatized companies to workers; and reducing the powers of the President of the Republic. In July, in spite of protests from workers' organizations, the government adopted a reform of the labour code that widened the possibility of hiring on a temporary contractual basis and liberalized firing conditions. Since certain provisions had been judged to be anti-constitutional by the courts, the government proclaimed a new decree law on these matters in February 1989.[17]

The improvement of certain economic and social indicators – the doubling of foreign investments, 5.4% growth, 5% drop in unemployment, reduction in infant mortality, illiteracy and crime – was offset, in 1989, by the persistence of economic imbalances. This situation led to a tightening of credit control measures. The constitutional revision was adopted. This sanctioned the elements of the 1988 PSDP–PSP agreement, abolished economic and social planning, authorized the disengagement of the state from the realm of social security, and enshrined certain democratic principles, such as recourse to a referendum and the right to petition members of parliament. Following this reform, the government was able to step up the privatization movement. Two laws were adopted towards this end. The first legitimized a certain degree of government monitoring over privatized companies,[18] whereas the second, adopted in 1990, sanctioned complete privatization of state companies, that is, the sale of over 51% of the shares to private interests. This legislation allowed the remaining public shares of UNICER and Centralcer, of the Tranquilidade and Aliança insurance companies, and of the *Trotta e Açores* and *Banco portuguese do Atlantico* banks to be ceded to the private sector. The second phase of the tax system reform aimed at modifying direct income taxes was implemented. On the whole, it discouraged tax evasion, simplified tax payments, and increased the tax burden of the majority of individuals, while reducing that of the poorest contributors.[19] In the area of labour law, the government was able to obtain the adoption of new, more flexible rules with regard to hiring and firing, but its project for setting a limit on salary raises in the public service was rejected by the Assembly of the Republic.

1989 was also marked by the commencement of a major reform of the social security system with the same objectives as that undertaken in Spain: harmonizing the country's social legislation with that of the most advanced countries of the EC in the social area, in order to promote the free circulation of workers. This reform should have come into force in 1993, in virtue of the membership treaties and the SEA. In March 1989, the government modified the unemployment insurance law. The minimum period worked to justify the payment of unemployment insurance benefits was reduced from 36 to 18 months. The length of the payment period was set at between 10 and 13 months, depending on the age of the beneficiary.[20] Under the new rules, the minimum monthly payment would be equal to the minimum wage paid in industry in May 1990 (US$710), and the maximum monthly payment equal to three times this amount (Campbell, 1990, 2–4). In September 1989, another law granted the government administrative control over private pension plans and harmonized private and public retirement plans, which had the effect of increasing pensions for the first category of plans. The retirement age was lowered to 60. In February 1989, the government consolidated the voluntary social insurance plans for categories of people not covered by social security, a measure which followed the conferring of universality in social security in 1989 (Campbell, 1990, 5–6). There were numerous other important measures adopted in 1989 aimed at improving professional training.[21]

1990 was marked by increased inflation, the government having quickly relaxed the credit control measures ratified in 1989. These price increases increased the BT deficit. Furthermore, the higher revenues generated by the tax reforms had no significant effect on public finances, since they were accompanied by increased spending in health, education, infrastructures and the civil service (the establishment of higher pay scales), and also by higher interest on the debt. The financing needs of public administrations rose by four points, to 9% of GDP, and the budgetary deficit climbed to FF25 billion, or 7% of GDP. In order not to compromise the entry of the escudo into the EMS and in response to the SEA convergence requirements, the Cavaco Silva government adopted a new stabilization plan: QUANTUM. The effectiveness of this plan was, however, compromised by an increase in public spending, following the social and economic agreement reached with the employers and unions in October. While claiming to support the goal of modernizing the economic system, the unions were demanding the implementation of various measures aimed at improving the standard of living of Portuguese citizens. In response to this request, the government increased the minimum guaranteed wage, adopted decree law 441 which applied the EC directives with respect to health and work security, and granted seniors a thirteenth month of pension payments. In order to improve the efficiency of its monetary policy, the government had undertaken a major structural reform of the banking system in 1990. The direct control of the Central Bank upon the total amount of money in circulation, in force since 1977, was replaced by a policy of indirect control (interventions in the money market).

The economic policy of the second PSDP majority government (1991–95) was characterized by the continuation of measures aimed at improving the living and working conditions of Portuguese citizens, while at the same time pursuing the structural reforms and tightening stabilization measures. The measures aimed at improving living and working conditions were aimed, on the one hand, at respecting the tripartite agreement of 1990, and, on the other, of harmonizing Portugal's legislation with the regulations resulting from the SEA. The measures instituted by the government included improving the professional training programs; adopting, in 1995, a deadline for reducing the working week from 48 to 40 hours; increasing the rate for overtime and limiting this to two hours a day; adjusting layoff compensations;[22] and improving the social security plan for self-employed workers and others excluded from the labour market. It also created the Economic and Social Council in order to ensure permanent consultation between the state, employers and unions on economic and social policies.

In order not to compromise the entry of the escudo into the EMS and in response to the SEA convergence requirements (see Chapter 1, note 15), the government increased direct taxes by 25% and indirect taxes by 35%, while limiting salary increases. The reform of the money market was followed up by the privatization of the two national stock exchanges and the creation of a new institution in charge of the control of the securities markets. At the end of 1991, it also adopted a new stabilization plan for the period 1992–95, the QUANTUM 2 (Q2), the main objective of which was to reduce the inflation rate to 4–5% in 1994–95. The entry of the escudo into the EMS in 1992 was followed by the adoption of annual budgetary programs aimed at attaining the convergence norms set for the completion of the first phase of the EMU (1990–95).

The effectiveness of Q2 was however lessened by the recession, whose effects on the Portuguese economy began to be felt in 1992, as was the case with the European economies as a whole. Between 1992 and 1994, the monetary policy was relaxed (devaluation of the escudo by 6.5%, relaxation of interest rates) and the weight of the budget deficit in relation to GDP grew from 4.7% (in 1992) to 8.5% (in 1993), primarily as a result of reduced revenues from VAT and taxes and to losses due to tax fraud. On the whole, however, the government remained faithful to its commitment to put Portugal's public finances on a healthy footing and gain acceptance into the EMU. In testimony to this are the objectives of the 1993–96 Revised Convergence Program (RCP) that was adopted in 1993 to replace Q2. The RCP set more modest economic performance targets than those established for 1994 by Q2, yet projected a reduction of interest rates to 5% and a reduction of the public debt to 35 and 60% of GDP (Léonard, 1994). In 1993, the government also ratified a new Regional Development Plan aimed at raising the living standard of Portuguese citizens to 70% of the European average through undertaking vast infrastructure projects within the framework of the EC's second SF aid package for the period 1993–99.[23] In 1994 and 1995, the recession forced the government to slow down the economic reforms. Nevertheless, it continued the privatization, monopolization and rationalization of the public banking sector, which had allowed the financial groups of the Salazar era to increase their control over the latter. Accordingly, the Champlinaud group increased its control over the *Banca Pinto e Sotto Mayor* to 80% and in the *Banca Totta e Açores* to 50%.

4 Greece: Timid and Fruitless Attempts at Adjustment

THE EXPANSIONIST POLICIES OF ND AND PASOK GOVERNMENTS: 1977–85

In Greece it was the forces of the moderate right, which, under the leadership of Constantin Caramanlis, took charge of the process of re-establishing democracy between July 24 and November 17, 1974.[1] It was also these forces, which, grouped together in Caramanlis' new party, New Democracy (ND), formed the first two majority governments of the post-authoritarian period (1974–77, 1977–81).

During this six-year period, the ND negotiated and signed the EC membership treaties (1976–79), and at the same time pursued an expansionist economic policy, in spite of the persisting economic crisis. It is important to stress here that although Greece received financial assistance from the EC[2] during the negotiation of the membership treaties, signature of these treaties was not conditional on reform of its industry and agriculture, as in the case of Spain. The expansionist policy of the Caramanlis and George Rallis governments[3] resulted in a strong growth in government spending, growth which was fed by the progressively higher external indebtedness and recourse to public deficits. In fact, major resources were invested in improving the education,[4] health and retirement systems in order to consolidate the fledgling democracy and to bring Greece's social policies into line with those of the EC states (Maravall, 1993). A massive nationalization program was also undertaken aimed at supporting economic sectors in difficulty. The state also bought up majority shares of banks, telecommunications and transportation companies, the petroleum industry and port installations. This policy, together with the impact of the recession following the second petroleum crisis of 1979, contributed to a worsening of the problems of the Greek economy. During the period 1975/76–80, the inflation rate rose from 15.8% to 24.7%; the annual average growth rate of GDP, which was at 7.7% between 1961 and 1973, fell to 3.5%; the average annual rate of net capital formation, which was 12.3% between 1970 and 1973, fell to 1.25%; the BT deficit reached

45

3998 mecus. In spite of the nationalization program, roughly 300 companies were driven into bankruptcy.

The election of a majority PASOK government in 1981, in a context marked by the continuing economic crisis and the coming into effect of the EC membership treaty,[5] did not bring about any significant change in direction with regard to the economic policy (see Table 7). The government of Andreas Papandreou persisted in its attempts to resolve the crisis by means of a Keynesian approach, while claiming to imitate the management methods of the new French socialist government rather than those of the Greek conservatives. During its first term in power (1981–85), the PASOK attempted to renew production through various demand-side measures financed by loans and foreign aid and by increased budgetary deficits: the earnings of the middle and lower classes were increased; access to state retirement plans was broadened;[6] social benefits were augmented and extended to a greater number of workers; low salaries were indexed retroactively to the cost of living;[7] and a vast public works program was undertaken, aimed at creating 270 000 jobs. In parallel with these measures, the government continued the ND policy of bailing out companies in difficulty by financing the deficits of 44 of them, by nationalizing Esso-Greece, and by creating a state pharmaceutical industry. With the exception of the devaluation of the drachma by 16% and 15% in 1983 and 1984 respectively, most of the SMs announced in the 1983–87 development plan remained dead letter. With regard to SCMs, government action was very limited. In 1982, the PASOK had ratified the framework law on higher education.[8] In 1983, in the domain of labour relations, it ratified in 1983, the law respecting 'the socialization of public enterprises'. This law limited the exercise of the right to strike by imposing the rule of absolute majority rather than of a simple majority in order to justify a strike. This restriction on the power of the unions was offset by giving workers' representatives continuous direct control over the management of companies. The expansionist policy of the first socialist government in fact brought about a 5.5% increase in demand, yet did not lead to renewed production growth; this levelled off at less than 0.5% between 1983 and 1985 because of an increase in salaries and the resulting drop in investments. Furthermore, it worsened macro-economic imbalances. After dropping from 24.7% to 18.2%, the inflation rate bounced back to 25% in 1985. Inflation remained high, in spite of a decrease from 24.7% to 18.4%. BT deficits increased considerably, as well as the weight of the central government's total and foreign debts.

THE SPORADIC AND LIMITED ADJUSTMENT MEASURES OF PASOK AND ND GOVERNMENTS: 1985–95

The PASOK was re-elected with an absolute majority of seats in 1985. Contrary to what it had led the electorate to believe during the campaign, it opted from the beginning of its second mandate for a more liberal economic policy, thereby continuing the trend begun with the devaluations of 1983 and 1984, concurrently with a reorientation to the right of the economic policy of its French emulators (Tsakalotos, 1987; Featherstone, 1994). This new attitude was primarily motivated by the socialists' desire to obtain a new loan from the EC (Pepelasis, 1990, 86). As soon as it came to power, the new Papandreou government adopted a stabilization program that targeted three objectives: reducing inflation, reducing the BT balance and reducing the budget deficit. This program resulted in higher interest rates, a 15% devaluation of the drachma, the imposition of partial pre-payment on certain imports, the adoption of a less generous salary indexation policy;[9] fixing the price of agricultural products below the inflation rate; a 4% reduction in the financing needs over public companies thanks to stricter control over public spending and tax fraud; the creation of a special tax on corporate profits, the incomes of self-employed workers and rents; a rise in interest rates, the closure of certain public companies showing a deficit and the conversion of the debts of several others into shared capital underwritten by the national bank of Greece and the Business Recovery Office. In parallel with these measures, the government intensified the process of structural reforms so as to bring them in line with the requirements of the membership treaties and the SEA.[10] It introduced the VAT system in 1987; it liberalized legislation on foreign investments and the regulation of the financial sector, it began the rationalization of the domain of public administration. In the domain of labour relations, the socialists adopted several pieces of legislation aimed at establishing equal rights between men and women (Tzannatos, 1987), and in 1989, created the National Council for Employment and Professional Training. This body, which came under the Ministry of Labour, was responsible for defining the major outlines of the employment policy and encouraging coordination among the departments managing the professional training and employment programs. In actual fact, this new bureaucratic structure turned out to be relatively ineffective, a fact which progressively led SMEs to assume the training of their labour force on their own (ECC, 1990a, III-3).

The PASOK adjustment policy contributed toward the improvement of several economic indicators between 1985 and 1988: the inflation rate went from 25% to 14%; the unit cost of labour fell from 22% to 11%; the financing needs of companies went down from 18% to 13%; the unemployment rate went down from 9.7% to 8%. Nevertheless, due to its limits, it neither succeeded in renewing investment and production nor in attenuating, to any significant degree, the major imbalances in the economy. The government debt and the budget deficit continued to grow; companies continued to experience problems of productivity and competitiveness, because of the insufficient decrease in labour costs. Inflation remained high because of the discrepancy between consumption and investment (see Table 8). In 1988, in spite of these mitigated results, the Papandreou government, undermined by corruption scandals and divided over the orientation of the economic policy, decided not to pursue its adjustment measures. This decision resulted in the resignation of the National Economy Minister, Kostas Simitis (Catsiapis, 1984–89; Pepelasis, 1990).

The period between June 1989 and April 1990 was marked by a deterioration in the economic situation and the inactivity of the political authorities, the primary cause of which was the frequent changes in governments. Since the election of June 1989 had only given the ND a relative majority, it formed a coalition government with the communist forces of the Synapismos[11] whose brief existence was to be focused exclusively on reconciliating left and right and sanctioning illegal acts committed by the leaders and friends of the PASOK.[12] Once the objectives of this historic compromise were achieved, the government resigned, resulting in new elections being held in November 1989. Since these elections once more obtained only a relative majority of seats for the ND, the new government concluded an ecumenical alliance with the KKE and the PASOK which was to survive for only a few months. A third electoral consultation in April 1990 allowed the ND to form a majority government led by Constantin Mitsokakis.

The positions taken by the ND in favour of a new liberal economic policy during the PASOK's years in power and the conditions attached to the award of a new community loan of 200 billion ecus – rehabilitating the economy and using this loan for major investment projects rather than as a tool to support consumption – contributed to the adoption of a major adjustment program by the Mitsokakis government. As soon as it assumed office the new cabinet announced several stabilization measures – reduction of the inflation rate by 10% before 1983, cutting the number of civil servants by 10%, increasing the tax burden for farmers, cutting public sector funding needs in half, and a vast program of privatization of public companies and bankrupt private companies that had come under state control. It also undertook a reform of social security which tightened the very generous conditions for access to retirement benefits[13] and continued the modernization of labour laws and national social laws through the adoption of certain limited-range legislative measures.[14] In practice, however, the implementation of this program came up against various obstacles and resulted in only partial improvements in economic imbalances.

In 1991, the inflation rate dropped by five points and the BP deficit was stabilized; however, the public deficit–GDP ratio increased from 20.6% to 23.2%, the employment rate rose from 8.7% to 9.2%, the GDP growth remained negative (–1.0%) and the level of investment continued to stagnate. The application of the stabilization plan, particularly the increase in public tariffs and the reform of social security, sparked various strikes by trade union organizations in the public sector (EDADY) and the private sector (GSEE). After 18 months of trial and error, the government succeeded in passing the law respecting 'the privatization and the strengthening of the rules related to competition' in December 1991.[15] This law instituted an interdepartmental privatization committee chaired by the Minister of National Economy, and specified three major procedures for ceding national corporations or state financial participation in public companies to the private sector: (1) sale to private investors through direct negotiations; (2) sale by public adjudication; and (3) sale through the intermediary of the stock market. Application of the privatization policy was, however, hindered by economic and social difficulties. Because of the persistent economic problems and the fact that most privatizable companies were running a deficit or were in the process of liquidation, private investors showed little interest in acquiring state-controlled companies. Their reticence was reinforced by the unions' demand that the privatizations must not infringe on the principle of employment security. Given these difficulties, the privatization process was not effectively begun until March 1992, with the sale of 70% of the shares of Aget-Heraklis, the country's major cement manufacturer, to the Italian group Feruzzi (Catsiapis, 1992).[16]

In 1992, the Greek parliament ratified the Maastricht Treaty (TEU) by 286 votes to 8. This ratification, like that of the SEA, was aided largely by the EC's commitment to increasing aid in the area of economic and social cohesion policies (ESCPs) (see Part Two). On this occasion, the Mitsokakis government stated its resolve to have the country accepted within the EMU. Most observers consider however that Greece, which did not manage to join the EMS, would be unable to meet the convergence criteria set for the implementation of the first phase of the EMU (see Chapter 1, note 15), unless it managed to restructure its economy dramatically and bring about a change in mentalities. The progress of the economic and social situation since 1992, however, shows no sign of such drastic changes. In 1992, the Greek economy was seriously affected by the crisis in Yugoslavia.[17] Furthermore, the progress made thanks to the austerity policy – lowering the inflation rate to 14.4%, a light improvement in the GDP growth rate of 0.9%, the elimination of the moving salary scale, tightening of fiscal controls and the social security deficit

– was counterbalanced by a 33.4% increase in the BT deficit and the refusal of several members of the government to apply the spending cuts stipulated in the stabilization plan. The privatization process, for its part, had made little progress, as the state only managed to sell one public company, the EAS, in charge of public transit in Athens. The government nevertheless announced 80 privatizations for 1993, including that of the telephone company (OTE) and various hotel complexes belonging to the Greek tourist organization (EOT) (Catsiapis, 1993, 221–2).

This vast operation aimed at dismantling the public sector was fated to remain at the project stage, however. Since the Mitsokakis government had already been reduced to a minority in September 1993 by the defection of three members who disagreed with its policy on Macedonia,[18] early elections were held in October 1993, which resulted in the PASOK returning to power with an absolute majority of seats. Having reproached the Mitsokakis government, during the period 1990–93 and the electoral campaign, of having provoked a recession and higher unemployment through its offer restriction measures, the PASOK abandoned the SMs instigated by the ND, upon its return to office. It proposed as an alternative a supply-side expansionary policy. The aim of this policy was to raise the level of capital investments from 17% to 26% before the end of the century, through increasing public spending and new resources allocated to the Southern European countries by the EC through the 'Growth Initiative', the 'Cohesion Fund' and the ESCPs of the Structural Funds (SFs) that are aimed at offsetting the negative effects of building the EMU (see Part Two). In an attempt to reduce inflation, the PASOK undertook the negotiation of a new social contract between the state, business and the trade unions, which would permit control over the prices of public services and goods while slowing down the rate of salary increases. It also promised a reform of the tax system, which consisted in increasing rates and levels of taxation while eliminating fraud. After denouncing the ND's privatization program, the Papandreou government renationalized the company EAS in 1993, but committed itself to privatizing the OTE telephone company and the DEH electricity company in 1994.

In fact, the economic policy of the PASOK between 1993 and 1996 was characterized both by the pursuit of SMs undertaken by the ND and the absence of significative SCMs. The illness and the retirement of Papandreou in fall 1995, that gave the opportunity to Kostas Simitis, the leader of the liberal faction, to be appointed as Prime Minister and to reshuffle the cabinet in order to entrust economic ministries to liberals elements,[19] did not bring about a radical change of the economic policy. Indeed, Simitis's room for manoeuvre remained limited because of the persistent influence of Papandreou and his nationalist and socialist supporters within the cabinet, the party and the state apparatus. Many observers believe that the death of Papandreou, in July 1996, as well as the reinforcement of external constraints inherent to the establishment of EMU in 1999, will favour the definitive conversion of the PASOK leaders to economic liberalism. However, the analysis of the conditions which have determined Greek economic choices since 1977 demonstrates that these prospects are probably too optimistic (see Part Two).

5 Comparative Results of Southern European Economic Policies

Specialists in the field do not necessarily all use the same criteria for measuring the success of the adjustment process. Nelson and colleagues (Nelson, 1990a) consider the latter to be successful when the government has managed to adopt and apply a coherent set of SMs and SCMs of a period of several years. The content of the preceding three chapters and Tables 2, 6 and 7 reveal that as regards this criterion, economic adjustment has been a failure in Greece and a relative success in Spain and Portugal.

Other authors, notably Haggard and Kaufman (1992) and Haggard and Webb (1994a) justifiably consider that the evaluation of the degree of success of the adjustment process must also take into account the attainment of the specific economic objectives targeted by the SMs and the SCMs. It should be remembered in this regard that the goal of the SMs is to offset, even eliminate, macro-economic imbalances, whereas that of the SCMs is to liberalize the laws and institutions which govern the functioning of the economic system, in order to increase its openness and competitiveness. Both series of reforms have as a final common goal the improvement of long-term growth. The major indicators in measuring the success of the SMs are the lowering of the inflation rate, the reduction of the public administration debt, the decrease in government budget deficits and the elimination or substantial lightening of negative BT and CAB balances. The primary instruments for measuring the effectiveness of the SCMs are the indicators of increased productivity of labour and the competitiveness of companies. In this chapter, I will verify whether the failure of adjustment in Greece and its relative success in the Iberian countries are confirmed by these indicators.

THE REDUCTION OF INFLATION

The figures in Table 9 show that the results in this respect obtained by Spain and Portugal are clearly superior to those of Greece, even though the latter made definite progress between 1992 and 1994. They indicate in fact that between 1980 and 1994, Greek inflation rates declined from 21.9% to 10.2%, whereas those of Spain and Portugal dropped from 16.5% to 4.8% and from 21.6% to 5.6% respectively. At the dawn of the convergence standard set by the EMU (3%), the performances of Spain and Portugal nevertheless appear in a less favourable light, since they, along with those of Greece, are the worst among the 15 member states (Table 8).

The fact that the Iberian countries have succeeded in controlling their inflation better than Greece can scarcely be explained by the adoption of more restrictive monetary policies, since Greek interest rates remained higher than Spanish and Portuguese rates during the period 1980–92 (Table 10). Nor can this be attributed to stricter control over public and private consumption, since these two components of the offer grew at a comparable rate in all three countries during the period under consideration (Table 10). It is due to the fact that because of a sharper increase in GDP growth rates during the second half of the eighties, the imbalance between supply and demand was less pronounced in Spain and Portugal (Table 10). The more positive progress of growth rates in these countries is itself linked to a more marked increase in direct foreign investment (DFI), of primarily European origin,[1] during this period (Table 12).

THE DECREASE IN PUBLIC DEBT AND DEFICITS

The figures in Tables 13 and 15 demonstrate that as a percentage of GDP, the total public debt and its primary component, the central government debt, grew by a far greater amount in Greece that in Spain and Portugal between 1980 and 1992. In 1994, the total public debt of Greece represented 121.3% of its GDP, whereas in Spain and Portugal, this was equal to 63.5 % and 70.4% of GDP (Table 8). Compared with the EMU norm, which is 60%, Greece was situated in the tail-end of the 15 member states along with Belgium and Italy, whereas Spain and Portugal were classed fifth and eighth respectively.

Moreover, the public debt of Greece constitutes a more serious source of concern for three reasons. On the one hand the share of loans negotiated with foreign financial institutions has risen sharply since 1986, to reach 20.7% in 1992, whereas in Spain this has progressed in far more limited manner and has dropped spectacularly in Portugal (Table 14). Given the unfavourable exchange rates of the Southern European currencies compared with those of more economically healthy countries, this externalization process makes the Greek public debt more costly. On the other hand, the interest rates that Greek public institutions have to pay are higher than those that are assumed by the Spanish and Portuguese institutions (Table 10). Finally the state's ability to repay is more problematic in the case of Greece.[2]

The uneven increase of public debt in the three countries is attributable to the different evolution of public deficits. Between 1980 and 1992, the central government deficit in percentage of GDP rose from 4.5% to 25.2% in Greece, while it fell back from 5.4% to 3% in Spain and from 10.9% to 7.8% in Portugal (Table 16). Despite a significative decline beyond 1992, the Greek public deficit still corresponded to 14.1% of GDP in 1994, which represented the worst performance among the 15 member states in relation to the EMU convergence standard, that is 3% of GDP. On the other hand, the 1994 Spanish and Portuguese public deficits were equal to 7% and 6.2% of their GDP, a more positive performance, yet one which remains below that of the majority of the countries in the European Union (Table 8).

It must be observed that if Spain and Portugal have seen the weight of their public debts lessened more than in Greece, it is mostly because of their higher growth rates, during the second half of eighties, rather than their budgetary policies. An examination of the national accounts (Tables 17, 18, 19) shows that the gap between expenditures and revenues was not in absolute value higher in Greece than in Spain between 1980 and 1993. It also indicates that the public deficit has increased almost continuously during the eighties in all three countries; however, the scope of the deficit and its progression were much less pronounced in Portugal than in Spain and Greece. In Spain and Greece the deficit has literally soared between 1988 and 1991: the Spanish deficit rose from US$9.1 billion to US$17.1 billion while the Greek deficit grew from US$6.1 billion to US$13.4 billion (no data are available for Portugal). The increase of Southern European public deficits is mainly due to the fact that the growth of revenues, generated by fiscal reforms, did not compensate the cost of social policies betterment. Portugal kept a tighter control on its deficit because it did not invest as much as Greece and Spain in the improvement of education, health and social security.

However, we cannot conclude that SMs did not help at all to lessen the weight of public deficits in Spain and Portugal. The fact that both countries have implemented austerity measures in a more coherent and systematic manner than Greece, during the second half of eighties, has without a doubt stimulated the foreign and domestic private investments and subsequently favoured the revival of internal demand.

IMPROVEMENT IN THE EXTERNAL TRADE BALANCE

According to the adjustment doctrine, the liberalization of trade constitutes a crucial condition for the improvement of BT and CABs. In this domain, Greece, Spain and Portugal have all respected the precepts of the doctrine by signing the membership treaties and the SEA. Analysis of the foreign trade figures for the three countries between 1980 and 1992 nevertheless shows that these agreements have not produced the anticipated beneficial effects.

It was foreseeable that membership in the EEC would reinforce the commercial dependence of the Southern European countries in relation to the community market. Figures 1 and 2 show that a major share of the imports and exports previously carried out with the rest of the world have been replaced by new trade with the states of the community. The United States, for its part, has remained a marginal trade partner. Between 1980 and 1992, the total share of imports from the EC rose from 40% to 62% in Greece, from 30% to 60% in Spain and from 40% to 75% in Portugal, whereas imports from the rest of world diminished during the same period, from 55% to 30% in Greece and Spain and from 48% to 28% in Portugal (Figure 1). The share of total exports towards the EC during this period increased from 48% to 65% in Greece, from 42% to 62% in Spain, and from 58% to 68% in Portugal, whereas those of exports to third countries fell from 48% to 38% in Greece, from 50% to 30% in Spain, and from 35% to 25% in Portugal (Figure 2). This more pronounced insertion within the European market contributed to and stimulated the foreign trade of the new member states, since the volume and value of their total imports and exports rose significantly between 1986 and 1991, to taper off somewhat during the recession at the beginning of the nineties (Table 21 and Figure 3). Nevertheless, these developments were accompanied by a dramatic deterioration in the intra-EC, extra-EC, and total BT balances of the three countries (Table 22). Thus between 1984 and 1994, the value of Greece's BT deficit had tripled, while those of Spain and Portugal quadrupled. These deficits are the sole cause of the negative CAB balance, since in all three countries the other CAB items – balance of services and invisibles – recorded surpluses. Relevant data show that the degradation of the BT balance is due essentially to an increase in the value of imports that is higher that of exports.

Analysis of the countries' trade structure (Figures 4 and 5) provides a better understanding of the causes of this imbalance. On the one hand, a drop in raw material imports (RM) related to a higher degree of energy self-sufficiency was accompanied by a marked increase in imports of manufactured goods (MG) with high-added value (machines and transportation equipment, IGE); on the other hand, exports of RM stagnated (in Greece) or declined (in Spain and Portugal) and exports of MG, made of primarily low added-value ECG in Greece and Portugal, either did not increase (in Greece) or increased to a lesser degree than those of imports of the same type (in Spain and Portugal). These observations reveal that membership in the EC did not allow the three new member states to compensate, as they had hoped, for the expected increase in MG imports through higher exports of agricultural goods and MG.

There are two factors primarily responsible for these disappointing results. On the one hand, the growth of MG imports was stronger than anticipated, due mostly to the boom in DFI (see above). Several studies (ECC, 1990b; Ethier, 1991; Heinz-Jurgen, 1991) have shown that the DFIs, a strong proportion of which were concentrated into construction and industry, stimulated production of, and demand for, equipment and consumer goods. The latter generated increased imports of MG, on the one hand because they came largely from the MNFs, and on the other because the Southern European countries were unable to satisfy it due to the limited range or higher prices of their industrial products.

On the other hand, the three economies were also unable to sufficiently improve the competitiveness of their exports particularly in the high added-value sectors, compared with those of the newly industrialized countries (NICs) and the EC countries (Ethier, 1991). The data in Table 23 are revealing in this regard. It shows that between 1970 and 1989, the contribution of the various industrial branches to the overall added value of the manufacturing sector remained the same in Portugal, whereas in Greece the share of added value produced by the machine and vehicle branch and that of 'other industries' (a category which includes intermediate and durable consumer goods) diminished in favour of those produced by the traditional industries, (agro-food, textiles, clothing). On the other hand, in Spain, the percentage of added value created by the machine and vehicle industries increased from 16% to 25%. However, the 'other industries' branch saw its share decrease from 45% to 39%. The annual average growth rate of productivity per employee in industry constitutes another indicator of the changing face of competitiveness of this sector. The data from the EC reveal that the average increase in these rates, for the decade 1980–90, was 2.3% in Spain and 2.4% in Portugal. Although not bad, these performances are insufficient, on the one hand because they are lower than those obtained by the majority of industrialized countries,[3] and, on the other, because the Southern European countries have to make up lost time in this area. The difficulties with regard to the growth of productivity and competitiveness of industry are linked to several causes. Three of these are particularly important. On the one hand, investments devoted to the purchase of new equipment goods were clearly insufficient in Greece and declined in Spain and Portugal after a period of strong growth between 1986 and 1989 (see Table 24). On the other hand, although the growth in the unit cost of salaries diminished in the three countries between 1980 and 1994, this decrease was less than that recorded in the EC countries, particularly in Greece and Portugal (Table 25), so that the countries of Southern Europe saw their only true comparative advantage being gradually eroded. Finally the structural reforms needed to improve the performance of the production system were either shelved (in Greece), or characterized by various limits which reduced their effectiveness (in Spain and Portugal).

THE IMPLEMENTATION OF STRUCTURAL REFORMS

The record of Greece in this regard is very negative, since no significant reforms of the institutions and the structure of the productive system were undertaken by the government between 1975 and 1995. It is true that Greece, together with Spain and Portugal, was one of the major beneficiaries of the ESCPs managed by the EC's SF, thanks to which several modernization projects – including those of agricultural structures and the transportation and communication infrastructures – were carried out on its territory during the eighties and nineties. In spite of the large sums of money invested (see Chapter 4, note 5 and Table 32), the impact of these projects was very limited, however; on the one hand, because they were not carried out in the framework of a coherent national structural change policy, and, on the other, because the authorities often avoided the objectives and the operating and follow-up rules of the projects that were established in Brussels (D'Auhert, 1994).

In this case, the economic system continued to be dominated by the traditional centres of activity and employment: agriculture, based on small, undermechanized and unproductive family operations, giving rise to low revenues and urban exodus; and the tertiary sector, made up primarily of the public administration and secondarily by small business and crafts (Tables 26 and 27). The industry underwent a certain degree of modernization with the decline of the ECG labour-intensive industries and the development of the IGE capital-intensive industries;[4] but this transformation was accompanied by a decrease of the manufacturing sector to the GDP and, even more serious, of decreased productivity in the capital intensive branches (Table 23). Overall, the situation of industry deteriorated, either because of the inaction of the government in response to the structural problems in the sector – small size of companies,[5] insufficient means of communication between major cities and regions, absence of synergy between small, medium and large enterprises, excessive centralization of economic activities in Athens, lack of institutions and brain power able to develop research and development (R&D) activities on the basis of knowledge transfer carried out by foreign firms – or because of the negative effects of the initiatives implemented by the governments. In fact, not only did the governments not carry out the structural reforms that were required, but, through a variety of inappropriate or irrational measures, they contributed towards amplifying existing problems. Among these measures should be mentioned the decrease in the relative share of investments aimed at the formation of fixed capital,[6] the choice of increasing imports of equipment goods rather than beefing up budgets devoted to R&D, state takeover of the lame ducks in the industry, and the increase in salary costs.

The case of Spain is very different. As we saw in Chapter 2, the UCD and the PSOE governments applied a set of consistent adjustment measures, which, in the context of membership in the EC, encouraged the MNFs to increase their direct investments considerably. These, however, were concentrated into branches that were already multinationalized (agro-food, automobiles, computers, chemistry, electronics),[7] whose production is primarily aimed at the local market. Consequently, the activity of the most competitive companies had no stimulating effects on exports; on the contrary, it brought about an increase in IGE imports which contributed towards a worsening of the BT deficit (Mougey, 1991; Mattei and Lacharme, 1992). Only an improvement in the competitiveness of the other industrial branches could have offset this tendency. In this area, government interventions, although very numerous, were unable to produce the desired effects. On the one hand, the measures adopted to slow the growth of salaries were too timid in comparison with those applied in the competing countries, with the result that Spain lost progressively its comparative advantage at the level of salary costs.[8] On the other hand, the transfer to the Autonomous Communities of a share of the intervention powers and the resources related to industry reduced the effectiveness of state action in this domain. Finally, the industrial reconversion measures that were applied between 1982 and 1987, in spite of considerable aid to industry, did not yield a sufficient improvement in the productivity and competitiveness of industry because they were designed with only short-term goals in view, because they only affected certain sectors, and because they were badly coordinated with the other instruments of the economic policy. The errors committed by the Spanish authorities are not attributable to them alone, since they applied the industrial reconversion measures prescribed by the EC which, for its part, had no alternative industrial policy to propose to the member states.

It was only at the end of the eighties, in the context of the SEA, that the Community availed itself of an overall industrial policy. This policy, which was liberal in inspiration, rejected the interventionist approach of the Keynesian model, according to which the state planned and supported the development of certain sectors. Rather, it recommended that governments create an environment favourable to increasing productivity and the competitiveness of all the industries, through the reorientation and coordination of various economic and social policies. Its primary objectives were:

1. to reform the education system, in order to increase the quality of training and its adjustment to the needs of the labour market;
2. to increase the availability of capital through taxing savings, the more effective use of public resources, the reform of the financial system and of the securities market;
3. to strengthen technological capability through increased R&D spending and the development of closer cooperation between the state and the companies operating in this domain;
4. to optimize the functioning of the markets through improvements in the circulation of information and communication between buyers and sellers; and
5. to develop solidarity between the various economic agents: governments, trade unions, management, and professionals.

According to Arancequi (1989), Myro Sanchez (1990), Vinals (1992) and Espina (1993), Spain began to implement this new policy during the period 1987–89. Under the direction of the Minister of the Economy, Carlos Solchaga, the government initiatives aimed primarily at reducing prices and production costs, at privatizing or reconverting enterprises and sectors in difficulty, increasingly gave priority to improving professional training, to increasing the quality of products, to strengthening industrial cooperation and to maximizing the R&D effort. These changes led to an increase in the export growth rate from 4.7% to 11.5% and a reduction in the growth rate of internal demand from 7.8% to 3.3% between 1989 and 1991 (Argandoña, 1991). Yet they were unable to slow the progress of the BT deficit, which rose from –19.3 billion ecus in 1989 to –27.9 billion ecus in 1992 (Table 22). This situation explains why the socialist government confirmed the change in direction of its industrial policy in the convergence plan of 1992. Several studies carried out that time, including that of ICEX (1992) concluded that this plan, in conjunction with the strengthening of the ESCPs of the EC's SF, would bring about an improvement in the competitiveness of companies and the external trade balance. These forecasts have been partly confirmed since the BT deficits have stabilized since 1992 (see Table 22).

In Portugal, the SCMs aimed at improving the productivity and competitiveness of the productive system were on a larger scale than those in Greece, but were tardier and more limited than those in Spain. Until 1986–87, they were essentially focused on the privatization of nationalized companies. It was only after membership in the EC that the PSDP government undertook the structural reforms. These reforms were primarily carried out through the ESCPs of the EC's SF, but they also benefited from support and considerable involvement on the part of the Portuguese government apparatus. The modernization of agriculture, viticulture and fishing began in 1986; as for the modernization of infrastructure and industries, this began in 1988 with the adoption of the *Programa especifico da desenvolvimento da industria portuguesa* (PEDIP), that got under way during the period 1988–93. The PEDIP has not had any significant impact to date on the performance of industry since the implementation of projects only started in 1989–90 and has continued at a slower pace than anticipated. Given its ambitious objectives and its large budget,[9] and considering that it was renewed with an equivalent budget for a period of five years in 1993, it would be highly surprising if this program does not result in an improved level of competitiveness for Portuguese industry and, consequently, a reduction in the exterior trade deficit in the future.

CONCLUSION

In a study devoted to the evaluation of the IMF stabilization programs, Remmer pointed that 'there is only a moderate correlation between the implementation of IMF prescriptions and the achievement of desired economic results' (Remmer, 1986, 7). The previous analysis confirms this diagnosis in two ways. On the one hand it shows that the adoption and the long-term application of a coherent set of SMs and SCMs does not necessarily guarantee the attainment of all the objectives aimed at by these measures. Although the performances of Spain and Portugal, from the point of view of reducing inflation, debt and public deficit, are better than that of Greece, they nonetheless remain below the convergence norms set by the EMU; furthermore, neither of the countries has managed to re-establish the BT balance. On the other hand, the analysis reveals that the progress recorded by Spain and Portugal is largely due to the increased economic growth generated by a more pronounced increase in DFI than in Greece. This is only partly ascribable to the governments' SMs and SCMs. A recent EC study reveals in fact that the decisions of the companies to invest more in Spain and Portugal than in Greece (ECC, 1994), were largely motivated by the greater geographical proximity of the Iberian markets and the existence within these of more modern and efficient telecommunications and transport infrastructures. Finally, the analysis indicates that the structural reforms cannot, in one decade, transform a semi-industrialized dependent economy into one capable of competing with the industrialized economies, with the result that the progress in growth feeds the external trade deficit instead of solving it. This observation tends to confirm the view put forward by Nelson (1990b), according to which the success of adjustment depends above all on the irreversibility of the adjustment policy. Measured in the light of this norm, the prospects for the adjustment process in Spain and Portugal are clearly better than in Greece, despite new hopes aroused by recent political changes in that country.

Part Two

The Determinants of
Successful Adjustment:
Lessons from Southern Europe

As indicated in the Introduction, the major conclusion that emerges from recent studies is that democracies – old and new – are no less likely than authoritarian regimes to succeed in the economic adjustment process. On the other hand, there are three conditions that are judged to be decisive for every type of political regime:

1. the determination of all members of government to adopt a consistent program of stabilization and structural change measures;
2. the support of a team of competent economists and managers, who are united and convinced of the soundness of these measures, within the higher bureaucracy or parallel structures; and
3. the ability of the government to apply these measures in a systematic, long-term manner without compromising the stability of the political system.

In this second part, I shall concentrate on the factors that determine the attainment of the first and third conditions *within democracies* in order to better understand the different economic choices and performances of Southern European countries during the post-authoritarian period. I will not deal with the second condition, since my research has not permitted the gathering of sufficient pertinent information on the attitudes and roles of the Greek, Spanish and Portuguese higher bureaucracies in regard to the adjustment process.

6 The Governments' Commitment to Undertaking Reforms

NON-DECISIVE DETERMINANTS

Comparative analysis of the decision making processes that determined the economic choices of the new democracies shows that most of the factors that are judged *a priori* to be favourable to a government's committing itself to undertaking adjustment measures do not in fact constitute a constant decisive influence in this regard. Governments are not necessarily more inclined to undertake a process of economic cleansing and liberalization when an economic crisis is serious or when they are at the beginning of an electoral mandate; they are not necessarily more resolved to adopt an adjustment program when they are in the majority, dominated by a party of the right or submitted to pressure on the part of their partners and foreign investors. The comparative analysis of the Southern European cases largely confirms these conclusions.

The extent of the economic crisis

As discussed in Chapter 1, Greece, Spain and Portugal, as a result of their similar prior economic development, were confronted with macro-economic imbalances of a comparable size and nature from the middle of the seventies (see Table 1). In spite of the persistence and worsening of these problems during the second world recession of 1980–83, neither the Greek nor Portuguese governments managed to reach a consensus on the justification for an overall, consistent adjustment program between 1975 and 1983. Only the Spanish UCD and PSOE cabinets demonstrated cohesion and determination in this regard, by ratifying and developing the program reforms developed in the *Pactos de la Moncloa* in 1977.

The fact that the economic situation deteriorated further in Greece and Portugal than in Spain in the years following 1983 – higher inflation rates (Table 9); weaker GDP growth rates (Table 10); less direct foreign investment (Table 12); a sharper increase in the size of the public debt in relation to GDP (Table 13), and so on – contributed towards convincing certain Greek and

Portuguese political leaders of the need for a reform. No Greek government, however, managed to attain a sufficiently solid consensus to push through the adoption of a comprehensive, consistent set of adjustment measures before 1990. The ND government of 1990–93 was the first – and the only – government that was able to propose a series of substantial reforms. In Portugal the impact of the worsening economic crisis seems to have been more profound, since the large majority of socialists and social-democratic leaders rallied around the adjustment objective after 1993. This permitted the PSP–PSDP coalition government to announce a set of stabilization and structural change measures between 1993 and 1995, which were continued and further developed by subsequent PSDP governments.

Government set-up and ideology

Analysis of the Southern European cases confirms that the composition – majority or minority – and ideology – whether of the left, the centre or the right – of the party in power are not decisive determining factors of the government's will to undertake the adjustments to the economy (Tables 2, 6, 7, 28, 29, 30).

Several minority or coalition cabinets successively came to power in Portugal between 1974 and 1987; several of these refused to contemplate economic adjustment measures (the first four provisional AFM governments (1974); the two AD governments (1979–83)); some, on the other hand, adopted certain liberalization measures (the fifth provisional AFM government (1975), the PSP minority government (1976–77), the PSP–CDS coalition governments (1978–79)), while others finally announced a relatively substantial and complete program of stabilization and structural change (the PSP–PSDP coalition (1983–85) the minority PSDP government (1985–87)). The choices of the Southern European majority governments were equally as diverse in economic matters. Although the majority PSDP cabinets (1987–95) of the UCD (1977–92) and of the PSOE (1982–93) opted resolutely for a policy of austerity, all the PASOK and ND majority governments (with the exception of 1990–93) either refused to ratify such a policy (1977–95), or adopted only a limited number of temporary adjustment measures (1985–90; 1993–95).

These very diverse attitudes among the Southern European governments cannot be explained by the ideological orientation of the ruling parties or whether they are located at the right, centre or left of the political spectrum. In Spain and Portugal, both the centre-right governments dominated or made up of socialists (PSP, PSOE), and the centre-right governments led by democrats and Christian democrats (PSDP, UCD) were resolutely committed to the path of adjustment. On the other hand, several rightist governments (those of the AD) and certain governments further to the left (those of the AFM), refused this option. In Greece, both the rightist ND governments and the leftist PASOK governments showed themselves to be highly resistant to any liberal economic policy until 1985. Subsequently, both types of governments effected a marked or limited changeover towards positions that were favourable to adjustment.

The electoral cycles

According to the Public Choice school, the political choices of governments are essentially motivated by the desire to retain their electoral support. According to this logic, political leaders would be more inclined to adopt unpopular measures at the beginning of an electoral mandate because they calculate that either the application of these decisions will produce beneficial effects in the short and medium term, or that the effects of these decisions will be of short duration, which will allow them to return to power in the next elections. In the case of adjustment measures, this logic is only partly applicable, since the costs of these measures are severe and long-lasting, and most of the positive effects are only realized over the long term and then only for certain groups of citizens. Although stabilization measures may reduce the inflation rate and improve the BP for a period of up to five years, they have recessionist effects which often extend beyond this time frame. Structural change measures, for their part, entail numerous severe social costs that will extend over a period of ten years or more; their positive effects, such as relaunching investments and economic growth, are felt more in the medium and long term than in the short term and do not benefit the entire population (Nelson, 1994b).

This no doubt explains why it has turned out to be impossible to establish a universal correlation between the electoral cycles and these governments' initiation of liberal reforms. On this question, Williamson and Haggard (1994, 571–2) observe that while certain governments profited from the honeymoon at the beginning of their mandate to launch their program of reforms (for example, Poland and New Zealand), others refused to undertake this step (Brazil) or postponed adopting unpopular decisions until the end of their mandate (Colombia). My analysis of the seven European cases totally corroborates this diagnosis. The first UCD government negotiated the *Pactos de la Moncloa* in October 1977, four months after the elections of June of the same year; the first PSOE government adopted a far wider and more radical program of stabilization and structural change measures in the first months following its accession to power, in December 1982. The

PSP–PSDP (1983–85), the PSDP (1987–97) and the ND (1990–93) governments announced and initiated liberal-style reforms as soon as they came to power. The second PASOK government, which was also a majority government, announced a number of stabilization measures after its election in 1985 but abandoned them in 1988. However, the third PSOE (1989–93) and the PSDP (1987–91) governments announced a new and more severe program of SMs and SCMs – the *Plano de Convergencia* (1992) and the QUANTUM 1 (1991) at the end of their mandate. Otherwise the ND and PASOK governments which were in power between 1975 and 1985 refused to adopt any adjustment measures.

External conditional aids

The studies devoted to economic adjustment policies do not accord any great importance to external factors, since they consider that the attitude of the decision makers in this regard is more determined by psychological and internal institutional factors. The only variable of this kind that has been explored in any depth is that of conditional external aid, that is, the various measures for rescheduling and relaxing the conditions for paying back the public debt, the loan guarantees and new loans awarded by international and national financial institutions (IMF, World Bank, United States Agency of International Development (USAID), and so on) to nations in difficulty, in return for their adoption of stabilization and structural change measures. The studies carried out by Remmer (1986), Nelson (1992), Kahler (1990, 1992), Mosley et al. (1991) and Haggard and Webb (1994b) indicate that these constraints have a relative, circumstantial impact on the attitudes of political leaders. They may convince a divided, recalcitrant government to undertake a process of reforms only if it is faced with a severe financial, economic crisis, if the state is highly dependent on external aid and if no opposition movements exist within the political system and civil society that are likely or judged to be likely to block the reforms. In cases in which the state is relatively autonomous with regard to external financial support or the economic crisis is less serious, or its market is important for foreign investors, or if it has to face challenges from various groups of actors, the conditional aids would be unable to modify the attitude of a government that is hesitant about, or opposed to, a neo-liberal shift.

The reactions of the seven European governments to the conditional loans obtained during the period following 1975 confirm these conclusions. In 1975, the IMF and the EC granted a 150 million ecu emergency loan to the Portuguese government of General Pinheiro de Azevedo, on condition that it adopted certain stabilization and structural adjustment measures. In 1977 and 1983, the IMF awarded new credits to the PSP and PSP–PSDP governments in return for stepping up economic austerity measures. In 1985, the PASOK government was awarded financial aid from the EC, conditional on its implementing a stabilization program. In all four cases, the government gave in to the demands of the creditors and ratified a certain number of SMs and/or SCMs, as a result of their worrisome financial situation and their dependence on the support of these financial backers. Nevertheless, these measures were totally or partially suspended a few months or years after the aid was received because of their denunciation by the opposition forces and/or by certain members of the government.

External support and non-conditional aids

On the whole, however, the Southern European cases are better suited to testing the impact of a conciliatory and cooperative international environment than the impact of coercive external aids on the economic choices of governments. In fact, whereas the new Latin American, Asian, East European and African democracies (NDs) were faced with demands for adjustment by western governments and international financial institutions during or immediately after their inauguration, the Greek, Spanish and Portuguese NDs retained, for almost 15 years, a substantial degree of autonomy with regard to their economic policy, while benefiting from non-conditional aids from the EC. The prescriptions of the Maastricht Treaty considerably reduced this autonomy, yet they did not put in question the non-conditional aids awarded by the EC.

The conciliatory EC attitude (1975–85)

Even though the democratic transitions (DTs) in Greece, Spain and Portugal (1974–78) took place in the context of economic crisis (see Chapter 1), the new democratic regimes were not submitted to strong external pressures with regard to the adoption of stabilization and structural change measures in the first years of their existence. The first explanation for this fact is the *timing of DTs in Southern Europe*. Indeed, from 1975 to 1983, the western governments continued to defend Keynesian growth strategies while the financial institutions continued with their liberal aid policies. During this period, the only conditional aid came from the IMF and other multilateral public loans aimed at the elimination of BP deficits that requested the adoption of short-term stabilization measures by the borrower states. It was only after the second oil shock of 1979, and the second global economic recession of 1980–83, events that provoked a dramatic increase in inflation combined with a severe drop in revenues, that the United States Federal Reserve and other financial institutions decided to increase their interest rates very substantially, a decision that sparked a financial crisis in most indebted nations, causing the IMF and other aid agencies to henceforth make their various aid measures conditional on the adoption, by the receiving states, of a series of stabilization and structural change measures.

The second factor that contributed to a reduction of external pressures in favour of adjustment was the main objective of the negotiations and requirements for membership in the EC (1975/78–1981/86). Indeed, the major outcome of these negotiations was *the consolidation of Southern European NDs*; the improvement in the economic climate and the economic benefits expected from the widening of the Common Market remained secondary objectives, at least until 1983. Political leaders in Greece, as well as in Spain and Portugal, hoped that integration into the EC would help to rapidly consolidate their fragile democracies, which were at that time menaced by plots and *putschs* by rightist elements in the army and, in Portugal, by the possible radicalization of a faction of the revolutionary forces of the left. For its part, the EC hoped for a stabilization of the political situation in all three countries (EEC, 1976, 1978a, 1978b), both to assure the security of its southern borders and to create a climate favourable to an anticipated speeding up of European integration.[1] The priority accorded to democratic consolidation and the existence, in Greece and Portugal (Verney, 1990; Ethier, 1994b), of strong opposition to EC membership and liberal economic policies explains why Brussels did not require austerity measures from the three candidate states during the negotiations.

There was another important factor motivating this attitude in Brussels. As discussed in previous chapters, the *EC wanted the Southern European countries to improve their social policies* before the end of the negotiations, in order to comply with the Community's social regulations[2] and to bring the cost of their social regimes in line with the average in other member states, so as to avoid a North–South transfer of capital, companies and jobs after entry into the Common Market.[3] It may appear surprising that the Community should ask the Southern European countries to increase their social spending while they were facing a serious economic crisis. One the one hand, none of the member states, except for Great Britain, was particularly concerned at that time about the growth of budgetary deficits (see above); furthermore, the EC considered that the reform of the tax systems (introduction of the VAT), which was also conditional on the finalization of membership negotiations, would allow the three candidate countries to substantially increase their revenues and to control the state of their public finances.

EC non-conditional aid (1985–1993)[4]

Upon entry into the EC, the three Southern European member states were obliged to abide by the provisions of the EC membership treaties. These provisions required the abolition of all barriers to the free movement of goods, capital, services and workers, and the harmonization of national legislations with the EC regulations ensuing from the Treaty of Rome during various transition periods, the longest of which extended over four years (1981–85) in the case of Greece and seven years (1986–93) in the case of the Iberian countries. However, apart from these liberalization measures, the treaties did not formally prescribe any program of stabilization or structural adjustment for the new member states (see Chapters 2, 3 and 4). On the other hand, they gave Greece, Spain and Portugal the opportunity to benefit from very substantial aids through the CAP (see Chapter 2, note 17), ESCPs and the Integrated Mediterranean Programs (IMPs) managed by the three SFs.

The adoption of the SEA in 1986, which required the abolition of all remaining technical, fiscal and physical barriers to the free movement of goods, capital, services and persons between member states by 1993 (Chapter 1, note 14) was accompanied, in 1988, by a reform of the SF (Ethier, 1993). This reform redirected the ESCPs toward five objectives:

1. the development of backward regions (70% of the credits);
2. the renewal of declining industrial areas;
3. the fight against long-term unemployment;
4. the upgrading of labour skills; and
5. the modernization of agriculture and the professional training of farmers.

It also doubled the budget devoted to ESCPs for the period 1988–93. Since, along with Ireland, they were the most backward regions in the EC, Greece, Spain and Portugal received 10 624, 11 350 and 7503 million ecus[5] respectively during the period 1988–93 (see Table 32). By means of this reform, the EC wished to limit the worsening of structural inequalities generated by the acceleration of market integration and to gain the political support of poorer member states to the SEA. These motivations, such as the new SF reform principle of 'additionality of spending' that obliged the recipient states to invest into the ESCPs equivalent amounts of money to those injected by the EC (see Table 31), explain why the latter did not make its aids conditional on the implementation of adjustment measures until 1991–93.

TEU constraints and aid

The adoption of the TEU by the Council, in 1991, modified the EC's non-interventionist attitude toward the economic choices of its member states.

Yet, as previously indicated (Chapter 1, note 15), the TEU foresees the establishment of an EMU for 1999. According to the TEU, entry into the EMU, which involves acceptance of a single currency (the Euro) and submission to the authority of a common central bank, requires the liberalization of national economic policies and adjustment measures before 1997 in order to comply with the convergence norms prescribing the reduction of inflation, public debts, government deficits and interest rates. Arguing that the enforcement of the EMU provisions would limit their ability to apply the principle of 'additionality of spending' and consequently compromise the alleviation of socio-economic and regional disparities, the poorer member states – Ireland, Greece, Spain and Portugal – warned the EC that they could not obtain ratification of the TEU by their parliaments or citizens[6] without adopting a new and more generous aid package for the period 1993–99. These requests were successful. In Edinburgh, in December 1992, the Council of Ministers agreed to double, in real terms, the aid conceded to the four countries during the 1993–99 period. This objective was reached by a 50% increase in the budget devoted to ESCP objective 1 and by the creation of a 15 billion ecu Cohesion Fund (investments in energy infrastructures and transportation). These allowances were not formally conditional on the progress of the economic reforms required by the TEU. Nevertheless, Greece, which did not undertake any serious steps toward complying with the EMU convergence norms, unlike Portugal and Spain, which respectively accepted QUANTUM in 1991, and the Convergence Program in 1992, received less aid from the EC than the other two countries for the period 1994–99 (see Tables 31 and 32).

In conclusion, it is undeniable that the Keynesian, rather than liberal, orientation of the EC policy between 1975 and 1985, as well as the non-conditional aid awarded concurrently to the SEA between 1985 and 1993, created conditions that were conducive to the rejection or postponement of the adjustment measures by the Greek government during the seventies and eighties, and by the Portuguese government between 1974 and 1985. Nevertheless, these external conditions cannot be considered decisive in determining the economic choices of the Southern European states, since both the Spanish and Portuguese governments subsequent to 1983 resolutely opted for liberal economic policies. Furthermore, the fact that the ND and PASOK governments continued to be divided over the adjustment question beyond the adoption of the Maastricht Treaty, reveals that sanctions (a smaller amount of aid) and threats (exclusion from the EMU), did not play a more determining role on the attitudes of the political leaders.

Overall then, the study of the Southern European cases shows that whatever the attitudes of the international actors, these did not in every case influence the cohesion and resolution of the political leaders with regard to liberal reform. In this regard, it confirms the thesis of Nelson and colleagues, who claim that internal factors are the most decisive determinants of the economic choices of governments.

The nature of these determinants stands in need of clarification, however. The literature consulted, as we have seen, clearly shows that several internal variables – the size of the economic crisis, the majority composition of the government, the conservative ideology of the parties in power, the beginning of an electoral mandate – have no major, universal effect on the commitment of political leaders to liberal reforms. The literature is not very explicit, however, about the other internal factors likely to promote such commitment in all the cases under consideration.

DECISIVE DETERMINANTS

The evaluation of political risks

The very large majority of authors cited assert that the evaluation of the political risks inherent in the application of envisaged adjustment measures, always has a crucial influence on the economic choices of those elected to office. If they judge that the risks of political dissent are small, they will necessarily be more inclined to adopt and undertake SMs and SCMs. This assertion, however, remains strictly hypothetical, since it is practically impossible to verify what the calculations, suppositions, and individual and collective conclusions of the members of the cabinet were in such cases. Neither interviews with the latter nor studies of the transcripts of meetings – usually confidential – have yielded any reliable information about this aspect of the decision making process.

The commitment of governing parties to economic liberalism

Most specialists, including Nelson (1990b), consider moreover that the cohesion and resolution of the governing powers with regard to liberal reforms is fundamentally and universally determined by their appreciation of the *effectiveness* of the SMs and SCMs. If *all* cabinet members believe that the latter will in fact allow for a resolution of the economic crisis and improve growth, the government will not hesitate to undertake a neo-liberal shift. However, the authors are not very explicit about the factors that determine such confidence in the efficiency of SMs and SCMs. I think that most of them consider that the perceptions of the political leaders, at this level, are mainly influenced by the convictions and opinions of their economic advisers within the higher bureaucracy. However, this causal relation is obscured by the fact that they treat the government's commitment to undertaking reforms, and the support of the higher bureaucracy to the latter, as two independent variables.

The analysis of the Southern European cases permits the completion of this analysis by showing that the opinions – positive or negative – of individual decision makers and their respective parties concerning the *values of economic liberalism* also largely condition the assessment that a government makes of the relative effectiveness of the SMs and SCMs. These opinions are independent of the make-up of the cabinet and the ideological orientation of the party or parties that compose them. A majority single-party cabinet is no more favourable to the precepts of economic liberalism than a unicoloured, minority or multiparty government. Moreover, no significant correlation can be established between the historical position of one party on the political spectrum and its attitude – whether favourable or unfavourable – towards liberal economic ideology. In the three decades following the Second World War, in fact, the majority of parties were opposed to this ideology, either defending a nationalist, protectionist and interventionist vision of capitalism (left, centre-left and centre-right parties), or a socialist model (parties of the extreme left). Only certain small centrist formations of the liberal, radical and republican type have, to varying degrees, promoted the values of economic liberalism. The cleavages between the capitalist parties of the right, centre-right and centre-left were more ascribable to political, moral,[7] and social concepts than to their vision of the economic system. In the period following 1975, however, the majority of parties in the various political families moved, more or less rapidly and to differing degrees, towards liberal positions. This development began with the crisis of the Keynesian model and accelerated concurrently with the worsening of this crisis, with the increasing liberalization of international economic relations and with the fall of the communist regimes.

Analysis of the Greek, Spanish and Portuguese cases indicates that the speed and degree of ideological change that characterize the various political parties depends on the *nature* and the *extent* of the sociological and organizational transformations to which they have been subject for the past 25 years. Two factors are particularly crucial: the accession to power of a leader and a team convinced of the soundness of economic liberalism, and the ability of the new leadership to impose its program on the organization as a whole. This second condition itself depends on several variables: the modification of the membership, the executive, and the decision making and operational rules; the party's rootedness within civil society; the popularity of the leader among the general population and the militants; and the support of foreign brother organizations.

Greece

The New Democracy

As indicated in Chapter 4, the first two ND governments (1977–79; 1979–81), led by Constantin Caramanlis and George Rallis, did not undertake any economic liberalization programs, whereas the majority government of Constantin Mitsokakis (1990–93) set out on this course without, however, being able to apply all of the adjustment measures that had been adopted. These differences in performance are primarily due to changes that occurred with regard to leadership, ideological orientation and power relationships within the ND during the eighties.

The ND was created in 1974 by Caramanlis upon his return from exile. Caramanlis was a well-known figure in Greek political life, as he had founded the National Radical Union conservative party (ERE) during the fifties and led the government between 1955 and 1963. During this period, he encouraged national industrialization through state intervention and protection of the domestic market. However, his party remained divided and lacked a distinct ideological orientation, particularly in the economic domain. More of a pragmatist technocrat than an ideologue, he never managed to unify ERE on the basis of a clearly articulated program (Katsoudas, 1987, 92). ERE, which was characterized by factionalism and clientelism in common with all Greek parties, essentially remained a body for uniting several tendencies of the right that were opposed to communism (Mouzelis, 1976). Caramanlis' political thought developed during his years of exile in France. When he founded the ND in 1974, his objective was to make it a party distinct from ERE: a pluralist, modernist, democratic party open to the legalization of the KKE, and a partisan of membership in the EC and the North Atlantic Treaty Organization (NATO). Beyond these few new ideas, however, Caramanlis had neither a platform of precise principles nor a structured action program to propose to his supporters. This ideological inconsistency, combined with a vacillating leadership, prevented unification of the various tendencies on the right. On the economic level, these remained divided between the protectionist, nationalist project of the previous governments and the liberal project. These divisions explain why the first two ND governments, led by Caramanlis and Rallis, defended a contradictory economic policy, characterized by anti-inflationist measures, the beginning of EC membership negotiations, an extension of the public sector (between

1977 and 1979) and increased public spending. The fact that public opinion was more favourable to the ideas of the left than of the right in the period after the junta of the colonels (Dimitras, 1987) and the electoral opportunism of the leaders and members of the ND (Katsoudas, 1987, 98) also explains this inconsistency in the conservatives' economic policy. The eclecticism and fickleness of ND orientations between 1977 and 1985 was, incidentally, such that they were unable to associate themselves with any of the pan-European groups of parties which formed or became consolidated after the inauguration of election of members of the European Parliament by universal suffrage, in 1979.

The replacement of Rallis by Evangelos Averoff, head of the ND traditional right, following the electoral defeat of 1981, did not bring about any significant modification to this situation. The new leader favoured a spectacular development of ND recruitment and organization at the local and regional levels. At the ideological level, however, his actions were primarily focused on the struggle against the leftist ideas of the Papandreou government. This deepening rivalry between left and right did nothing to contribute towards an attenuation of the conflicts between the various clans and tendencies within the ND, nor did it do anything to help the development of an economic program that offered an alternative to that of the PASOK. In 1984, however, when the ND became a member of the European Democratic Union (EDU), a group of European Christian democratic parties, a wider dissemination of liberal ideas was encouraged within the party, thereby creating conditions favourable to a change in its economic orientations. This change began with the accession of Constantin Mitsokakis to the head of the party in 1985.

Unlike Caramanlis and Averoff, Mitsokakis was a liberal of long standing. Upon his return to Greece, this former minister of the 1964–67 Enosis Kentrou (EK) government – the centrist party of George Papandreou, Andreas Papandreou's father – founded the New Liberal Party. He left this party in 1978 to rejoin the ND and occupy the post of Minister of Economic Coordination and Foreign Affairs. Under his leadership, the ND converted to the liberal doctrine and set about restructuring itself by making consistent gains in the legislative elections of 1985, 1989 and 1990 (Catsiapis, 1990, 1991). During the 1984 leadership race, Mitsokakis presented militants with a manifesto that was to become the party's official ideological platform. This manifesto criticized state intervention, demanded more severe anti-inflationary measures, and pushed for more freedom for the private sector in order to combat unemployment (Katsoudas, 1987). During the 1985 electoral campaign, the party supported the inauguration of a 'Liberal New Democracy'. According to Dimitras (1987), Katsoudas (1987, 101) and Catsiapis (1987, 200) it would be a mistake to believe that the ND's defeat at the polls in 1985 was caused by its commitment to liberalism (see Table 29). A large segment of the population had in fact been hoping for such a change after its disappointment with the results of the expansionist policy defended by the first PASOK government. This change in public opinion was, moreover, not foreign to the – partial and temporary – reorientation of the PASOK's economic policy during its second mandate (see Chapter 4). The ND's failure was more attributable to Mitsokakis' inability to rally his party's right around his program and to the consequent distrust of the latter by a section of voters, who saw certain ND representatives registered on the electoral lists openly associating with extremist groups that were nostalgic for the authoritarian regime.

The divisions within the ND persisted beyond 1985. Stéphanopoulos and his supporters split off to form the Democratic Renewal Party and the other factions of the right that had remained within the party obliged Mitsokakis to water down his liberal program. In fact, Mitsokakis never managed to achieve solid party unity around his ideas. On the eve of the 1989 elections, an internal enquiry showed a persistent current of criticism of his leadership and his ideas, both at the executive level and within the subordinate bodies (Catsiapis, 1990, 203). During the period 1990–93, the majority Mitsokakis government was constantly torn by internal quarrels, certain of which were centred on the direction of the economic policy. Several ministers resigned in protest against the adoption of this adjustment program, which had no precedent in Greece. These confrontations hindered the implementation of the economic stabilization measures, contributing to electoral defeat in 1993 and the resignation of Mitsokakis as president of the ND (Catsiapis, 1992, 1993).[8]

PASOK

The refusal of the Panhellenic Socialist Movement (PASOK) majority governments to adopt and pursue a comprehensive, in-depth adjustment program in 1993 or at any other time, is due largely to the rejection of the liberal economic doctrine by the 'leftist' nationalist and populist wing of the party, which, thanks to the support and the authoritarian leadership of Andreas Papandreou, had maintained its hegemony over the organization ever since its creation in 1974. Although a more liberal current had always existed within the PASOK, it had never succeeded in imposing itself. As I have pointed out before, the accession of its chief, Kostas Simitis, to the leadership of the party and of the government, following Papandreou's retirement and death, could mark a turning point in the history of the PASOK, but it is still too early to speculate about this with any degree of certainty.

The PASOK was a new party created in 1974 by Andreas Papandreou, whose father was the historic leader of the non-communist centrist and leftist forces in Greece between 1935 and 1967. After the example of his father, who founded various parties including the Centre Union Party (EK), during the sixties, Papandreou formed the PASOK in order to bring together the intermediate classes that were hostile both to the capitalist project of the conservative right and the communist project of the KKE. In spite of his years of study and teaching in the United States and Canada, however, Papandreou was always more radical than his father, denouncing western and American domination with more virulence and compromising himself with the groups of the extreme left in Greece, upon his return to the country and through his participation in the EK government between 1964 and 1967 (Featherstone, 1987a). After 1974, Papandreou succeeded in making the PASOK one of the two major Greek political parties by representing it as the party of all the 'under-privileged who are exploited by the monopolistic, foreign oligarchy', and as the defender of a 'third path to socialism' based on the socialization of the means of production, co-management of enterprises, the decentralization of economic planning, national affirmation and the diversification of external alliances (between the western, Soviet and Third World blocs) (Lyrintsis, 1989). Once in power, however, even though he was officially identified with the new French socialist party created by François Mitterrand in 1971, he tended to defend a rather vague platform of change (*Allaghi*) of a nationalist and populist inspiration (Featherstone, 1987a; Lyrintsis, 1989; Kapetanyannis, 1993). His nationalism was made evident through an increased state involvement in the economy between 1981 and 1986, a foreign policy that was focused on solidarity with the nationalist states of the Third World, the denunciation of American military bases in Greece, the rejection – until 1981 – of the EC membership plan (Verney, 1990), and his support for opposition to Turkish, Macedonian and Albanian threats during the nineties. His populism took the form of the adoption of a speech making style that was purposely vague and changing, unsupported by a consistent set of policies whose aim was to rally all of the intermediate levels of society (Lyrintsis, 1989). This demagogic discourse turned out to be effective, on the one hand because of the sheer numerical weight and the high degree of fragmentation and interpenetration of the middle classes, and on the other because of the fickleness of public opinion. According to Dimitras (1987, 68–9), between 1974 and 1985, the intermediate classes supported the values of nationalism and socialism, while showing themselves to be hostile to the traditional right and to a rapprochement with the EC and the United States. After that time, attachment to socialist ideas weakened concurrently with the espousal of democratic, liberal and Europeanist values (Morlino and Montero, 1991; Ethier 1994b). Nevertheless, the rejection of the traditional right and the promotion of nationalism persisted. The evolution in the PASOK's policies, particularly its economic policies, between its first (1981–85) and second (1985–89) mandates, represented little more than an opportunist, electoralist response to changes in public opinion. In neither case was it ever guided by a determination to apply the principles of socialism or liberalism in any consistent manner.

The PASOK's adoption of the authoritarian organizational methods of populism and the communist left during the era of resistance and the civil war (Kapetanyannis, 1993) contributed towards the marginalization of the modernist and liberal elements. From the very beginning of the PASOK, in 1974, Papandreou had manoeuvred in order to impose his authority on the party as a whole, which subsequently allowed him to conduct an opportunist policy of compromise between the various tendencies in the party and the electorate, while limiting the influence of the liberals. Featherstone (1987a, 121) referring to Clogg (1984, 14), recalls in this regard how, in 1974, Papandreou pronounced himself in favour of the cooptation, rather than the election, of members of the party's subaltern bodies. Confronted with opposition from a majority of militants, the Central Committee was dissolved and reconstituted at the time of the preliminary congress of March 1975. At the meeting of the new Central Committee, Papandreou announced that as head of the party he would henceforth name the members of the executive bureau who in turn would designate the members of the disciplinary council. This indirect control over the disciplinary council permitted him to expel a few hundred opponents to his policy from the PASOK, which precipitated several thousand defections during 1975 and facilitated the subsequent recruitment of militants who were more obedient to the populist and nationalist doctrine of the chief. Papandreou's domination over the party apparatus was perpetuated and reinforced through the maintenance of hierarchical organizational structures, through the submission of the parliamentary group to the executive bureau, through the leadership's creation of a vast network of local committees, through the imposition of strict party discipline, and through the power of the disciplinary council. During the PASOK's terms in power, the government carried out a number of sanctions (suspensions, demotions or expulsions) against those opposed to Papandreou's leadership, citing violations of disciplinary rules (Featherstone, 1987a, 121).

Thanks to such authoritarian methods and to patronage, Papandreou maintained a great measure of control over the PASOK during its passage into power. This control allowed him to rid the cabinet of all opponents to his economic policy without the risk of a protest movement forming within the executive or the junior bodies. Accordingly, in 1985, Papandreou asked for the replacement of eight of the eleven members of the executive bureau who were opposed to his stabilization program (Featherstone, 1987, 123). On the other hand, he fired ministers Koutsogioros and Gennimatas because they had first criticized the timidity, then the abandonment (1988), of these adjustment measures (Catsiapis, 1986).[9]

Spain

In Spain, both the UCD and the PSOE governments showed consistency and determination in the adoption and implementation of the adjustment measures, since the leaders and members of the two parties were committed to the values of liberal economic idealism. The conditions favouring such an adherence were quite different within each formation, however.

The Union del Centro democratico

The UCD, a new party created by interim Prime Minister Adolfo Suarez in 1977, a few months before the first democratic legislative elections of June 1977, brought together the modernist, reformist elements of the Francoist regime, which had supported the opening-up and social modernization of Spain since the end of the fifties. Conservative Francoists, in fact, shunned the UCD and joined the *Alianza Popular* (AP) of Manuel Fraga Iribarne. It was these people, several of whom had been trained in American universities, who between 1973 and 1976, faced with a worsening economic situation and the repeated refusal of the EC to consider Spain's membership request because of its authoritarian political regime, progressively accepted the idea of negotiating a peaceful transition towards democracy with the parties of the left. Considering that their support for DT had been primarily motivated by a desire to stimulate growth and socio-economic modernization in Spain through membership in the EC, it is not surprising that the great majority of them recognized the virtues of economic liberalism and the need for adjustment measures. The fact that the first UCD government had initiated discussions with the PSOE and the PCE aimed at the adoption of the *Pactos de la Moncloa*, only a few months after its inauguration, without this initiative raising any significant opposition in its ranks, is eloquent testimony to the unity of Suarez's partisans in this regard.

This is an important point, since, as a number of specialists (Gillespie, 1990a; Gunther, 1992; Maravall, 1992; Bermeo, 1994a and Heywood, 1995) have stressed, the UCD as a coalition of various political groups – including the conservative Christian democrats, reformist civil servants linked with the *Tacito* network, the social-democrats of the Francisco Fernandez Ordonez clan, the liberal sub-groups patronized by Joaquim Fernandez Ordonez, former heads of the *Movimiento*, was deeply divided. It was, moreover, these divisions which led to its electoral defeat in 1982 and to its subsequent disappearance. Nevertheless, these facts were not economically motivated. They were, on the one hand, the result of power and interest struggles among the various clans in the party, and, on the other, of ideological cleavages over constitutional, social and moral questions. The issues which gave rise to the most opposition within the UCD during its passage to power were the negotiation of the autonomy statutes, the separation of the Church from the state, the secularization of the education system, the legalization of abortion and the reform of the army (Gunther, 1990).

The Socialist Party

The commitment of PSOE leaders and militants to economic liberalism was due to the organizational and ideological restructuring of the party, under the leadership of a new group of reformist militants during the 1970s.

Created in 1879 by Pablo Iglesias, the PSOE underwent a transformation during the twenties and thirties after the schism which gave birth to the PCE, a radical socialist Marxist organization characterized by the coexistence of a revolutionary tendency supporting armed struggle as a strategy for political change, and a moderate, legalistic tendency favouring accession to power by the electoral means. During the Second Republic (1931–39), the PSOE – which now numbered over 1.4 million members and controlled the *Union general de los Trabajadores* (UGT), the *Casas del Pueblo* and several municipalities – played a political role of the first importance. However, the victory of the Francoists, which sanctioned the end of the civil war (1936–39), brought about the near disappearance of the party. Forced into clandestine existence like the PCE, the PSOE remained for several years a much less influential organization than the latter because of its internal ideological divisions and the exile of its leaders.

The progress of industrialization and social modernization during the sixties favoured the emergence of new socialist groups, notably in Andalusia, Astoria and Bilbao. This new generation of militants to which Felipe Gonzalez and his colleagues of the University of Seville's Faculty of Law belonged, did not share the concepts of the exiled leadership in Toulouse (France). Unlike the latter, it favoured an alliance with the communists to overthrow the Franco dictatorship. During the 1972 congress, 80% of militants gave their support to the political platform of the 'young Turks of the interior'. This support resulted in a breakdown within the old guard leadership of the exterior, and the formal recognition of the new leadership by the German Social Democratic Party (SDP) and the Second Socialist International. In 1974, at the congress of Turesne, Felipe Gonzalez was elected Secretary General. This change of leadership and ideological orientation, combined with the adoption in 1973 of the Euro-communist platform by the PCE,[10] favoured the creation of a union of the left between the PSOE and the PCE. This took shape in 1976 with the establishment of the *Coordinacion democratica* and the adoption of a new strategy of political change focused on the negotiating of a peaceful transition towards democracy with reformist elements among the Francoists (Ethier, 1986).

As Heywood (1995, 194) points out, the objective of the new reformist PSOE leaders was to use the union of the left to re-establish democracy, marginalize the PCE and to come to power. Gonzalez and his disciples (including Nicolas Redondo, Secretary General of the UGT, Enrique Mujica, Pablo Castellano and Alfonso Guerra) knew that they could not attain the last two objectives without a profound transformation of the party. Opposed to the Euro-communist ideas of Santiago Carillo and his party, they wanted to turn the PSOE into an organization that was multiclass, pluralist, Europeanist and democratic on the political level, social-democratic on the social level and more liberal on the economic level. In order to pave the way for this restructuring, they encouraged the sociological transformation of the party that began towards the end of the sixties. Between 1969 and 1979, the majority of working members and officials were replaced by militants from the middle class. At the 1979 congress, workers represented no more than 7.5% of the delegates, whereas white-collar workers, professionals and entrepreneurs represented 36.65%, 28.9% and 10.1% of delegates respectively. Furthermore, only 11.2% of total delegates had been members of the party for more than 10 years.[11] These changes, combined with the introduction of new operating rules – the reduction of the number of delegates from 1000 to 50, the introduction of a block vote, and 25% of votes controlled by the Andalusian delegation (Heywood, 1995, 195) – permitted the *felipista* current to consolidate its hold over the party and to ensure acceptance of a rethinking of its ideological orientations (Craig, 1994).

After the signing of the *Pactos de la Moncloa* in 1977, thereby committing itself to a capitalist liberal economic program for Spain, the party leadership proposed, at the XVIII congress of May 1979, to expunge all references to Marxism from the party's statutes and program in conformity with the undertaking made in this regard by Gonzalez in 1974. This proposal was overturned by opposition from the left wing of the party. Gonzalez and the members of the executive reacted by resigning *en masse* and by launching a vast campaign aimed at raising awareness of their ideas in the base organizations. This campaign permitted them to rally the majority of party members to their point of view. The extraordinary congress of September 1979 marked the return to power of Gonzalez and his team, the definite break with the party's Marxist past, and the marginalization of the radicals. At the congress held at the beginning of the eighties, the period during which the PSOE came to power, the left, which was henceforth concentrated within the *Izquierda socialista* (IS) current, no longer represented more than 8% of the delegates.[12] This consolidation of their political-ideological hegemony allowed the partisans of the reformist current to enjoy wide autonomy in political and economic matters particularly after their accession to power in 1982. The internal cohesion of the party was also maintained, thanks to patronage, limitations on membership and control over local party organizations.

> The iron control exercised by the PSOE leadership and the refusal to brook internal dissent provoked ever-greater criticism from disaffected militants ... Nevertheless, the dissaffection of a critical minority was easily outweighed by the loyalty of the majority of party members. Such loyalty was the more easily ensured by the small size of party membership and the ample opportunities for political rewards afforded by electoral victory after 1982. Patronage became a basic practice in the hold of PSOE leaders over militants: it had been estimated that about 50,000 public posts were given to PSOE members between 1982 and 1984, during which time the party's total membership reached only just over 150,000 (Perez-Diaz, 1987). In addition, the speed with which the PSOE achieved its national pre-eminence ensured that local and provincial networks were established only after the centre had become firmly entrenched, making it easier for the leadership to impose its decisions and guarantee discipline (Julia, 1990).
> (Heywood, 1995, 197)

However, the PSOE had never been a monolithic party. During its various mandates, it was the theatre of numerous internal rivalries, in particular between the populist current of Vice-President Alfonso Guerra and the liberal current, represented notably by Miguel Boyer, Carlos Solchaga and Jorge Semprun. These rivalries did not, however, pose a serious threat to the party at the economic level, since the liberals retained their hold over the orientation of the cabinets' policies and progressively rallied the majority of militants to their view. The 1989 congress sanctioned the triumph of their ideas over the more opportunistic discourse of the *Guerristas*. The latter's opposition was in fact less a criticism of the liberals' ideas than an attempt to prevent them extending their authority over the party apparatus that they controlled thanks to the powerful Andalusia federation. In return for the liberals' ideological victory at the 1989 congress, the *Guerristas* obtained their exclusion from the party's leadership organs (Bon, 1990).

Portugal

As indicated in Chapter 3, the PSP was the only party, in the period from 1975 to 1983, which supported the adoption of adjustment measures during its mandates. The AFM, the CDS, the PSDP and the *Partido popular monarquico* (PPM) – components of the AD – refused to ratify this orientation, either because of their allegiance to leftist, socialist ideas, or because of their attachment to the nationalist, protectionist model of the *Estado novo*. The PSP's adherence to liberalism is explained by the fact that this was an entirely new party, created in 1973 by Mario Soares under the auspices of the German Social Democratic Party (SDP). Unlike the *felipistas* in Spain, the *soaristas* did not, however, succeed in unifying the PSP behind the banner of liberalism. The division among the socialists over the economic policies is a major reason why the governments led by Mario Soares, both between 1976 and 1983, and 1983 and 1985, were unable to adopt and to implement a complete, consistent program of SMs and SCMs. This task was to be achieved by the PSDP during the period following 1985, as a result of the profound transformation of the party that occurred under the leadership of Cavaco Silva.

The Armed Forces Movement

The AFM, which was responsible for the revolutionary *coup d'état* in 1974 and led the transition towards democracy, was profoundly divided between a radical left wing close to the PCP and the sub-groups of the extreme left, and a moderate wing that was relatively sympathetic to the views of the socialists (McLeod, 1990, 158). The first five provisional governments of Palma Carlos and Gonçalves (April 1974–September 1975) belonged to the first tendency, which explains their nationalist, expansionist and socialist economic policies (see Chapter 3). The problems engendered by these policies gave rise to an antagonization of the relations between radical and moderate members of the military. In August 1975, the moderate members of the AFM published the famous 'Document of the Nine', which denounced the adventurist policy of the leftist and PCP military. In September 1975, they succeeded in dislodging radicals from power and formed a new government led by General Azevedo (September 1975–April 1976). Azevedo adopted a certain number of SMs at the end of his mandate, but overall his economic policy was a continuation of that of his predecessors (see Chapter 3), due to the persistence of profound divisions within the AFM. In November 1975, in fact, the moderates had to intercede to crush an attempted *coup d'état* orchestrated by the radical elements with the support of the communists (McLeod, 1990, 158).

The Socialist Party

The PSP is not an old, renovated socialist party like the PSOE, but an entirely new party created by Mario Soares on the eve of the Revolution of the Carnations in 1973, while he was in exile in France. His founding congress, held in Germany, was financed by the Friedrich Ebert Foundation, which had close ties to the SDP and Second Socialist International. During this congress, the PSP adopted a non-dogmatic Marxist program that supported the inauguration in Portugal of a pluralist democracy rather than a socialist system. Emigrant Portuguese workers in Germany were excluded from this congress. Recruitment of founding members was essentially conducted among exiles whose roots were in the middle classes (Gallagher, 1989). These conditions must have been conducive to a certain ideological homogeneity in the party as well as more or less widespread adherence, among its members, to the values of economic liberalism. However, when the PSP established itself in Portugal after the revolution of April 1974, the composition of its membership and its electoral base was highly diversified. As Kedros (1986, 262) reports, 'when in 1975 the first PSP congress was held in Portugal, Mario Soares himself publicly remarked that his followers were "extremely diverse" even "hybrid"'. The degree of ideological divergence, particularly on economic orientations, was such that it caused the popular socialist movement of Manuel Serra, who had joined the PSP after the fall of the Salzar regime, to secede. In 1978, these divisions induced the government of Mario Soares to integrate 50 leftist intellectuals formerly from the socialist intervention group within the organs of the party leadership in order to reinforce the influence of the *soaristas*. It was under the influence of these new leaders that the liberal-inspired 'Ten years to change Portugal' program was adopted, at the congress of 1979. However, this program was only truly accepted by leadership circles in Lisbon. Since the PSP had developed no major organic links with grass-roots members and its own electorate, it was unable to convince them to support this new ideological orientation. Numerous defections occurred within the party and the electorate following the PSP's adjustment efforts, both in 1976–77 and 1983–1985.

In the period 1985–95, the PSP was consigned to the opposition benches, and it continued to be torn both by the power struggles between the leadership personalities – including Mario Soares, who, in spite of being elected President of the Republic in 1985, wanted to maintain control over the party – and by ideological dissention between the liberal-conservative, social-democratic and socialist blocs. Then in 1986, Vittor Constâncio, former Finance Minister, Governor of the Central Bank and a convinced partisan of liberalism and European integration, was elected to the post of Secretary General. Repudiated by Mario Soares, he resigned in 1988 to be replaced by Jorge Sampaïo, the leader of the socialist group (Rudel, 1989). These divisions explain why the PSP gave inconsistent and often mitigated and/or conditional support to the liberal reforms of the PSDP governments during this period.[13]

The rightist parties

The CDS and the PSDP were rightist conservative parties with close ties to the Catholic Church whose supporters came from the same social and geographic milieu: small property owners, farmers, craftsmen, tradesmen – concentrated in the centre and North of the country and in the archipelagos of Madeira and the Azores. Competition between the two formations was more motivated by the struggle for power than by ideological divergences. This explains why the two parties were able to unite within a coalition – the AD – which controlled the government between 1979 and 1983. Beyond their internal divisions and their rivalries, the CDS and the PSDP shared convergent points of view in economic matters: they more or less defended the orientations put forward by the *Estado novo* under the direction of Caetano (1968–74), that is, a relatively introverted policy of open import substitution (see Chapter 1). Although more open than the radical – and nationalist – forces of the left to the prospect of membership in the EC, they remained reticent toward the precepts of orthodox economic liberalism. This fact, together with the numerous divisions and leadership crises which characterized the two parties between 1980 and 1983, following the accidental death of PSDP chief Sa Carneiro in 1980, and the resignation of the leader of the CDS, Freitas do Amaral, in 1983 (Rudel, 1984), explained why the AD seemed to be in no hurry to adopt an adjustment program between 1979 and 1983 (Table 6).

During the period after 1983, this configuration of rightist forces was profoundly modified by the transformation of the PSDP under the leadership of Anibal Cavaco Silva and the subsequent decline of the influence of the CDS, a party whose rootedness within the rural regions had always been less developed and less structured than that of the PSDP (McLeod, 1990).

Profiting from the internal crisis in the PSDP, the growing discontent among the populace over the economic and political instability of the country and the end of the EC membership negotiations,[14] Cavaco Silva, former minister and *dauphin* of Sa Carneiro, who had returned to a university career after the latter's death, succeeded in getting himself elected to the party leadership in 1985 by denouncing the rivalries of the *baronatos* and by proposing to reunify the party around the liberal platform, the only orientation likely to maximize the gains of the imminent entry into the EC (Rudel, 1986; Gladdish, 1990). As soon as he was inaugurated, Cavaco Silva showed his determination to go through with his program by breaking the alliance with the PSP, which he considered too hesitant in the area of economic reforms,[15] a decision which led to early elections and allowed him to form a minority, yet homogeneous, pro-liberal government. The new cabinet formed in 1985 was in fact rather small – it contained only 30 ministers – and was completely renewed. Cavaco Silva only returned three of the social-democratic ministers of the leaving coalition government to their portfolios. The new Prime Minister then undertook the unification of the PSDP. He revitalized the party's local structures, which, in particular, allowed him to increase the number of municipalities controlled by the social democrats from 88 to 137 during the 1985 municipal elections. He imposed strict discipline on the militants of the party, not hesitating to punish opponents to leadership and government policies. Proceedings were instituted against several militants who, during the 1985 presidential elections, supported candidates other than those of the PSDP. In 1986, three unionists were expelled for their criticism of their leadership policy. This authoritarianism aroused the disapproval of certain leaders, including Francisco Pinto Balsameo, former leader and Prime Minister, President of the Bureau of the National Council, who resigned from his post. But overall, Cavaco Silva's firmness and liberal convictions did not weaken his popularity, either among voters or within his party. In June 1986, he was re-elected to the post of Secretary General, and in 1987 and 1990 he won the legislative elections with an absolute majority of seats (Table 30), a performance that no other party had been able to achieve since the establishment of democracy (Rudel, 1986, 1987, 1988, 1989; Léonard, 1990).

CONCLUSION

The comparative study of the attitudes of the Greek, Spanish and Portuguese governments confirms that the unity and determination of political leaders to adopt a consistent program of SMs and SCMs depends, fundamentally, neither on the size of the economic crisis, nor on electoral cycles, nor on the homogeneous and majority composition of the cabinet, nor on the rightist tendencies of the party/parties in power, nor on the coercive or cooperative behaviour of foreign partners and financiers. On the other hand, it reveals that the leadership of the government as regards the development and promulgation of the reforms, is linked decisively to the degree of adherence of the decision makers and the members of their parties to the values of economic liberalism (EL).

Insofar as the large majority of political parties supported other options besides EL before 1975, the attainment of this condition supposes either the unification of liberal elements within new formations (UCD, PSP), or the ideological transformation of the existing parties (PSOE, PSDP, ND). Both changes demand the presence, at the head of the organization, of a leader and a team convinced of the merits of economic liberalism, who are equipped with a well-designed program, and who are determined and able to get it accepted by all of the militants. The examples of the PSOE and the PSDP show that when a party is divided – a situation which can exist in both a new or reconstituted party, as shown by the cases of the PSP and the ND – the leaders may be led to resort to rather draconian methods – certain of which find their inspiration in authoritarianism and corporatism rather than in democracy – in the attempt to unify the organization around a liberal program: marginalizing working-class elements in favour of representatives from the middle classes and the elite; modifying operating and decision making rules in order to promote the domination of the partisans of liberalism within the local, regional and national bodies of the apparatus on the one hand, and the modification of the party's program, on the other; adopting coercive measures to deal with dissidents and tightening discipline in the parliamentary group, and so on. The popularity of the party leader and his team among the general public is a crucial factor. By voting them into office with a strong majority, it bestows upon them an enormous hold over the state apparatus, thus making it possible for them to use the resources of the latter to 'buy' the support of militants and sympathizers who are unresponsive to their policy, through the distribution of posts, subsidies, contracts and other favours. The comparison of the evolution of the ND, PSP, PSOE and PSDP also indicates that a party's conversion to economic liberalism has more chance of success when that party has deep roots in all the regions and sectors of society and when it benefits from the active support of foreign sister parties. Finally, the PASOK, PSOE and PSP's various trajectories reveal that the conversion of socialist or social-democratic parties to economic liberalism is easier when the communists are themselves engaged in a process of ideological reconversion.

7   The Governments' Ability to Implement Reforms

MAIN DETERMINANTS

The third decisive condition of the success of adjustment is a government's ability to apply the SMs and the SCMs in a systematic manner for at least a decade. This means that it has to be able to avoid the development of opposition movements that are likely to hinder its progress, in spite of the many serious transition costs (TCs) – unemployment, higher interest rates, increased tax burden, reduced social spending, precariousness of jobs, lowering of real income, and so on – generated by SMs and SCMs.

As pointed out in the Introduction, most of the authors cited consider that the realization of this condition is mainly determined by the nature of the relations existing between the executive, the major institutions of the political system and the civil society, on the one hand, and by the harshness and the duration of TCs, on the other. In every case, the room to manoeuvre of the executive or its autonomy toward main political actors (army, bureaucracy, parliament/parties) and interest groups (IGs) decisively conditions the implementation of SMs and SCMs. The executive benefits from a large autonomy when it controls the political institutions and the organizations of civil society or when it is supported by the latter. Most of the authors cited prefer by far the second pattern for it implies the existence of a democratic consensus. There is no unanimity among scholars about the factors that favor such a consensus. Many of them recognize that the political leadership, that is the government's determination to undertaking reforms, contributes over time to convince citizens and institutional actors of the necessity of the reforms. Some authors like Przeworski (1990, 1995) and Nelson (1995) maintain that the consolidation of democracy that supposes the enlargement of the representation and the participation of various interests within the political system incites main institutional actors to adopt a more conciliating attitude toward adjustment policy.

However, almost all specialists admit that the alleviation of TCs largely contributes to the acceptation of SMs and SCMs in every case. The strategies for attaining this objective are nonetheless a matter of controversy. As seen in the Introduction, the most liberal theorists, such as Sachs (1994), Aslund (1995) and Balcerowitz (1995), argue that the best way to reduce TCs is shock therapy. In their view, such a strategy reduces the length of TCs while rapidly generating some beneficial economic effects (reduction of inflation, decrease of interest rates, resumption of investment, creation of new jobs, and so on) that contribute to changing public opinion. For their part, more social-democratically inclined authors like Nelson (1994, 1995), Bresser Pereira et al. (1993), Haggard and Kaufman (1992), Smith, Acuna and Gamarra (1994), Desai (1995) Graham (1995), and Przeworski (1995) consider that TCs can best be alleviated by an heterodox strategy of adjustment characterized by the gradual implementation of SMs and SCMs, the adoption of measures of compensation for the social groups most affected by reforms and the betterment of social policies, notably the universal programs of health, education and pensions. Finally, some social-democrat authors believe that concertation or the negotiation of periodic and recurrent economic agreements between state, employers' associations and Labour Unions help to build a large consensus toward reforms.

THEIR RESPECTIVE IMPACTS IN SOUTHERN EUROPEAN COUNTRIES

A comparison of the conditions that in Spain and Portugal favoured, and in Greece compromised, the application of SMs and SCMs, confirms that the progress of the reforms depends both on government leadership and its autonomy within the political system and civil society.[1] On the other hand, it shows that most of the factors judged to be necessary or favourable to the constitution of a wide coalition of interests regarding the adjustment process have played a significant role in Southern Europe.

Spain

In Spain the UCD (1977–79) and PSOE (1982–96) governments were able to implement the programs of reforms (Chapter 2 and Table 2), through their consistency and determination (Chapter 6) on the one hand, and the benefit of support from the principal political and social actors, on the other. During the period 1977–96, in fact, the Spanish leaders enjoyed greater freedom of action than other Southern European leaders because of earlier, more consistent support for the process of economic liberalization from the major political parties (UCD, PSOE, AP–PP, PCE), from the business sector (CEOE) and the trade unions. This consensus permitted the conclusion of the *Pactos de la Moncloa* between the UCD, PSOE and PCE in 1977, and the signing of the various tripartite or quadripartite socio-economic agreements between the UCD or PSOE governments, the CEOE and certain trade union organizations between 1979 and 1992 (see Table 33).

However, the size and speed of the reforms, particularly at the structural level, was more modest under UCD leadership than under the PSOE (1982–96) governments. These differences are ascribable to factors which limited or widened the executive power's freedom to manoeuvre in relation to political institutions and civil society during the two periods in question.

UCD (1997–82): strong leadership and limited autonomy

Many of the economic reforms promised by the UCD governments were never fully implemented. The tax reform which had started in 1977 was only partially carried out, attempts to liberalize the financial system were delayed, many institutional reforms were never confronted and the labour market reforms which were made 'protected most rigidities'. Despite the parts of the Moncloa pact that promised to reduce state intervention in industry and 'build a market economy comparable to Western Europe', state spending went up dramatically and the large and generally inefficient public enterprise sector actually increased in size. Despite the UCD's sincere commitment to restructuring Spanish industry to make it more competitive, 'the majority of state aids' to industry during this period were dedicated to the maintenance of jobs and the real role of the state in industry appeared to be the protection of the most depressed sectors of the economy.

(Bermeo, 1994b, 10)

The inability of the Adolfo Suarez and Calvo Sotelo governments to implement the major structural reforms on their agenda, particularly those related to the public sector industries, cannot be imputed to their minority position in the Cortès, since they already had the support of the opposition parties, particularly those of the PSOE, which controlled almost a third of members' seats (Table 28). It was as much a result of their lack of control over the army and the bureaucracy, which harboured several factions opposed to the weakening of the state enterprises created under the Francoist regime, as to their weak hold over a civil society in disarray, which was, moreover, divided between several rival, weakly institutionalized union organizations. These observations demonstrate that the absence of consolidation within the new democratic regime largely determined the limits of the UCD governments' economic action (Bermeo, 1994b).

Both the governments of Adolfo Suarez and Calvo Sotelo retreated before the prospect of reforming the civil service, as a significant number of their party members came from this bastion of Francoism (Buse, 1984). Since they had no real authority over the army, they also refused to go ahead with the budget cuts and with a rationalization/clean-up of their personnel, for fear of increasing the risk of rebellion among elements of the upper military hierarchy. The latter, in fact, had found it hard to accept the new liberal economic orientations, the disappearance of the Francoist regime and the climate of social turmoil which reigned in Spain at the end of the seventies. As Bermeo (1994b) points out, this period was characterized by a major increase in strikes and work stoppages;[2] workers contested the effects of the government's austerity policy or demanded an improvement in their economic situation and an extension of their political rights and liberties. UCD leaders postponed several of their projected restructuring measures, particularly in the declining industries of the public sector, so as not to aggravate the social mobilizations, which, moreover, they were unable to contain through the intervention of their union allies, the UGT and the USO.

During that period, in fact, the workers' movement was divided among several organizations (UGT, CC.OO, CNT, USO, ELA–STV) whose membership was more or less similar[3] and which competed among each other, less for ideological motives than to consolidate their positions. In such a situation, neither the UGT nor the USO was able to support the government SCMs, for fear of being discredited in the eyes of the workers and seeing a part of their membership join other union organizations. The latter, propelled by the same logic of competition, actively supported the popular mobilizations in order to strengthen their influence and their organization, and in the case of the ELA–STV, to persuade the government to grant more powers to the future Basque community in the context of the ongoing discussions on Autonomy Status. This situation explains the limits of social concertation during this era. On the one hand, only the UGT and the USO agreed to sign tripartite agreements with the CEOE and the government, agreements whose content was limited to liberalizing certain aspects of the labour relations system and slowing down rising salary costs (see Table 33). On the other hand, reaching agreements within the context of national concertation institutions, such as the Institute for Social Security and Employment, remained difficult because of fragmented union representation. This representation was in fact established on the basis of the percentage of delegates controlled by each union organization on the company committees. The McElrath data (1989) show that in 1978, 1980 and 1982, 95% of the delegates were shared between the UGT, the CC.OO and the ELA–STV.[4] Although the ELA–STV delegates were concentrated exclusively in Basque companies, they retained major representation at the level of national concertation institutions, because of the high number of companies in the Basque region.

The limits of consensus and social concertation, which compromised the application of the SCMs between 1977 and 1982, are perhaps also related to the factors which prevented the attenuation of TCs and the widening of the political rights and freedoms of the various interest groups. Due to the recession of 1979–83, the UCD's political stabilization policy did not permit any improvement in the difficult economic situation. Tables 9, 10, 11 and 34 show that inflation and unemployment grew, whereas the growth rate declined. Furthermore, the cabinets of Suarez and Sotelo were unable to get their party to accept the reforms aimed at improving social policies and widening democratic rights and freedoms. It should be recalled in this regard that the government's plan to increase access to the education system by reducing the privileges of private Catholic institutions and increasing funding to public institutions was rejected by the conservative elements of the UCD. The same happened with the project aimed at legalizing abortion and divorce within the framework of bolstering equality between men and women.

PSOE (1982–93): strong leadership and wide autonomy

Even though they adopted a wider set of SMs and SCMs than the preceding government, the first three PSOE cabinets were able to honour the majority of their commitments. As shown in Chapter 2, the socialists not only further stabilized macro-economic imbalances but they proceeded with major structural reforms in every sector of the economy in the period 1982–93. This success is due to the fact that the cabinet of Felipe Gonzalez exerted a veritable hegemony over the political system and civil society thanks to its having secured an absolute majority of seats in the Cortès, to the weakness of the opposition parties, which incidentally were largely in agreement with the orientations of their economic policy, to the submission of the army and the bureaucracy to their authority, to the cooperation of the employers, to the strengthening of the influence of the UGT within the union movement and to the social dialogue with the CEOE, the UGT and CC.OO.[5]

Autonomy towards the parties, the army and the bureaucracy. The data in Table 28 shows that the PSOE enjoyed the support of almost half the Spanish population in 1982 and 1986 and that it obtained many more than the 176 members needed to control an absolute majority of votes in the lower house. In 1989, the relative decline in its popularity caused it to lose its absolute majority by one seat, but it easily won this back through an agreement with the *Partido nacionalista vasco* (PNV), *Convergencia i Unio* (CiU) and the *Centro democratico y social* (CDS).[6] The PSOE's majority in parliament would not have allowed it to apply its reforms as deeply as it did, if it had been obliged to confront powerful political parties that were opposed to its program. Now, except for the communists, some of whom had become increasingly critical over time toward the adjustment measures, all the political parties, including the PNV and the CiU, preserved the favourable attitude that they had adopted towards the economy liberalization program upon the development of a new constitution and the signing of the *Pactos de la Moncloa* in 1977. The finalization of the Status of Autonomy in 1982 contributed towards strengthening cooperation between the PSOE, the PNV and CiU. None of the parties represented in the Congress of Deputies in the period 1982–93 would have been able, in any case, to mount an effective opposition to the socialist government, owing to its marginal influence and/or its internal divisions. Between 1982 and 1986, the PCE, whose popularity among voters had dropped dramatically, underwent two successive splits and was reduced to the status of a sub-group. It survived thanks to the formation of a coalition, *Izquierda Unida* (IU),[7] with various sub-groups of the extreme left. But it did not manage to impose its leadership on this group, which remained constantly torn by ideological and political dissention. The UCD, a factionalist and very heterogeneous party from the sociological and ideological standpoints (see Chapter 6), did not survive the resignation of Calvo Sotelo. The CDS, the new social-democratic formation created by the former founder of UCD, Adolfo Suarez, for the 1982 elections, remained marginal due to the similarity of its program to that of the PSOE. *Alianza Popular* (AP), the conservative party created and led by ex-Francoist Manuel Fraga Iribarne, profited from the disappearance of the UCD by rallying its most conservative members and supporter. In 1982, this widening of its membership and its electoral clientele allowed it to become the major opposition party, yet it remained profoundly divided as it was made up, after the fashion of the UCD, of clans with opposing interests and positions. The AP, which was renamed the *Coalicion Popular* (CP) during the 1986 elections only, underwent a true transformation under the new leadership of José Maria Aznar, after 1989. After his dizzying rise to the head of the organization, Aznar, who, although he originated from a Francoist family, was a modernist yet a liberal, changed the name of the party to *Partido Popular* (PP); he imposed on the party a markedly more centrist program that was in many respects similar to that of the PSOE, an operation which allowed them to make the PP a far more pluralist formation, more representative of the various regional and social interests in the country.

Unlike the UCD, the PSOE was able to impose its authority on the army by proceeding with a reduction and a clean-up of the army personnel, by limiting the growth of their military spending and by modernizing their rules of operation. These reforms were greatly aided by the failure of the attempted *coup d'état* led by Colonel Tejero in February 1981 and the unprecedented mobilization of political and social forces for respect of democracy that the aborted *putsch* had triggered. They were also helped by Spain's membership in the North Atlantic Treaty Organization (NATO), in 1986. Membership in NATO in fact obliged the Spanish government to undertake a process of modernization, not only of its army's equipment but also of its rules of operation. This process contributed toward eliminating from the army elements that were nostalgic for the former regime and attached to its economic model.

Unlike the UCD, the PSOE was able to impose its hegemony on the bureaucracy. During its first mandate, as noted in Chapter 6, it created 50 000 new jobs in the civil service, most of which were assigned to members or sympathizers of the regime (Heywood, 1995, 197). By investing it with control over management personnel, this renewal of the work force subsequently allowed it to proceed with the deregulation, rationalization, modernization and partial privatization of the public sector, measures which would have the effect of reducing the political power and resistance of the state administrative apparatus. These changes were to be completed after Spain's entry into the EC in 1986, by new reforms that were this time aimed at harmonizing the procedures and operating rules of the bureaucracy with those of the other member states. Yet, the participation of the central government in the elaboration, application and follow-up of the projects carried on in the framework of ESCPs, constituted an major driving force in this harmonization process (Ethier, 1993, 1994b). According to Petras (1990), socialist control over the public sector was not limited to the bureaucracy since they managed, through four major families of the regime – the Solano, Fernandez, Ordonez, Yanes-Barrionuevo and Rodriguez de la Borbolla families – to create a new elite to head the administration and the state companies. This elite, together with the former financial oligarchy, constituted the new ruling class that, through the intermediary of the CEOE in particular, became the principal supporter of the PSOE's economic reforms.

The determinants of social concertation. Social concertation proved to be more fruitful during the reign of the PSOE than under the UCD government. Although the social dialogue, which became formally institutionalized, experienced successes and failures, particularly at the end of the socialist mandate, it gave rise to six multipartite social economic agreements that were more far-reaching and more closely linked to the SCMs than those concluded under the UCD between 1982 and 1993 (Table 33). This relative success was due to several factors. First, the PSOE, unlike the UCD, had very close political and ideological links with one of the major union organizations, since the Secretary General of the UGT sat on the executive board of the PSOE and the members of PSOE were obliged to be members of the UGT. Second, the UGT became Spain's major trade union organization. Finally, the CC.OO, whose influence was also consolidated, agreed to cooperate more with the government.

In fact, the period following 1982 was characterized by falling memberships in all union organizations except for those of the ELA–STV; nevertheless, this drop was far more pronounced within the USO and the CNT than within the UGT and the CC.OO, with the result that these two organizations became, except in the Basque region, the two major organizations for the defence of Spanish workers, with the UGT nevertheless outclassing the CC.OO both in terms of the size of its membership and the percentage of delegates on company committees (this Chapter, note 3). This new situation led the CC.OO to adopt a more conciliatory and cooperative attitude towards the government's economic policy. It should be recalled that the leadership of the CC.OO, particularly its Secretary General Marcelino Camacho, was not opposed to the adoption of a liberal economic program for Spain in spite of the concessions it implied for the labour movement, since it had supported the decision of the PCE's allies to sign the *Pactos de la Moncloa* in 1977 (Camacho, 1979). Nevertheless, the leadership did not want these concessions to compromise the position of its organization at the level of the companies and the national concertation institutions. In the context of the fragmentation of the trade union movement which prevailed under the UCD government, this risk was higher than in the new climate created by the consolidation of the double hegemony of the UGT–CC.OO. From then on, the communist organization faced competition solely from the UGT, which incidentally was more popular among workers. Within the framework of this new situation, the CC.OO also adopted a position of support for the PSOE program of reforms, but they modulated this support in line with reaction from the base. When this support was positive or neutral, their support was open and formal (signing of multipartite agreements of 1990, 1991 and 1992 – Table 33); when it was negative and critical, their support was more discreet and mitigated (pursuit of the social dialogue and/or organization of demonstrations and sporadic short-lived strikes). This opportunist and corporatist attitude was also adopted by the UGT, particularly in 1987–88.

The most eloquent indicator of the climate of labour peace which prevailed for the major part of the three mandates was the limited number and size of strikes organized against the government reforms. Moderne (1983–89) and Bon (1990–93) count three 24-hour general strikes initiated by the UGT and CC.OO in 1985, 1988 and 1992, and about a dozen sectorial and local work stoppages, instigated primarily by the CC.OO, including one in 1983, three in 1987 and more than five in 1988. The stoppages of 1987 and 1988 were angry protests organized by several social groups (social workers, doctors, professors and students, workers) against various aspects and consequences of the government policy (reform of public teaching, freeze in salaries, liberalization of the labour relations system, increased unemployment, the youth employment plan, the restructuring of the iron and steel industries, and so on). The other work stoppages were directed against specific objectives of the socialist program (the restructuring of the Mediterranean blast furnaces in 1983, the modification of the retirement plan in 1985, the reduction of the length and the amount of unemployment insurance benefits in 1992) and were, in the case of the general strikes, partially followed through.

In fact, the only period for which it is appropriate to speak of a significant deterioration in the social climate was 1987–88. Nevertheless, it would be a great exaggeration to assert, like Gillespie (1990a), that the strikes of 1987–88, and the general strike of December 14, 1988 in particular, led to a 'rupture in the relations between the PSOE and its union allies' and to a 'split in the socialist family'. It is true that the general strike of 1988 followed a failure of social concertation, since neither the CC.OO nor the UGT wanted to endorse the government proposals in a climate marked by generalized discontent. It is also true that this strike amplified the current of support within the UGT for autonomy *vis-à-vis* the PSOE; this pressure led Secretary General Nicolas Redondo to resign from the PSOE executive committee in 1988 and to successfully press, during the 1990 PSOE congress, for the abandonment of party members' obligation to belong to the UGT. Nevertheless, these events did not prevent an agreement in principle on resuming the social dialogue at the end of 1988 and renewing the dialogue between the PSOE, the CEOE, the UGT and the CC.OO after the PSOE's third electoral victory in the fall of 1989, which testified to the limited social impact of the 1988 general strike on public opinion. This new phase of concertation was marked by the signing of a quadripartite agreement from 1990 to 1991 and the acceptance, by the UGT and the CC.OO, of the 1992 Plan for Economic Convergence. The anger of the UGT and the CC.OO was provoked by the adoption by decree of the emergency youth employment program and by the reform of the unemployment insurance system (see Chapter 2) – less because of the content of these measures than because they were promulgated outside the context of concertation. Two general strikes were planned for May and December 1992, but the second was cancelled due to the mitigated success of the first. In the meantime, the two organizations signed a new tripartite agreement limiting the right to strike (Table 33). This agreement clearly shows that, faced with the choice between the strategy of collaboration and that of confrontation, the UGT and the CC.OO preferred the former.

The ideological and organizational transformations that occurred at the highest levels of the union movement were not the only factors capable of explaining the preservation of social peace and the pursuit of dialogue between the government and the social actors. The decline of socialist ideals among unionized workers and their commitment, like the great majority of citizens, to the liberal, democratic project,[8] contributed significantly toward weakening the combativeness of the union leaders. While there were several factors that determined these cultural changes, it is probable that the improvement in the economic situation brought about by the end of the cycle of recession at the beginning of the eighties and the combined positive effects of the adjustment measures and membership in the EC (see Tables 5, 9, 10, 12, and Chapters 2 and 5)[9] played a considerable role in this regard. In fact, the percentage of citizens 'very satisfied or somewhat satisfied with the economic situation' increased by 70% in 1985, to 81% in 1989 (Eurobarometer, December 1989, Table B1).

The fact that the socialist leaders were able to offer the population and the trade unions social and political compensations in return for their economic sacrifices also facilitated the social dialogue. The PSOE, in fact, instituted universal accessibility to the education, health and social security systems while reducing the social contributions of companies and individuals (see Chapter 2). The SCMs were also accompanied by initiatives aimed at offsetting transition costs. Thus the restructuration programs in the declining industrial sectors were accompanied by various measures (lowering retirement age, increasing pre-retirement and retirement benefits, the creation of professional training programs) aimed at lightening the burden of the layoffs. The professional mobility incentives introduced in the 1992 Plan for Economic Convergence were accompanied by new programs aimed at improving the housing and professional training conditions of workers in outlying regions (see Chapter 2). Finally, the socialists awarded new political rights to the trade unions in order to compensate for the losses incurred as a result of the adjustment measures. In return for their acceptance of the new standards for relaxing the rules related to hiring and firing and making the regulations regarding unionization more severe – which led to a very significant drop in the rate of unionization (see this Chapter, note 3) – the trade union organizations managed to get the PSOE to recognize the rights of workers' representatives to participate in company management. They also obtained the right to negotiate collective agreements in the civil service, and they convinced the government to facilitate the unionization of part-time workers in the service sector (see Chapter 2). The trade unions' major political gain, however, was the institutionalization of social dialogue and the formalization of the multipartite negotiation process as a major tool for developing government policies. It is noteworthy that all the strikes and demonstrations organized by the CC.OO and the UGT against the government's economic policy either followed the failure of concertation or a decision on the part of the government to circumvent this process by decree or by submitting draft legislation to the Cortès that had not previously been negotiated with their social partners.

As for the EC aid programs (the CAP, ESCPs), it can be presumed that these contributed toward attenuating criticism originating in public opinion and the unions concerning the cost of the economic reforms, because of the size of the sums earmarked by the EC, the national public administrations and the private sector for providing support to agriculture, backward regions, declining industrial regions, and professional training and reinsertion of the chronically unemployed (Tables 31 and 32). Nevertheless, it would be difficult to claim that their actual impact increased support among the population and the interest groups for the PSOE adjustment policies. The evaluations currently available, in fact, provide only very fragmentary data on the topic, and these data tend to show that the positive effects of the ESCPs were minor both on the plane of economic growth and on the plane of employment.[10]

PSOE (1993–96): strong leadership and restricted autonomy

During the period following the 1993 elections, the PSOE saw its independence seriously reduced in relation to parliament. As it only managed to have 159 members elected, it had to conclude a much more constrictive alliance than the one formed in 1989 with the PNV and the CiU, since it involved the support of 16 deputies from the two parties. Furthermore, it was confronted with far more formidable opposition, as the PP of José Maria Aznar had increased its share of votes from 25.8% to 38.4% and the number of its seats from 106 to 141 (Table 28). Nevertheless, the government of Felipe Gonzalez managed to implement the provisions of the 1992 Plan for Economic Convergence – in spite of the onset of a new cycle of recession in 1991 – due to the support of the opposition parties for the plan, and to the consolidation of the liberals' position within the cabinet and the PSOE deputation.[11] However, the deterioration of the economic situation, and the new adjustment measures adopted by the government aimed at minimizing its effect, particularly with regard to employment, provoked a stiffening in the union leadership and a failure of social dialogue in 1993 and 1994, a failure sanctioned by the calling of a general strike on January 27, 1994. In the face of the mitigated success of the latter, and strengthened by the support of the opposition parties, the government, which incidentally was more convinced than ever of the soundness of its liberal program, decided to act unilaterally. It had parliament adopt a series of executive decrees that contained emergency measures against unemployment and a new ambitious review of the Status of Workers.[12]

The continuance of the adjustment process in spite of the economic recession and the protests of the trade unions and the organizations of the left (the IU and the IS), was not a major cause of the PSOE's electoral defeat in 1996 (Table 28). This resulted primarily from the socialists' loss of legitimacy following numerous conflicts of interest, influence peddling and political scandals (the *Grupos anti-terrorista de Liberacion* (GAL) affair)[13] which tarnished their two last mandates. The fact that the PP had been elected on the basis of a program aimed at reinforcing austerity measures and cleaning up administrative structures shows that it was much more the socialists' ethics than their economic program that earned them public disfavour at the elections of March 3, 1996 (Craig, 1994).[14]

Portugal

In Portugal, it was the absence of will of the governments in power or their internal discord combined with the opposition from other political parties (the PCP, the CDS) the AFM, the army and a number of social forces (the Catholic Church, SMEs, the *Confederacion general de los Trabajadores Portugueses-Intersyndical* (CGTP-IN), controlled by the PCP) that explain why it was not possible to apply a significant set of SMs and SCMs in any lasting manner before 1983. It was only when the leadership and the autonomy of the governments were strengthened in subsequent years, that the most rapid progress was achieved with these reforms.

PSP (1976–79): weak leadership and narrow autonomy

In spite of ideological dissention within the PSP (Chapter 6), its minority position in the Legislative Assembly (Table 30), the rejection of the liberal option by a high proportion if not all of the members of the opposition parties (PSDP, CDS, PCP), the army, the bureaucracy and numerous interest groups, the first Mario Soares government decreed a halt to the nationalization and collectivization procedures and various anti-inflationary measures at the beginning of its mandate; the latter were reinforced in January 1978 in order to obtain a new emergency loan from the IMF (see Chapter 3, 36–7). This unilateral attempt at imposing austerity would not last long, however. At the beginning of 1978, the government was obliged to resign as the result of a no-confidence motion. The *soaristas* then tried to remain in power and continue their stabilization policy through an alliance with the most liberal elements of the CDS, but this new strategy was as unproductive as the first. The PSP–CDS coalition only survived a year (1978–79) and was twice overturned in the meantime following a tightening of anti-inflationary measures. The latter were subsequently abandoned by the AD governments (an alliance of the CDS, PSDP and PP) (1979–83) (see Chapter 3 and Table 6).

PSP–PSDP (1983–85): shaky leadership and relative autonomy

The second experience of the socialists in power, thanks to the formation of a coalition government with the PSDP (1983–85), was more fruitful than the first, since it was formed for the implementation of a more substantial series of SMs and the beginning of a true process of structural change (Chapter 3, 37–9). There are several reasons for this relative success.

First of all, the fact that the liberals had progressively widened their influence, both within the PSP and the PSDP, in the period 1980–83, strengthened the cohesion and determination of the government in relation to the adjustment process. Nevertheless, because of persistent divisions in socialist ranks and electoral rivalries between the two formations, the PSP–PSDP alliance remained fragile and proved to be of short duration. Second, the PSP–PSDP coalition benefited from far wider autonomy in relation to parliament, on the one hand, because it obtained an absolute majority of 169 seats, 20 seats more than the PSP–CDS government (Table 30), and, on the other, because it faced less formidable opposition. Since its participation in the AD government, the CDS was more inclined to cooperate with the PSDP; it was also weakened by the resignation of its chief, Freito Amaral, and by internal dissention (Mcleod, 1990; Graham, 1992). The PCP, for its part, was unable, with only 44 members, to overturn the cabinet's liberal policy, in spite of the fierce opposition it mounted against it. It was the limited yet significant margin of manoeuvre enjoyed by the PSP–PSDP government with regard to the National Assembly which allowed it to ratify the constitutional reform in 1982, a reform which, by abolishing the powers of the Revolutionary Council over the executive power and by authorizing the adoption of a law on national defence, contributed to widening its autonomy in relation to nationalist, protectionist and socialist elements in the army (Bruneau, 1990; Gladdish, 1990; Graham, 1992). Third, the government of Mario Soares tightened its control over the bureaucracy by instigating, at the very beginning of its mandate, a vast anti-corruption operation. It gave a High Authority the mandate of warning, confirming and denouncing to the relevant authorities all acts of corruption and fraud committed in the exercise of public and administrative services, at the national, regional and local levels and in the armed forces (Rudel, 1984, 212).

Finally, the government was able to benefit from a climate of relative social peace. Although the PCP and various groups, particularly the Catholic Church and the CGTP-IN, denounced the costs of the austerity policy – higher prices, delays in salary payments,[15] higher unemployment (see Table 34) – no strikes or large-scale mobilizations were organized between 1983 and 1985 (Rudel 1984, 1985, 1986). This situation was in line with the progressive reinforcement of the PSP and PSDP new unions (grouped together within the *Union general de los Trabajadores* (UGT)), notably within the service, chemistry and textile sectors and the creation of the Permanent Council of Social Concertation (PCSC). This body, which was instituted at the instigation of Mario Soares and inspired by other European concertation experiments, notably that of the PSOE, brought together, in addition to government representatives, the UGT and the major owners' associations: the Confederation of Portuguese Industry (CPI), the Confederation of Portuguese Merchants (CPM) and the Confederation of Portuguese Farmers (CPF). Its mandate was to negotiate multipartite agreements on the orientations and modes of application of SMs and SCMs. Even though it did not result in any formal agreement in the period 1983–85, this institutionalization of social dialogue encouraged the various social partners, including the CGTP-IN, to adopt a more moderate, tolerant attitude toward government action (Marques, 1990, 187–8). The preservation of labour peace was also helped by the changes which took place within public opinion at the beginning of the eighties. Observing that nationalist and socialist policies had not improved the economic situation (Tables 9, 11 and 16) and considering that membership in the EC was now inevitable, an increasingly larger proportion of citizens turned away from the project of the left and gave their support to the Europeanist and liberal policy of the PSP and the PSDP,[16] in spite of its costs. One of the most eloquent indicators of this development is the victory, in the early elections of 1985 (Table 30), of the PSDP, which had broken off its alliance with the socialists because the latter were slowing down the application of the structural reforms.

PSDP (1985–95): strong leadership and wide autonomy

The social-democrats' accession to power in 1985 sanctioned Portugal's irreversible commitment to the road of economic liberalization. Both the minority PSDP government of 1985–87 and the majority PSDP governments of 1987–91 and 1991–95 firmly and rapidly adopted a wide range of SMs and SCMs (see Chapter 3) that allowed Portugal to join the nucleus of EC member states that were most likely to join the EMU in 1999 (Table 8). It was the intensification of the governments' cohesion and determination and their increased autonomy in relation to the political system which were the most decisive determinants of this major shift. The finalization of negotiations for EC membership in 1985, and Portugal's official entry into the EC in 1986, certainly created conditions favourable to the liberalization of the Portuguese economy (Torres, 1994), but this would not have been possible without a transformation in internal political factors. The preponderance of these factors is, moreover, clearly demonstrated by the fact that in Spain, the adjustment process was initiated several years before its entry into the Europe of the Twelve, whereas in Greece, membership in the Community did not further the economic reforms.

The strengthening of solidarity and the resolution of the Portuguese leaders with regard to the economic reforms is linked to the ideological transformation and unification of the PSDP under the new leadership of Cavaco Silva (see Chapter 6). Their greater freedom to manoeuvre in the application of SMs and the SCMs can be ascribed both to their obtaining important absolute majorities in the parliament in 1987 and 1991 (Table 30) and to the support that the social-democrats received from a large number of PSP and CDS deputies, as the influence of the liberals within these two formations continued to increase in the period following 1995. In fact, the PCP is the only opposition party that unilaterally and consistently denounced the PSDP liberal policy. The effectiveness of this opposition, however, remained very limited due to conspicuous continual weakening of the communists' position in the National Assembly (Table 30). This decline, incidentally, is largely attributable to the ideological rigidity of the PCP, which in effect remained faithful to its Marxist-Leninist program, in spite of the failure of the nationalization, collectivization and self-management measures experienced by its allies in the AFM, Portugal's membership in the EC, the fall of the communist regime in the USSR and Eastern Europe and the emergence of currents of renewal (the Third Way, the Group of Six) within its ranks. Alvaro Cunhal and the PCP leadership responded to these changes by excluding dissidents from the Central Committee, by recognizing Portugal's membership in the EC and agreeing to democratize the party's internal operating rules.[17] They refused, however, to undertake any modifications to the party's communist platform.

The control exerted over parliament by the PSDP was a crucial factor in the advancement of these reforms; first of all because it allowed for the abolition in 1988 of the provisions of the 1976 constitution that prohibited reprivatization of public enterprises and retrocession to its former owners of farming land that had been collectivised following the April 1974 revolution (Bruneau, 1990); second, because it made possible in the same year the adoption of a new organic law on national defence which consolidated the authority of the executive power and its policies over the army (Bruneau, 1991–92); third, because it facilitated the continuance of the modernization and democratization of the public administration. This reform, which was made necessary by Portugal's membership in the EC and its participation in the latter's various aid programs, permitted it, in conjunction with the measures for privatizing and restructuring the public sector, to strengthen the domination of the executive over the bureaucracy and to weaken that institution's resistance to the neo-liberal shift.

Finally, the PSDP's control over parliament allowed it to adopt the stabilization and structural change measures that the trade unions had refused to ratify and had, in several cases, contested by means of strikes and other forms of pressure. This strategy was used more in Portugal than in Spain, as social concertation proved more difficult due to the less cooperative attitude of the CGTP-IN and of the existence within the UGT of a wing of the radical left which had quite close ties to the CGTP-IN. These divisions in the trade union movement, accentuated by the more rapid pace of reforms and the necessarily greater severity of their costs, explain the limited nature of social dialogue under the Cavaco Silva governments after 1997. While labour peace was maintained during the first PSDP minority government (1985–87), it degenerated significantly under the majority governments of the Social Democratic party (1987–95).

Although the political leaders pursued discussions with the representatives of management and union parties, primarily within the PCSC, and they managed to conclude episodic *Pactos laborales* with the UGT, and in certain cases, with the CGTP-IN, these agreements remain partial, as the unions only gave their support to certain government reforms.[18] As of 1988, in spite of continued concertation and the signing of new ad hoc multipartite agreements, the CGTP-IN, supported by the leftist wing of the UGT, the PCP and the Catholic Church, organized several sectorial strikes against the economic reforms.[19] In concert with the UGT, it also organized two 24-hour general strikes against the reform of the labour code (in 1988) and against the QUANTUM (in 1992), which received wide support. In spite of these protests, these social-democratic governments refused to amend their draft legislation,[20] which they had ratified by the National Assembly, made strong by their absolute majority, by the strict vote discipline imposed on the deputies in their party, by the support of several socialists and Christian Democrats, by the support of the moderate wing of the UGT and by the support of a large share of public opinion.

According to the Eurobarometer survey of December 1989 (Table B1), the percentage of Portuguese 'very satisfied or rather satisfied with the economic situation' in fact increased from 56% in 1985 to 71% in 1989. This change is no doubt ascribable to the improvement in the economic and social situation during this period, which was the result of the end of the 1979–83 recession, the beneficial effects of the adjustment measures, of membership in the EC, and of the investments made through the community aid programs (Tables 31 and 32; this Chapter, note 10). The period following 1985 was in fact characterized by lower inflation (Table 9), a resurgence of investment (Table 12) and of growth (Table 11) and a decrease in the unemployment rate, which, moreover, was markedly lower than in Spain (Table 34). The improved level of public satisfaction with the economic situation is perhaps also ascribable to the improvements in social policies. Within the context of the constraints created by membership in the EC, the Portuguese governments improved accessibility to the education system and the protections offered by the various social security plans. However social expenditures remained far below those of Greece and Spain (see Tables 17, 18 and 19).

Analysis of the case of Portugal shows that the existence of conditions favourable to the attenuation of TCs may increase the level of satisfaction among the general public without at the same time convincing all the trade union organizations to go along with government reforms. It seems that the attitude of the Portuguese trade unions was in the final analysis more influenced by their ideology, their corporate interests, their position *vis-à-vis* their competition and the political gains obtained in exchange for their economic concessions (a variable about which which we possess no pertinent information in the case of Portugal) than by the general interest and the opinions of the population.

Greece

PASOK (1985–89) and ND (1990–93): autonomy without leadership

As discussed in Chapter 4, it was only after 1985 that the PASOK (1985–89; 1993–96) and the ND (1990–93) governments adopted a set – very limited in the first case, much wider in the second case – of SMs and SCMs. Actually, the SMs were only applied in a partial, temporary manner, and most of the SCMs were never implemented, with the result that the imbalances and structural problems within the economy continued to worsen (Chapter 5; Tables 8–16). Three major factors led to the poor performance of the Papandreou and Mitsokakis governments in their attempts to carry through an economic adjustment program: first, opposition from the majority of members and leaders of the PASOK and a large percentage of militants and leaders of the ND to the neo-liberal shift (Chapter 6); second, domination by the PASOK, the ND and several anti-liberal elements over the major institutions of the political systems (parliament, the bureaucracy, departmental administrations); and third, the control exerted by PASOK and the KKE over the major popular interest groups, particularly ADEDY, the civil servants' association and the major labour trade union (GSEE).

Thus, as Featherstone (1987, 1990), Diamandouros (1993) and others have pointed out, the democratic regime established in 1975 did not signal a break with the period prior to the junta of the colonels (1967–74), since it reinstituted the traditional polarization of political forces between a party of the right (the ex-ERE that had become the ND) and a centre-left party (the ex-EK that became the PASOK). The results of the legislative elections since 1974 clearly illustrate this bipartisan domination. Table 29 shows that every parliament elected in this period was largely dominated by the PASOK and the ND, each of the two parties having alternately come to power with absolute or near absolute majorities, except in 1989. This situation did not, however, make the progress of the adjustment process any easier. Due to opposition from several cabinet members and several deputies in their party, the liberal ministers of the Papandreou (1985–89; 1993–) and Mitsokaksis (1990–93) governments either put their reform projects on the back burner, or were unsuccessful in having them adopted by the Legislative Assembly. During its first term in power, officially with the goal of consolidating democracy, the PASOK adopted a constitutional reform that reduced the power of the president in favour of parliament; it replaced enhanced proportional representation (PR) by simple PR in 1985; it increased parliamentary control over the public administration (Featherstone, 1990)[21] and it proceeded with a limited transfer of administrative powers from the state to the departments (Papageourgiou and Verney, 1992). These changes, in fact, increased the control of the two major parties over the legislative process,[22] the administrative process and the regional entities, but at the same time extended the influence of PASOK and ND members who supported the nationalist and interventionist economic model of the preceding political regimes within these bodies for developing and applying public policies. Also, the influence of PASOK supporters over the bureaucracy and its clientelized networks received a strong boost when the first Papandreou government awarded 100000 new posts for civil servant to militants and sympathizers.

PASOK failed completely to reform an overinflated and notoriously inefficient public administration. Not only was the public sector expanded but the bureaucracy was also enlarged with the addition of more than

100,000 to the public payroll. The state apparatus was colonised from top to bottom by the party faithful, other hangers-on and voters in the best Greek traditions of patronage, clientelism and the distribution of the spoils of power ... many party members took governmental positions of other public posts and the party machine was thrown into some disarray.

(Kapetannyannis, 1993, 81)

During its first mandate, the PASOK also adopted a wide range of legislation officially aimed at democratizing the functioning of these interest groups (IGs). In reality, this legislation primarily intended to limit the influence of the ND in the interests of the other political parties, and above all the PASOK, within the organizations of civil society. As Mavrogordatos (1993) emphasizes, rather than consolidating democracy by favouring the self-reliance of the IGs *vis-à-vis* the political system, as in Spain and Portugal, the PASOK strengthened the corporate links between them and the parties. One of these pieces of legislation obliged all IGs to elect their leaders by PR. By allowing the lists of candidates to be partisan lists, this new regulation transformed these organizations into mini-parliaments, which, just like the parliament in Athens, were dominated by the PASOK, the ND and the KKE. The PASOK also, under the threat of dissolution or exclusion, imposed on all IGs a tripartite structure (local organization, regional federation, national confederation) and new rules and statutes.[23] An analysis of the percentage of posts held by each party within the leadership of each IG (see Table 35), shows that these reforms in fact preserved the ND's control over the major employers' associations – the confederation of large commercial enterprises (EESE) and the associations of Greek industries (KEE, SEV), while breaking up the leadership of the IGs in the 'popular bloc' – PASEGES, the farmers' federation, GSEE, the workers' trade union organization, ADEDY, the civil servants union, GSEVEE, the small and medium enterprise association[24] – among the PASOK, the ND and the KKE.

The fact that the PASOK and the KKE, the two major parties opposed to the stabilization and liberalization of the economy,[25] had more influence than the ND, particularly within the GSEE and ADEDY, contributed towards the postponement of several SCMs contemplated by the Mitsokakis government (1990–93).[26] Thus, in 1992, the GSEE, the ADEDY, the PASOK and the KKE organized a series of strikes, certain of which turned into confrontations with the police, in protest against the government's austerity policy (Catsiapis, 1993, 222). Nevertheless, the PASOK itself experienced a backlash from its strategy of 'democratizing' the IGs when it wanted to modify the orientations of its economic policy. In 1985 and 1986, the KKE, the ADEDY and the GSEE organized major protest movements against its stabilization program in which numerous PASOK militants, members of ADEDY and GSEE, participated. Following this contestation, the PASOK lost its majority position on 45 GSEE councils, and several hundred militants broke off their membership of the PASOK (Catsiapis, 1986, 202). On February 27, 1986, the GSEE and the KKE organized a general strike against the PASOK's austerity policy that affected banks, industry and transportation. The Papandreou government reacted by excluding a dozen unionists from the left wing of the PASOK, who in turn reacted by forming a new organization with several GSEE dissidents: the socialist workers and employees' union movement (SEER) (Catsiapis, 1987).

The case of Greece and, in particular, the experience of the PASOK in power, demonstrates that the degree of autonomy or control of the executive over political institutions and civil society is a variable that depends on government leadership; it is favourable to the success of adjustment only when the majority of the members and leaders of the government party support this process. It is also evident that the tightening of external constraints, such as the threat of being denied EMU membership, has had no effect on the liberals' determination to pursue reforms when they were repudiated by their colleagues in the cabinet, the militants in their party, and the political and social actors. The case of Greece also indicates that the existence of conditions favourable to the attenuation of TCs, such as the enhancement of social programs and the intioduction of programs aimed at reducing regional and social economic inequalities, does not necessarily guarantee that a social consensus will be reached on the process of economic liberalization. Although, just like Spain and Portugal, Greece extended the accessibility and the universality of education and social security systems concurrently with gaining membership in the EC (see Chapter 4); although it went ahead, in concert with the EC, with extremely large investments in the area of economic and social developments in the context of IMPs, the ESCPs and the Cohesion Fund (see Tables 31 and 32); and although these programs had more significant positive effects on economic growth than in Spain (this Chapter, note 10), both the social actors and a large segment of public opinion remained resistant to the SMs and SCMs. Finally, the case of Greece demonstrates that the deterioration of the economic situation did not necessarily incite IGs and citizens to lend increased support to the adjustment measures. While this variable contributed towards changing public opinion in Portugal, such was not the case in Greece. In fact the Eurobarometer survey of December 1989 revealed that the rate of satisfaction of Greek citizens with regard to the economic situation in their country increased from 63% in 1984 to 68% in 1989 in spite of the negative effects of abandoning its – limited – stabilization program.

In the last analysis, the failure of the adjustment process in Greece originated fundamentally in the rejection of the liberal project by a large sector of the population and the majority of the political and social actors. While the period following 1975 had been characterized by growing support for democracy among citizens (Dimitras, 1987; Morlino and Montero; 1991; Diamandouros, 1993) and gradual acceptance of the positive effects of EC membership (Verney, 1990; Spourdalakis, 1992), mistrust of the values and implications of economic liberalism – the opening and integration of markets, the need to compete with other economies – persisted within various social strata and their organizations, with only the elites linked to the ND involved in activities of an international nature firmly adhering to this ideology. This attitude is doubtless related to the persistent influence of several values of the traditional culture that Diamandouros (1993) characterizes as 'the underdog culture': nationalism turned in on itself; fear of foreigners and the liberal, capitalist west; dependance on a paternalist state; and an emphasis on egalitarianism. According to this author, this rigidity of the cultural substratum can be partially explained by the long-term predominance within the economy of small family enterprises, a factor that is conducive to the centralization of political power, corporatism and nationalism. This explanation, which is also defended by other authors (Dimitras, 1987; Boutilier and Uzundis, 1991) is validated by the antithetical case of Spain, where the capitalist industrialization of the sixties and seventies encouraged the expansion, at every level of society and the various nationalities, of a new liberal political and economic culture (Maravall, 1982; Hermet, 1984; Maravall and Santamaria, 1986; Perez Diaz, 1993). It is, on the other hand, partially invalidated by the case of Portugal, where the persistence of pre-capitalist structures in several regions of the country, comparable to those in Greece, did not prevent a large part of citizens abandoning their nationalist, corporatist and egalitarian values in favour of pro-democratic, pro-capitalist and liberal attitudes towards the mid-eighties. It seems then, as Diamandouras himself states (1993), that one would need to refer to other factors, particulary geo-political and historical considerations, to explain both the relative imperviousness to change of the traditional Greek culture and the more or less precocious and rapid metamorphosis of the Iberian culture.

Conclusion

On the whole, the comparison of Southern European cases either confirms or challenges and complements the main findings of the studies that have analyzed the process of economic adjustment and the determinants of its success, in various authoritarian and democratic regimes of Latin America, Asia, Eastern Europe and Africa since 1990.

It corroborates the thesis in accordance with which new democracies are not less or more able than authoritarian regimes to take up the challenge of economic liberalization. Indeed, the assessment of Southern European countries' economic performances, during the post-authoritarian period (1975–95), with the help of the three criteria mostly used by the specialists – (1) the adoption of a coherent set of SMs and SCMs by the governments; (2) the implementation of this program in a systematic way during several years; and (3) the attainment of the objectives aimed by SMs and SCMs (correction of macro-economic disequilibrium, improvement of the economy's opening and competitiveness, resumption of growth) – reveals that Spain and Portugal have achieve their economic adjustment with relative success while Greece could not take up this challenge. The thorough assessment of Spain and Portugal's economic reforms shows that they have been overestimated by many observers. It cannot be denied that both countries have succeeded in curbing inflation and reducing the weight of their public debts and deficits while improving their growth rates (between 1983 and 1990) and their res-distributive policies. However, the success of this heteredox or social-democratic strategy of adjustment is largely due to the boom of FDI and EC transfers after their entry into the Community. This massive inflow of capital was only partially determined by the liberalisation of Iberian economic policies. Other variables, like the proximity of their markets and the lower costs of their labour force, have contributed to this movement. Otherwise, structural reforms were insufficient in both countries and thus did not permit a significant betterment of the enterprises competitiveness and external trade balances. In fact, economic adjustment can be qualified as a success mainly because it seems henceforth to be irreversible. Since the beginning of the nineties, all the governments have committed themselves to reinforcing SMs and SCMs in order to comply with the EMU convergence norms, despite the lessening of growth and investment rates.

The study corroborates the conclusion according to which the success of adjustment, in democracies as in authoritarian regimes, is mainly determined

(1) by the government's commitment to undertake reforms, a condition that implies the cohesion and the resolution of all the cabinet members; and (2) by the government's ability to implement reforms in a systematic and lasting way while avoiding major social unrest related to transition costs.

As far as it concerns the first point, Chapters 2, 3 and 4 show that in Greece (before 1990), as in Portugal (before 1983), economic reforms were rejected or limited to few SMs and SCMs, because of the liberals' dissident minority within governments. On the other hand, in Spain as in Portugal (after 1985), the adoption of a coherent set of SMs and SCMs resulted from the solidarity and the determination of all the cabinet members. Chapter 6 confirms that the favourable attitude of political leaders toward economic adjustment is decisively determined neither by the seriousness of the economic crisis, nor by the majority or minority composition of the government, nor by the rightist or leftist orientation of the governmental party/parties, nor by the electoral cycles, nor by the conditional aids of international institutions. Furthermore, it brings new insights about the role of external factors, showing that neither EC membership, nor the conciliating attitude of the Community toward the economic choices of its new partners, nor its generous non-conditional aid, have contributed to change the resistant attitude of the PASOK and the ND leaders. If in Spain, and later in Portugal, the prospect of joining the EC has reinforced the support of citizens and elites toward economic reforms, it was not the case in Greece: most of the PASOK leaders as well as a large proportion of the ND rulers never agreed to economic austerity and liberalization, despite their acceptance of Greece's entry into the Community. The conciliatory attitude of the Community and the generous non-conditional aid conceded to the new member states – through the CAP, IMPs and ESCPs – have encouraged the persistence of these resistent attitudes. Indeed, if in Spain and in Portugal, the Community's subsidies have been effectively employed to alleviate the integration and economic adjustment transition costs, in Greece they have rather been used to consolidate the clientelist networks of governing parties and to justify the profitability of corporatist and interventionist economic policies.

Recent publications pay more attention to the above-mentioned non-decisive variables, than to the factors that influence a government's cohesion and resolution in all cases. Many authors maintain that the political leaders' attitudes are always greatly determined by the way each of them evaluates the political risks and economic efficiency of SMs and SCMs. However, they do not question in more depth the foundations of these evaluations. Chapter 6 brings new insights on this topic. It postulates that the cabinet members' stances on the efficiency of SMs and SCMs, that is, their ability to solve existing economic problems, are mainly determined by their own party's/parties' degree of adherence to the values of economic liberalism. The comparison of Southern European governing parties' attitudes reveals that new parties, created during transitions towards democracy and neo-liberalism, are not necessarily more favourable to this ideology than old renovated organizations. If most of the UCD's members shared the liberal beliefs of their leader Adolfo Suarez, the PASOK membership remained largely hostile to liberalism, as well as an important proportion of the PSP's members, even though both organizations were created during the seventies as the UCD. On the other hand, old parties like the PSOE, the PSDP and the ND (under Mitsokakis, 1990–93) have experienced a more or less thoroughly ideological metamorphosis during the seventies and/or eighties. These changes permitted them to adopt more complete programs of SMs and SCMs when they acceded to power. On the whole, my analysis indicates that program choices, which characterized the various new and old political parties, depend on two factors: the accession to directorship of a leader and a team convinced of the soundness of economic liberalism, and the ability of the new leadership to impose its views on the organization as a whole. This second condition itself depends on several variables: the selection or the modification of the rank and file and managerial membership; the change of decision making and operational rules, sometimes by authoritarian and corporatist methods; the party's rootedness within civil society; the popularity of the leader among the general population and the militants; and the support of foreign brother organizations. Among all these variables, the party's rootedness within civil society is particularly crucial. Mitsokakis and Mario Soares did not succeed in rallying the vast majority of their militants and executives behind their liberal platform, unlike Felipe Gonzalez and Cavaco Silva, largely because the basic organizations and influence of the ND and the PSP, within various social strata and regions, were less developed than those of the PSOE and the PSDP.

With regard to the second decisive condition of the success of adjustment, that is, the governments' ability to implement SMs and SCMs in a systematic and lasting way despite their transition costs, my analysis only partially confirms the thesis of Nelson and colleagues.

Chapter 7 shows that, in democracies, the leadership of the government – that is, its cohesion and determination – constitutes a necessary prerequisite for the advancement of reforms. Indeed, the Greek case demonstrates that political leadership is a more decisive condition than executive's autonomy (Figure 6). Despite their parliamentary majority and their control over state apparatus and IGs, neither the ND nor the PASOK could apply their programs of reforms, for both governing parties were deeply divided over the validity of adjustment.

This being said, the unequal achievements of the UCD, on the one hand, and of the PSOE and PSDP, on the other hand, demonstrate that a united and resolute executive cannot pursue the adjustment process, notably the SCM, without a large autonomy *vis-à-vis* the main political institutions. In this regard, an absolute majority in the parliament is a very important asset, given that it facilitates the reform and the control of the bureaucracy and the army by the governing party. Furthermore, the PSDP case indicates that such a majority can counter-balance the absence of a strong and large support from other political parties and IGs.

In other respects, Chapter 7 shows that neither the betterment of social policies, nor the allowance of generous non-conditional external aids, nor the institutionalization of social concertation, nor the progress of democratic consolidation can be considered as decisive determinants of the acceptance of economic reforms by political parties, popular interest groups and citizens.

The three Southern European democracies have significantly improved their education, health and social security policies during the eighties, to comply with the EC's requests and to consolidate their still fragile democracies. These reforms have contributed to improving the living conditions of the poorer and less powerful social groups, while permitting a reduction in the costs of structural changes in Spain and Portugal. However, I cannot conclude from these acknowledgements that there exists in all cases a causal relation between social improvements and the increase of popular IGs and citizens' support for economic adjustment. In Greece, labour unions and popular associations upheld their opposition to adjustment despite social reforms. In other respects, various polls indicate that the population continued to be satisfied with the economic situation, despite the failure of liberal reforms. In Spain and Portugal, the uneven support given by labour unions to economic adjustment cannot be attributed mainly to social reforms, even if these organizations have strongly encouraged the latter (see below). It must be noted that in Spain all the parties and the IGs, as far as the majority of citizens, agreed to the new liberal model of development during democratic transition (1975–78) before the achievement of social reforms (1982–92). In Portugal the reversal of public opinion about adjustment occurred between 1983 and 1987, before the implementation of social reforms; it mainly resulted from the disillusion of the population about socialist and nationalist policies on the one hand, and from the imminence or the irreversibility of Portugal's entry into the EC, on the other. Otherwise, a large proportion of labour union leaders and militants and other IGs remained hostile to adjustment measures despite the betterment of social programs.

Chapter 7 also indicates that the EC and Southern European countries allocated large amounts of money, from 1988, to prevent an increase of economic and social disparities, in the framework of the completion of the Single Market and the EMU. The assessment of their outputs indicates that these investments have unevenly contributed to the resumption of economic growth in all three countries. On the whole, the EC's aid has undoubtedly created favourable conditions for a heterodox or less painful adjustment. Nevertheless, it is difficult to maintain that this support has helped to alleviate transition costs, and reinforce the support of IGs and citizens toward adjustment.

In Spain and Portugal, the PSOE as well as the PSP–PSDP and PSDP governments have established a permanent and institutional framework of multiparty negotiations between the state, the employers' associations and the labour unions, in order to conclude compromises about the SMs' and the SCMs' content and modes of application. However, only the socialist labour bodies (Spanish and Portuguese UGT) participated in these negotiations on a regular basis. The collaboration of the communist unions (CC.OO in Spain, CGTP-IN in Portugal) was only episodic and both refused to sign many of the agreements concluded by other social partners. Nevertheless, until 1987–88, they did not mobilize their members against these agreements. From 1987–88, the communist and socialist labour unions became quite less cooperative and jointly organized strikes and mobilizations against some of the government's measures. The analysis of the motivations that underlay these behaviours tends to demonstrate that the Spanish and Portuguese labour bodies' positions toward economic reforms and social concertation were mainly influenced by their ideological convictions – and their privileged links with one or other political party – as well as by their own corporatist interests, rather than by their members' or workers' interests. The communist unions never fully collaborated with the socialists or social-democrats, given their ideological hostility to liberalism, especially in Portugal, and because of the political and electoral competition between leftist parties in both countries. In other respects, before 1987–88, all the unions accepted officially or tacitly many SMs and SCMs which implied a deterioration of the general working and living conditions, not only because the latter were accompanied by social improvements and measures of compensation, but also because they did not seriously threaten their membership and influence. After 1987–88, the communists together with the socialist unions mobilized their members against the new labour legislations – such as aiming to promote early retirement, mobility of workers and flexibility of employment (part-time and temporary jobs) – deemed likely to reduce the size of their membership and the extent of their influence within civil society. Being mainly preoccupied by their own power and interests, Iberian labour unions always paid careful attention to the opinions of their rank and file militants and members. The fact that the Spanish and Portuguese workers later progressively adhered, from a pragmatic point of view, to the new liberal credo of the democratic governments, has had a great impact upon the unions' behaviour. During the period after 1987–88, this factor incited them to limit their contestation to sporadic 24-hour strikes, while pursuing a more or less open and official collaboration with the political authorities. On the whole, Spanish and Portuguese cases demonstrate that social concertation, even when it is accompanied by social improvements and measures of compensation, is not sufficient to guarantee the collaboration of unions in economic reforms. Such a strategy is fruitful only when it does not threaten the corporatist interests of the unions and when the radical and moderate parties of the left support economic reforms.

Finally, the Southern European case studies do not corroborate the assertion that there exists a necessary relation between democratic consolidation and social consensus about economic reforms. First, although the legitimation or the popular support for democracy has constantly progressed in the three countries from the end of seventies, it was more pronounced in Greece than in Spain and Portugal (Morlino and Montero, 1991; Ethier, 1994b). Yet most Greeks and a significant proportion of the Portuguese remained opposed to liberal reforms. Second, if in all the three countries the democratic governments succeeded in establishing their control over army and bureaucracy, in Greece this process did not change the negative attitudes of the military forces and civil servants toward economic reforms. Given that the ND and the PASOK themselves were divided about or opposed to these reforms, they did not carry out changes intended to rally both institutions to economic liberalism, as in Spain and Portugal. It is interesting to note that the three countries, and especially Spain and Greece, imposed their authority over bureaucracy by expansionist and corporatist measures rather than by liberal methods – budget and staff cutbacks, privatization of services, and so on. Nevertheless, the results of these similar strategies were quite different, as far as the attitudes of bureaucrats about adjustment are concerned. Thus, it appears that the ideology of the reformers is more decisive than the reforms themselves. Third, it is a matter of fact that the autonomization of civil society – development of interest groups independent from the state and parties – and the stabilization of the party system – consolidation of bipartisanism, reinforcement of the cooperation or consensual unification among parties – have been more pronounced in Iberian countries than in Greece during the post-authoritarian period. The second element has without doubt favoured the growth of consensus about economic liberalization in Spain and Portugal. On the other hand, Iberian cases show that the autonomization of civil society is not necessarily a favourable condition to successful adjustment.

In Spain as in Portugal it is the dependence of some main IGs (like the employers' associations and socialist unions) on the PSOE and PSP–PSDP, rather than their autonomy, which has notably permitted these parties to build a coalition in favour of reforms.

In the final analysis, the study of the Southern European cases shows that the governments' commitment to undertake reforms, and their ability to implement the latter through the building of a wide social consensus, depends mainly on three factors: the leadership of the government, the beneficial effects of adjustment measures and the ideology of the major political parties, since the latter are the agents for the transformation of the army and the bureaucracy, the actors in parliament and a major instrument for shaping the attitudes of IGs and citizens. In this regard, a fundamental question still remains unanswered: why did all the Spanish political parties adhere so quickly to the liberal model, whereas the Portuguese parties converted only later and partially, and the Greek political parties continued in very large measure to reject them? Although comparative research on democratic transitions in Southern Europe may shed a certain amount of light in this regard (see Schmitter and Karl, 1991, Schmitter, 1986), the primary response to this question can only be found in a deeper analysis of the culture of the elite. In fact, as Pridham (1990b) and Morlino (1995) pointed out, if the recent political development of the Southern European countries has been marked by a certain consolidation of their democratic regimes, the major political parties have remained elitist organizations. To understand the evolution of the attitudes of the political parties towards economic liberalism, it is thus necessary to study in greater depth the socio-economic and cultural characteristics of these social strata.

Appendix: Tables and Figures

Table 1 Greece, Spain, Portugal: Socio-economic Indicators (1960–75)

Indicators/Country	Greece 1960	Greece 1975	Spain 1960	Spain 1975	Portugal 1960	Portugal 1975
External Trade Balance[1]	−311	−2916	57	7386	−106	1674
Current Account Balance[1]	−103	−1009	361	3488	−13	−819
Public Deficit[1]	96,5	1053	1600	1742	49	1072
Annual Average GDP Growth Rate[2]	6,9	5,2	7,3	5,4	6,3	5,2
Annual Average Inflation Growth Rate[2]	3,2	13,3	6,3	12,8	2,9	11,9
Unemployment Rate[2*]	0,05	4	0,01	5,2	n.a.	13,5
Imports[3]:						
Raw Materials	8	8	22	26	10	15
Manufactured Goods	65	64	37	44	47	53
Exports[3]:						
Raw Materials	91	52	78	30	45	29
Textile and Clothes	1	17	7	6	18	26
Other Manufactured Goods	9	32	15	63	37	42

1   in millions of US Dollars
2   1960–70; 1970–76
2* 1960–70; 1970–76. In % of the working population
3   in % of the global trade volume

Sources: The World Bank, *World Development Report*; OECD, *Economic Studies*.

Table 2 Spain: Economic Reforms Under Democratic Governments (1977–95)

Sector/Government	Minority UCD Govt. 1977–79	Minority UCD Govt. 1979–1982	Majority PSOE Govt. 1982–86	Majority PSOE Govt. 1986–89	Majority PSOE Govt. 1990–93	Minority PSOE Govt. 1993 …
Monetary and Budgetary Policies	*					
Taxation	*		*	*		
Social Policy	*	*	*	*		
Financial Institutions	*	*	*	*	*	
Foreign Investments	*		*	*		
Industrial Relations		*	*	*	*	
Pension Plans				*	*	
External Trade	*		*	*	*	
Public Sector		*		*	*	*
Industry		*		*	*	
Agriculture						

Sources: Bermeo (1996) and the author.

Table 3 Spain: Examples of Privatizations of INI Companies (1984–90)

Enterprise	Sector	Buyer	Year	% Privatized
Textile				
Tarazona	Textiles	Cima Eursa	1984	70
Secoinsa	Electronics	Fujitsu CTNE	1985	69
SKF Espanola	Ball Bearings	Aktiebolaget SKF	1985	99
Viajes Marsans	Travel	Trapsa	1985	100
Motores MDB	Veh. Engineering	Klockner Umbolt	1986	60
Olcesa	Food	Mercosa	1986	51
Seat	Vehicles	Volkswagen	1986	75
Dessa	Shipbuilding	Forestal del Atlàntico	1987	80
Purolator	Vehicles	Knecht Filterwerke	1987	95
Carcesa	Food	Tabacalera	1988	100
Lesa	Food	Tabacalera	1988	100
Astican	Shipbuilding	Italmar	1989	91
Ateinsa	Engineering	GEC-Alsthom	1989	85
Enfersa	Fertilizers	Ercros	1989	80
MTM	Engineering	GEC-Alsthom	1989	85
Oesa	Food	Grupo Ferruzzi	1989	100
Pesa	Electronics	Amper, SA	1989	97
Enasa	Vehicles	Fiat	1990	60

Source: Salmon (1991), p. 36.

Table 4 Spain: Restructuring Programmes (1980–91)

Sector	Dates	Number of Companies	Labour Force*		
			A	B	C
Integrated Iron and Steel	1980–90	3	42,837	22,761	24,715
Special Steels	1980–90	11	13,744	5,016	6,119
Semi-processed Copper	1981–84	4	4,503	3,430	3,401
Heavy Forgings	1981–84	2	1,277	970	915
Fertilizers[1]	1984–88	10	8,541	7,232	6,517
Shipbuilding (GA)	1984–90	2	21,920	9,972	11,249
Shipbuilding (PM)[2]	1984–90	27	15,427	8,198	9,162
Textiles	1981–86	683	108,844	98,919	98,919
Domestic Electrical Appliances[3]	1980–88	18	23,869	11,258	12,272
Vehicle Electrical Equipment	1981–85	2	6,720	5,378	5,269
Electronic Components	1981–85	17	3,744	2,200	2,314
Alcatel-Standard Eléctrica	1983–91	1	16,133	7,756	11,459
ERT Group	1983–87	10	10,304	7,811	7,811
Marconi Espanola	1983–91	1	2,548	450	1,283
Total		791	280,411 (100%)	191,351 (68%)	201,405 (72%)

*   Labour Force: A Initial, B Planned, C Actual December 1988
1   The fusion of ERT and Cros has resulted in further reductions in employment
2   GA are large shipyards, PM are small shipyards
3   Of the 18 firms initially covered in the domestic electrical appliance sector, six closed and one left the sector. The labour force refers to the whole sector, including two firms that were not part of the reconversion program.

Source: Salmon (1991), p. 117.

Table 5 Spain : Net Foreign Investments (1982–89) (in billions of pesetas)

Year	Total	Direct	Portfolio	Property	Other
1982	199	106	1	73	19
1983	243	117	7	114	6
1984	322	156	37	138	–9
1985	413	164	82	159	7
1986	717	284	235	191	7
1987	997	322	435	221	19
1988	1,064	521	246	267	29
1989	1,730	667	733	303	27

Source: Salmon (1991), p. 20.

Table 6 Portugal: Economic Reforms Under Democratic Governments (1976–95)

Sector/Government	Minority PSP Govt. 1976–77	PSP/CDS Coalition Govts. 1978–79	AD Coalition Govt. 1979–83	AD Coalition Govt. 1980–83	PSP/PSDP Coalition Govt. 1983–85	Minority PSDP Govt. 1985–87	Majority PSDP Govt. 1987–90	Majority PSDP Govt. 1990–95
Monetary and Budgetary Policies	*	*			*	*	*	*
Taxation					*	*	*	
Social Policy					*		*	*
Financial Institutions					*		*	
Foreign Investments						*	*	*
Industrial Relations					*	*	*	*
Pension Plans						*	*	
External Trade						*	*	*
Public Sector	*					*	*	*
Industry					*	*	*	*
Agriculture	*					*	*	*
Constitution				*				

Source: author's compilation.

Table 7 Greece: Economic Reforms Under Democratic Governments (1975–95)

Sector/ Governments	Majority ND govt. 1977–79	Majority ND govt. 1979–81	Majority PASOK govt. 1981–85	Majority PASOK govt. 1985–89	ND/KKE Coalition govt. 1989	ND/KKE/ PASOK coalition govt. 1989	Majority ND govt. 1990–93	Majority PASOK govt. 1993 …
Monetary and Budgetary Policies				*			*	*
Taxation				*			*	
Social Policy		*					*	
Financial Institutions				*				
Foreign Investments			*	*				
Industrial Relations				*			*	
Pension Plans		*					*	
External Trade			*	*				
Public Sector							*	
Industry								
Agriculture								
Constitution								

Source: author's compilation.

122

Table 8 Attainment of EMU Convergence Norms (1994)

	Annual inflation rate (in %)	Public deficit (in % of GDP)	Public debt (in % of GDP)	Interest Rates (in %)
Convergence norm	**3**	**3**	**60**	**9,8**
Luxemburg	2,1	1,3	9,2	6,4
Germany	3,0	2,9	51	7
France	1,6	5,6	50,4	7,2
England	2,4	6,3	50,4	8,1
Ireland	2,4	2,4	89	7,9
Netherlands	2,7	3,8	78,8	6,9
Austria	3	4,4	65	7
Denmark	2	4,3	78	7,8
Finland	1,1	4,7	70	9,1
Belgium	2,4	5,5	140,1	7,7
Sweden	2,4	11,7	81	9,5
Spain	4,7	7	63,5	10
Portugal	5,2	6,2	70,4	10
Italy	3,9	9,6	123,7	10
Greece	10,8	14,1	121,3	20

Source: European Monetary Institute data reproduced in *La Presse*, April 5, 1995, p.D6

Table 9 Greece, Spain, Portugal: Inflation Rates (1980–94)

	1980	1982	1984	1986	1988	1990	1992	1994
Greece	21,9	20,7	17,9	22,1	14,2	19,2	14,6	10,2*
Spain	16,5	14,5	11	9,4	5	6,5	6,4	4,8*
Portugal	21,6	20,3	28,5	13,8	10	12,6	9,8	5,6*
Eur.12	13,4	10,7	7,2	3,8	3,8	4,7	4,4	3,2*

*: Estimates.
Source: Eurostat, *Économie Européenne, Supplément A*, 1994.

Table 10 Greece, Spain, Portugal: Consumption, Growth
and Interest Rates (1980–90)

	Annual average growth of private consumption 1980–90	Annual average growth of public consumption 1980–90	Annual average growth of GDP rate 1980–90	Interest rates	
				1980	1990
Greece	3,4	2,8	1,8	21,3	27,6
Spain	3,0	5,1	3,1	16,9	16,0
Portugal	5,0	2,5	2,7	18,8	21,7

Source: World Bank, *Report on World development*, 1992, pp. 215, 227, 337.

Table 11 Greece, Spain, Portugal: GDP Growth Rates (1980–94)*

	1961–73	1974–85	1986	1988	1990	1992	1994
Greece	7,7	2,5	1,6	4,4	–1,1	0,9	0,7
Spain	7,2	1,8	3,2	5,2	3,6	0,8	1,1
Portugal	6,9	2,2	4,1	3,9	4,4	1,1	1,1
Eur.12	4,8	2	2,9	4,3	3	1	1,5

*: Variation in constant prices.
Source: Eurostat, *Économie Européenne*, *Supplément A*, 1994.

Table 12 Greece, Spain, Portugal: Net Direct Foreign Investments
(in millions dollars)

	1980	1982	1984	1986	1988	1990	1992	1994
Greece	672	436	485	471	907	1005	n.a.	n.a.
Spain	1182	1272	1523	3073	5786	10904	n.a.	n.a.
Portugal	143	136	187	238	842	2447	2021	n.a.

Source: World Bank, *World Debt Tables*.

Table 13 Greece, Spain, Portugal: Total Public Debt/GDP Ratio (in %) (1980–94)

	1980	1982	1984	1986	1988	1990	1992	1994
Greece	28,53*	32,9	39,53	54,24	68,88	83,64	98,1**	n.a.
Spain	19,4*	21,48	37,9	41,12	39,78	37,11	38,05	n.a.
Portugal	n.a.	n.a.	58,76	64	63,9	59,36	55,09	n.a.

*: 1981 data.
**: Estimate.
Source: Eurostat, *Statistiques de Base de la Communauté, Monnaie et finances*.

Table 14 Greece, Spain, Portugal: External Public Debt/GDP Ratio
(in %) (1980–94)

	1980	1982	1984	1986	1988	1990	1992	1994
Greece	1,45*	1,52	2,18	21,6	21,48	18,53	20,71**	n.a.
Spain	1,17*	1,59	2,99	1,41	1,68	2,37	5,36	n.a.
Portugal	n.a.	n.a.	22,27	15,55	12,68	6,86	4,16	n.a.

*: 1981 data.
**: 1991 data.
Source: Eurostat, *Statistiques de Base de la Communauté*, and *Monnaie et finances*.

Table 15 Greece, Spain, Portugal: Central Government Debt
(in % of GDP) (1980–94)

	1980	1982	1984	1986	1988	1990	1992	1994
Greece	28,8*	34,5	40,7	58,6	71,1	89	96,3**	n.a.
Spain	18,3*	24,1	36,7	42,2	38,4	37,5	39,9	46,1***
Portugal	28,8*	n.a.	53,7	59,9	64,5	59,9	55,4	67,7***
Eur.12	33,8*	36,1	43,4	47,2	50,1	50,7	51,9	n.a.

*: 1981 data. **: 1991 data. ***: 1993 data.
Source: Eurostat, *Statistiques de Base de la Communauté*, *Monnaie et Finances*, mars 1994.

Table 16 Greece, Spain, Portugal: Central Government Deficit
(in % of GDP) (1980–94)

	1980	1982	1984	1986	1988	1990	1992	1994
Greece	4,5	6,8	9,2	9,4	16,6	21,4	25,2	n.a.
Spain	n.a.	5,4	5,4	4,6	3,4	2,7	3	6,5*
Portugal	10,9	9,4	11,4	12	12	11,8	7,8	n.a.

*: 1993. data.
Source: Eurostat, *Statistiques de Base de la Communauté*, *Monnaie et Finances*, Mars 1994.

Table 17 Greece: Expenditures and Revenues of Central Government
(1980–94) (US$ billions)

	1980	1982	1984	1986	1988	1991	1993
Expenditures							
Total expendit.	14.2	20.2	16.8	19.2	28.0	31.9	31.4
General public services	1.7	–	–	–	–	1.9	2.0
Defence	1.7	–	–	–	–	2.6	2.8
Public order and safety	–	–	–	–	–	0.7	0.7
Education	1.4	–	–	–	–	2.5	2.6
Health	1.4	–	–	–	–	2.5	2.3
Social security & welfare	4.1	–	–	–	–	4.8	4.2
Housing & Comm. Amenities	0.3	–	–	–	–	0.3	0.4
Recr. cult., relig. affrs	0.2	–	–	–	–	0.3	0.2
Ec. Affairs & Services	2.3	–	–	–	–	3.2	2.9
Agr. Foresty, Fish, Hunt	0.7	–	–	–	–	1.4	1.2
Mining, Manuf., Constr.	0.7	–	–	–	–	0.5	0.3
Transp. & communic.	0.9	–	–	–	–	0.9	1.0
Revenues							
Total revenues & grants	10.8	13.1	12.1	15.0	19.9	18.5	20.0
Tax.on Inc, profits, cap.gains	1.6	2.5	2.1	2.7	3.5	5.2	5.3
Social security contributions	3.2	4.3	4.1	4.6	5.7	0.08	0.2
Taxes on payroll & workforce	0.01	0.01	0.02	0.02	–	–	–
Taxes on property	0.2	0.3	0.2	0.3	0.8	1.1	1.0
Dom.taxes on goods & services	3.6	4.3	4.3	5.8	7.6	11.2	12.1
Taxes. Int'l, trade, trans.	0.3	0.2	0.1	0.02	0.02	0.02	0.01
Other taxes	0.4	0.8	0.5	0.7	0.5	0.6	0.7

Source: IMF, *Government Finance Statistics Yearbook*, 1992, pp. 266–8;1994, pp. 320–2.

Table 18 Portugal: Expenditures and Revenues of Central Government
(1980–94) (US$ billions)

	1980	1982	1984	1986	1988	1991	1993
Expenditures							
Total expendit.	9.5	9.4	7.8	13.5	17.3		
General public services	0.6	0.6	0.5	0.8	1.1		
Defence	0.7	0.6	0.4	0.7	1.0		
Public order and safety	–	–	–	–	–		
Education	1.0	0.9	0.7	1.2	1.9		
Health	0.9	0.9	0.6	1.0	1.5		
Social security & welfare	2.4	2.4	1.9	3.0	4.4		
Housing & Comm. Amenities	0.1	0.1	0.05	0.19	0.19		
Recr., cult., relig. affrs	0.05	0.06	0.05	0.09	0.15		
Ec. Affairs & Services	1.8	1.6	1.3	2.4	1.8		
Other expenditures	1.5	2.0	1.9	3.8	4.6		
Revenues							
Total revenues & grants	7.6	7.6	6.5	10.7	14.8	–	
Tax. on Inc, profits, cap. gains	1.4	1.6	1.5	1.7	2.8	6.4	
Social security contributions	1.9	1.8	1.4	2.6	3.8	6.6	
Taxes on payroll & workforce	0.1	0.1	0.1	–	–	–	
Taxes on property	0.09	0.1	0.1	0.1	0.09	0.1	
Dom. taxes on goods & services	2.5	2.4	2.1	4.2	5.5	8.6	
Taxes. Int'l, trade, trans.	0.3	0.3	0.2	0.3	0.4	0.2	
Other taxes	0.3	0.3	0.4	0.3	0.4	0.7	

Source: IMF, *Government Finance Statistics Yearbook*, 1992, pp. 454–5;1994, pp. 536–7.

Table 19 Spain: Expenditures and Revenues of Central Government
(1980–94) (US$ billions)

	1980	1982	1984	1986	1988	1991	1993
Expenditures							
Total expendit.	56.5	54.5	49.8	76.8	114.4	183.7	
General public services	2.4	2.3	3.4	–	3.4	5.7	
Defence	2.4	2.1	2.1	–	6.2	7.7	
Public order and safety	–	–	–	–	3.9	6.2	
Education	4.5	3.5	3.0	–	6.4	8.6	
Health	0.3	0.2	6.5	–	14.6	11.1	
Social security & welfare	33.3	35.0	23.8	–	42.3	70.2	
Housing & Comm. Amenities	0.7	0.6	0.3	–	0.7	0.9	
Recr. Cult. Relig. Affairs	0.5	0.3	0.3	–	0.7	1.1	
Econ. Affairs & Services	6.7	6.3	5.8	–	12.3	16.2	
Agr., Foresty, Fish, Hunt	1.8	1.7	1.3	–	1.5	1.4	
Mining, Manuf., Constr.	0.9	0.8	0.3	–	1.4	0.6	
Transp. & communic.	1.7	1.9	2.1	–	4.4	8.2	
Revenues							
Total revenues & grants	51.2	45.9	41.8	67.3	105.3	166.6	
Tax.on Inc, profits, cap. gains	11.8	8.7	9.2	15.0	29.3	52.9	
Social security contributions	24.5	21.5	18.3	25.4	39.2	62.2	
Taxes on payroll & workforce	–	–	–	–	–	–	
Taxes on property	2.1	1.3	0.7	0.8	1.1	0.6	
Dom.taxes on goods & services	6.4	5.9	6.3	18.4	24.8	35.7	
Taxes. Int'l, trade, trans.	1.9	1.8	1.6	1.8	2.5	1.7	
Other taxes	0.1	0.1	0.1	–	–	–	

Source: IMF, *Government Finance Statistics Yearbook*, 1992, pp. 490–2; 1994,
pp. 587–9.

Table 20 Greece, Spain, Portugal: Balance of Payments (1980–94)
Balance of trade (in US$ millions)

	1980	1982	1984	1986	1988	1990	1992	1994
Greece	−5566,53	−4799,59	−4231,22	−4447,68	−6063,66	−10855,9	−10692,2	n.a
Spain	−5765,33	−9280,79	−4272,26	−6441,26	−18033,7	−26585,7	−28550,8	n.a
Portugal	−2674,66	−4863,28	−2027,60	−1682,64	−5511,66	−7288,20	−8684,10	n.a

Balance of current account (in US$ millions)

Greece	−1918,63	−1903,57	−2132,58	−1734,79	−859,31	−3877,22	−1998,61	n.a
Spain	1157,02	−4241,16	2017,34	3943,87	−3705,57	−12981,3	−17112,9	n.a
Portugal	−57,08	−3239,9	−515,38	1137,5	−1024,79	204,49	−73,97	n.a

Balance of capital (in US$ millions)

Greece	2482,52	1733,10	2495,6	2061,48	2041,31	4069,45	2020,08*	n.a
Spain	5221,23	4198,05	−2614,8	12081	19679,1	39145,8	20033,8*	n.a
Portugal	1052,6	666,2	634,5	−87,57	3508,2	5087,8	n.a	n.a

*: Balance of long-term capital only.
Source: Eurostat, *Statistiques de base de la communauté*, 1991 data.

Table 21 Greece and Spain: Volume of Imports and Exports (1980–90)
(1985=100)

	1980	1981	1982	1983	1984	1985	1986	1987	1988	1989	1990
					Greece						
Volume of exports	85.5	72.1	72.2	82.5	100.2	100.0	116.9	132.1	88.8	122.2	115.8
Volume of imports	72.2	72.3	80.1	87.6	88.0	100.0	93.7	116.5	92.8	125.0	160.4

Source: FMI: *Statistiques financières internationales*, 1991, p.F367

				Spain			
Volume of exports	68.0	72.1	79.0	82.5	83.2	100.0	91.7
Volume of imports	97.5	91.2	94.2	94.4	93.8	100.0	116.3

Source: FMI: *Statistques financières internationales*, 1991, p. F407.

Table 22 Greece, Spain, Portugal: Trade Balances (1980–94) in billions of ecus

	1974–84	1986	1987	1988	1989	1990	1991	1992	1993	1994
Total										
Greece	–4,1	–5,8	–5,6	–5,9	–7,8	–9,2	–10,4	–9,6	–10,9	–12,1
Spain	–7,6	–6,3	–8,7	–11,9	–19,3	–20,1	–21,3	–27,9	–27,6	–28,7
Portugal	–3,1	–2,3	–3,7	–5,8	–5,6	–6,7	–7,9	–8,9	–10,6	–12,3
INTRA–EC BT										
Greece	–1,7	–3,1	–3,1	–3,6	–4,7	–5,9	–6,0	–5,0	–5,7	–6,4
Spain	–0,2	–0,6	–3,5	–5,3	–8,9	–9,2	–9,3	–11,6	–11,6	–12,1
Portugal	–1,0	–0,7	–1,7	–3,5	–	–4,1	–5,3	–6,3	–7,6	–8,8
EXTRA–EC BT										
Greece	–2,3	–2,7	–2,6	–2,3	–3,2	–3,3	–4,4	–4,6	–5,2	–5,6
Spain	–7,5	–5,9	–5,7	–6,9	–10,8	–11,5	–12,5	–16,3	–16,0	–16,6
Portugal	–2,1	–1,7	–2,0	–2,4	–2,3	–2,8	–2,8	–2,6	–3,0	–3,4

Source: CEC, *Economie européenne, supplément A*, nos 1/2, January–February 1993.

Table 23 Greece, Spain, Portugal: Distribution of Value-added Within Industrial Sector (in % at current prices)

	Food, Tobacco and Drinks		Textiles and Clothes		Machines and Vehicles		Others	
	1970	1989	1970	1989	1970	1989	1970	1989
Greece	20	22	20	24	13	10	40	36
Spain	13	17	15	8	16	25	45	39
Portugal	18	17	19	20	13	14	39	39

Source: World Bank, *Report on World Development*, 1992, Table 6.

Table 24 Greece, Spain, Portugal: Contribution of Equipment Expenditures to Internal Demand (1986–94)

	1986	1987	1988	1989	1990	1991	1992	1993	1994
Greece	–12,6	–7,7	8,4	18,1	7,9	3,3	4,5	6,0	7,5
Spain	15,8	24,2	16,5	12,9	1,4	–2,5	0,2	0,3	2,2
Portugal	14,2	26,8	23,2	10,0	5,5	1,0	4,8	3,8	6,0

Source: *Économie européenne ECC, supplément A*, no. 5, May 1991 and no. 1/2, January–February 1993.

Table 25 Greece, Spain, Portugal: Evolution of Labour Costs (1980–94)

	Wage earning by salaried worker (variation in % in comparison with previous year)					
	1974–84	1986	1988	1990	1992	1994
Greece	21,5	12,5	21,1	19,7	12,3	10,7
Spain	18,8	9,5	6,8	7,9	9,0	5,7
Portugal	24,4	21,6	13,4	18,7	14,9	8,7
Europe	13,3	6,3	5,8	7,5	5,8	4,4

	Unitary nominal labour force cost (whole economy)				
	1980–85	1986	1988	1990	1991
Greece	22,2	12,3	14,5	17,3	15,1
Spain	9,7	8,5	4,3	7,3	6,3
Portugal	19,7	13,6	9,1	12,9	12,3
EUR 12	8,6	4,3	3,3	6,2	5,3

Source: *Économie européenne ECC, supplément A*, nos 1/2, January–February 1993 and no. 1, January 1991.

Table 26 Greece, Spain, Portugal: Structure of GDP (in %)

	Greece		Spain		Portugal	
	1980	1993	1980	1993	1980	1993
Agriculture	17,7	17,0	7,1	4,6		9*
Industry	31,1	27,1	38,6	34,8		40*
Services	51,1	55,9	54,3	60,6		51*

*1987
Sources: *l'État du Monde*, 1995; World Bank, *Report on World Development* 1989.

Table 27 Greece, Spain, Portugal: Distribution of the Labour Force (in %)

	Greece		Spain		Portugal	
	1980	1993	1980	1993	1980	1993
Agriculture	30,9	22,3	18,9	10,1	28	–
Industry	28,8	26,8	36,1	30,7	35	–
Services	40,3	50,9	45,1	59,2	37	–

Sources: *l'État du Monde*, 1995; World Bank, *Report on World Development* 1989.

Table 28 Results of the Parliamentary Elections in Spain (1977–96)

	1977		1979		1982		1986		1989		1993		1996	
	Seats /350	% of votes	Seats /350	% of votes	Seats /350	% of votes	Seats /350	% of votes	Seats /350	% of votes	Seats /350	% of votes	Seats /350	% of votes
Union del Centro Democratico (UCD)	165	34,5	168	35										
Centro Democratico y Social (CDS)[1]					12	9,8	19	9,2	14	7,9				
Alianza Popular (AP)/ Partido Popular (PP)[2]	16	8,1	9	6	107	26,5	105	26	106	25,8	141	38,4	157	38,9
Partido socialista obrero espanol (PSOE)	118	28,5	121	30,5	202	48,4	184	44,1	175	39,5	159	38,6	140	37,4
Partido communista espanol (PCE)/Izquierda Unida (IU)[3]	20	9	23	10,8	4	4,1	7	4,6	18	9	18	9,5	21	10,4
Regional Parties[4]	31	19,9	29	17,7	25	11,2	35	16,1	37	17,8	32	13,5	32	9,5

1 The CDS is a new social-democratic party created by Adolfo Suarez after the dissolution of the UCD.

2 As a coalition of rightist forces, the AP has participated in periodic elections under different names: Alianza Popular (1977, 1982), Coalicion Democratica (1979), Coalicion Popular (1986). After 1986, the AP gave rise to a new, more centrist conservative party: the Partido Popular (PP). In 1993, the CDS and the PP concluded an electoral alliance. Of the 141 seats won by the alliance, 14 went to the CDS and 127 to the PP.

3 After DT, the PCE suffered many splits and defections that dramaticaly reduced its membership and electorate. In 1986, the PCE created a new leftist coalition – the IU – with six small groups of the radical left – see Chapter 7, note 7.

4 PNV, CiU, Herri Batasuna, etc.

Sources: Grosser (1977–93); the Europa World Yearbook (1996); El Pais, March, 4 1996.

Table 29 Results of the Parliamentary Elections in Greece (1974–93)

	1974		1977		1981		1985		1989 I		1989 II		1990		1993	
	Seats /300	% of votes	Seats /300	% of votes	Seats /300	% of votes	Seats /300	% of votes	Seats /300	% of votes	Seats /300	% of votes	Seats /300	% of votes	Seats /300	% of votes
New Democracy (ND)	220	54,3	172	41,8	115	35,8	126	40,8	145	44,3	148	46,2	150	46,9	111	39,3
Panhellenic Socialist Movement (PASOK)	12	13,5	93	25,3	172	48	161	45,8	125	39,2	128	40,7	123	38,6	170	46,9
Communist Party of Greece (KKE)	8	9,4	11	9,3	13	10,9	13	11,7							9	4,5
Progressive Left Coalition (Synaspismos)									28	13,1	21	11	19	10,2	0	2,9
National Front (EM)	0	1,1	5	6	0	1,6										
Centre Union of New Forces (EKND)	60	20,4	15	11,8	0	1,5										
Independents and other parties			4	5,8					2	3,4	1	2,1	8	4,3	10	6,4

Sources : Grosser (1975–94).

Table 30 Results of the Parliamentary Elections in Portugal (1976–95)

	1976		1979		1980		1983		1985		1987		1991		1995	
	Seats /263	% of votes	Seats /250	% of votes	Seats /250	% of votes	Seats /250	% of votes	Seats /250	% of votes	Seats /250	% of votes	Seats /230	% of votes	Seats /230	% of votes
Social Democratic Party (PSDP)	73	24,4	7	2,4			75	27,2	88	29,8	148	50,2	135	50,6	88	34
Social Democratic Centre (CDS)	42	16	–	0,4			30	12,5	22	9,8	4	4,4	5	4,4	15	9,1
Democratic Alliance (DA)			121	42,2	134	47,1										
Portuguese Socialist Party (PSP)	107	35	74	27,4	66	27,4	94	36,2	57	20,8	60	22,3	72	29,1	112	43,9
Portuguese Communist Party (PCP)	40	14,6	47	19	41	16,9	44	18,7	38	15,5	31	12,1	17	8,8	15	8,6
Democratic Renewal Party (PRD)									45	17,9	7	4,9	1	1,7		
others	1		1	2,2	9	8,6	7	5,4								

Sources: Grosser (1976–90); *The Europa World Yearbook* (1995).

Table 31 Greece, Spain, Portugal: Total Resources Devoted to ESCPs (1988–99) (in millions of ecus)[1]

| | EC Grants | | | | | National public expenditures[2] | | | | |
	Total	EFRD	ESF	EAGGF	Other	Total	State	Region	other[4]	Private sector	EC loans[3]
Greece											
1989–93											
Objective 1	5,886	3,662	1,098	600	526	5,102	–	–	–	997	1,410
Objectives 3&4	630		630			339	312	26			
Objective 5a	677			677		360				349	
Total	7,193	3,662	1,728	1,277	526	5,802				1,346	1,410
1994–99											
Objectives 1,3& 4, 5a[5]	6,520	5,668	321	531		6,000				670	
Spain											
1989–93											
Objective 1	8,037	6,199	1,083	755		6,048	3,930	2,118	–	1,901	2,206
Objective 2	723	564	159			1,130	581	444	194	93	
Objectives 3&4	1,828		1,828		–	1,931	576	104	–	–	–
Objective 5a	477			477		–	–	–	–	–	–
Objective 5b	285	61	39	185		348	181	167		60	
Total	11,350	6,824	3,109			9,457	5,268	2,833		2,054	2,206
1994–99											
Objectives 1,3,4,5a[5]	26,300	15,944	6,047	3,314	995	12,700					
Portugal											
1989–93											
Objective 1	6,280	3,757	1,550	563	410[6]	6,112	3,304	1,236	1,572	3,802	2,805
Objectives 3&4	478		478			257	257				
Objective 5a	609			609		288	288			641	
Total	7,368	3,757	2,028	1,173	410	6,658	3,849	1,236	1,572	4,443	2,805
1994–99											
Objectives 1,3,4,5a[5]	13,980					–	–	–		–	–

(1) Figures rounded off to the nearest thousand. One ecu= US$ 1.25 (Nov. 1995). (2) Forecasts of the 'Provincial Financing plans'. (3) Loans from EIB and ECSC. (4) Local governments, public institutions and companies. (5) Backward regions. (6) Program PEDIP.

Sources: ECC (1989a, 1989b, 1990c, 1990d, 1990e, 1991, 1992); *Europe* (1994).

135

Table 32 Greece, Spain, Portugal: Total Community Grants (1988–99)
(in millions of ecus)[1]

	Greece(G)	Spain(S)	Portugal (P)	EC	Share in % of G,S and P
1988–1993					
Objective 1[2]	7,193	9,779	7,368	41,715	58.3
Objective 2[3]	NIL	723.6	NIL	7,205	10
Objectives 3&4[4]	NIL	563	NIL	7,450	7.5
Objective 5b	131.8	285	135.6	2,795	19
Sub Total	7,324.8	11,350.6	7,503.6	60,315[6]	43
IMPs	3,300	NIL	NIL	–	
Total	10,624.8	11,350.6	7,503.6[5]		
1994–1999					
Objective 1[2]	6,520	26,300	13,980	102,493	45
Objective 2	NIL	3,109	NIL	15,316	20
Objectives 3&4[4]	NIL	1,843	NIL	15,840	11
Objective 5b	NIL	269	NIL	6,134	4.3
Sub Total	6,520	31,521	13,980	141,470[7]	
Cohesion Fund	2,727	8,787	2,727	13,450	
MIT[8]	20	300	15	1,530	
Total	9,267[9]	40,608	16,722	156,450[7]	42.5

(1)　In November 1995, an Ecu was equivalent to US$1.25. Community grants include credits from the three structural funds (EFRD, ESF, EAGGF) and from other financial institutions (notably the ECSC). For information about EC aid prior to 1988, see Chapter 7, note 10.

(2)　Credits for objective 1 include amounts devoted to objectives 3, 4 and 5a in backward regions.

(3)　For 1989–91.

(4)　For other regions not eligible for objective 1(1990–92).

(5)　This amount does not include the 1988–92 EC aid (about 4.6 billion ecus) allocated to the *Programa específico de desenvolvimento da industria portuguès* (PEDIP).

(6)　Total Europe of Twelve.

(7)　Total Europe of Fifteen.

(8)　Measures of innovation and transition.

(9)　This amount does not coincide with the data of Catsiapis (1995, 225). According to this author, Greece will received 13.9 billion ecus from the EC for the 1994–99 period.

Sources: ECC (1989a, 1989b, 1990c, 1990d, 1990e, 1991, 1992) ; *Europe* (1994).

Table 33 Spain: Social Agreements (1977–92)

Name	Year	Participants	Content
Pactos de la Moncloa	1977	Govt. UCD, PSOE, PCE	4 series of SMs and 5 categories of SCMs
Estatuto de los Trabajadores	1980	Govt. UCD, CEOE, UGT	New framework for industrial relations system
Interconfederal Frameworks Agreements (IFA)	1980–81	Govt. UCD, CEOE, UGT, USO	Percentages of salaries indexing to inflation
Accuerdo nacional sobre el Emplo (ANE)	1982	Govt. UCD, CEOE, UGT, CC.OO	Various measures intended to limit the growth of salary costs
Interconfederal Agreement	1983	Govt. PSOE, CEOE, UGT	Percentages of salaries indexing to inflation
Economic and Social Accord	1985–86	Govt. PSOE, CEOE, UGT	Percentages of salaries indexing to inflation
Interconfederal Agreement	1990	Govt. PSOE, UGT, CC.OO	Pensions indexing, civil servants collective agreement, union's control over work contracts, etc.
Pacto social de Progresso	1991	Govt. PSOE, CEOE, UGT, CC.OO	Measures intended to reduce inflation and to improve competitivity
Interconfederal Agreement	1992	Govt. PSOE, UGT, CC.OO	Limits to the exercise of the right of strike

Sources: McElrath (1989); Bermeo (1994b); Bon (1990–95).

Table 34 Greece, Spain, Portugal: Unemployment Rates (1980–94)

	1980	1982	1984	1986	1988	1990	1992	1994
Greece	2,8	5,8	8,1	7,4	7,7	7,0	8,7	10,1
Spain	11,6	16,3	20,0	21,1	19,4	16,2	18,2	23,3
Portugal	7,6	7,2	8,5	8,3	5,7	4,6	3,9	6,5
Eur 12	6,0	9,0	10,5	10,7	9,8	8,4	9,4	11,3*

* Estimates.
Source: Eurostat, *Economie européenne, Supplément A*, no. 5, May 1994.

Table 35 Greece: Comparative Influence of Political Parties Within
Main Interest Groups (1990)

IG/PARTY	ND	PASOK	KKE
PASEGES	50%	41%	
GSEE		39%	38%
GSEVEE	30%		58%
EESE	77%		
KEE/SEV	70%		
ADEDY	35%	41%	16%

Source: Mavrogordatos (1993, 51).

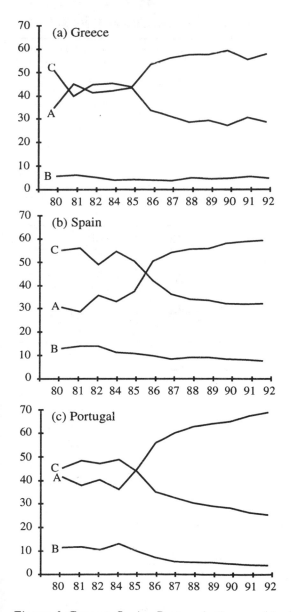

Figure 1 Greece, Spain, Portugal: Geographic distribution of imports (1980–92)

A: European Community; B: United States; C: Rest of the World
Source: Eurostat, *Statistiques de base de la Communanté 1980–94*

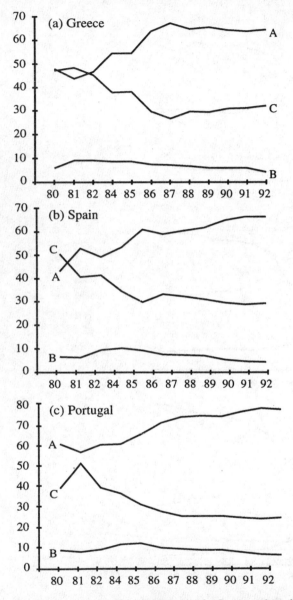

Figure 2 Greece, Spain, Portugal: Geographic distribution of exports (1980–92)

A: European Community; B: United States; C: Rest of the World
Source: Eurostat, *Statistiques de base de la Communanté 1980–94*

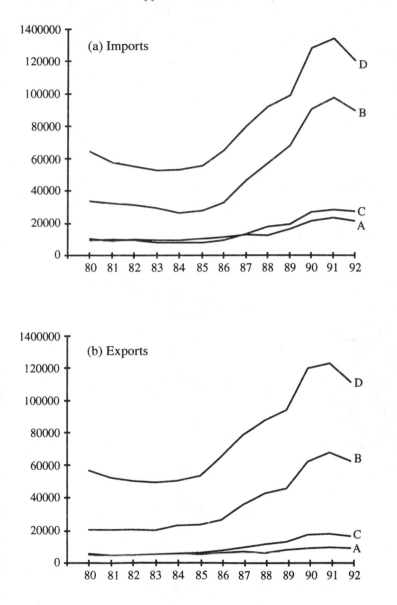

Figure 3 Greece, Spain, Portugal: Value of imports and exports (1980–92) (in millions of US dollars)

A: Greece; B: Spain; C: Portugal; D: European Community (average)
Source: Eurostat, *Statistiques de base de la Communanté 1980–94*

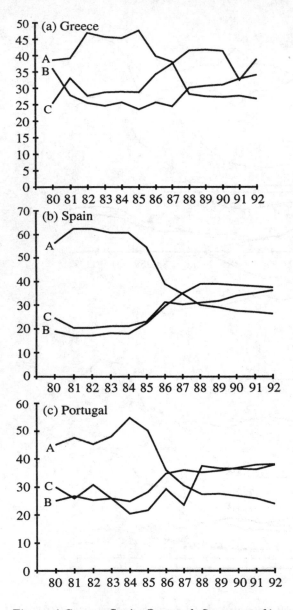

Figure 4 Greece, Spain, Portugal: Structure of imports (in % of the global trade volume) (1980–92)

A: Raw materials; B: Machines and transport equipments; C: Manufactured products
Source: Eurostat, *Statistiques de base de la Communanté 1980–94*

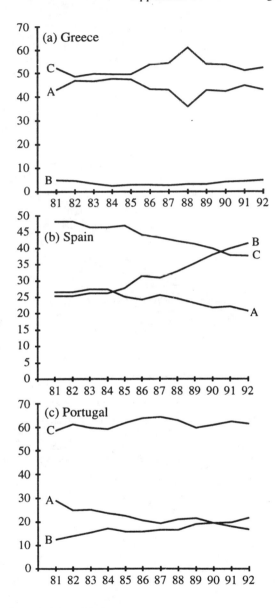

Figure 5 Greece, Spain, Portugal: Structure of exports (in % of the global trade volume) (1980–92)

A: Raw materials; B: Machinery and transport equipments; C: Manufactured goods.
Source: Eurostat, *Statistiques de base de la Communanté 1980–94*

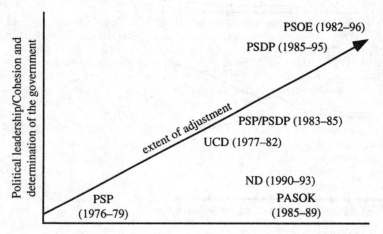

Autonomy of the executive towards political system and civil society

Figure 6 Southern European governments' ability to implement SMs and SCMs

Source: data of the author.

Notes

INTRODUCTION

1. The content of these measures is defined in Chapter 5.
2. The literature on the subject is far too vast to list extensively here. See in particular: Pridham (1984); O'Donnell, Schmitter and Whitehead (1986); Baylora (1987); Diamond, Linz and Lipset (1989); Ethier (1990); Huntington (1991).
3. I should nevertheless mention the commentaries of G. De la Dehesa (1994) and F. Torres (1994), which suggest that membership in the EC favoured the success of economic adjustment in Spain and Portugal; the work of Köves and Marer (1991), which argues that the prospect of membership in the EU favourably influenced the economic reforms in Eastern Europe; and the chapter by D. Rodrik (1994), which attempts to demonstrate that the adjustment processes compromised the pursuit of the liberalization of markets, since they limit the possibilities of redistribution, thereby strengthening opposition by protectionist lobbies.
4. To my knowledge, the two chapters of Maravall (1993, 1995), the Introduction of Hudson and Lewis (1985) and my recent text (Ethier, 1995) are the only studies that compare – if only briefly – Southern European economic policies during the post-authoritarian period. There exist no comprehensive analyses of Greek and Portuguese economic policies between 1975 and 1995. On the other hand, many more or less extensive studies have been devoted to Spanish democratic economic policies (notably: Garcia Delgado, 1990; Salmon, 1991; Holman, 1993; Bermeo, 1994a; Heywood, 1995, ch. 10). These ignore the period 1988–95, however, or only deal with it schematically.

CHAPTER ONE

1. Essential consumer goods include textiles, clothes, shoes and processed foods. Intermediate goods are the processed raw materials that are used for industrial production: chemical and petrochemical products, steels, pulp and paper, and so on. Equipment goods include machine tools and transportation vehicles used in industry.
2. Greece, Spain and Portugal began the process of industrialization at the beginning of the twentieth century through a classical strategy of import substitution, that is, development, by the national bourgeoisie, of small and medium ECG industries whose products are aimed at the local market and protected from competition by rigid protectionist barriers. However, as in the majority of countries which opted for this model, the growth of such industries was conditioned by the limits of internal demand, due to the low income level of the population and the high cost of importing IGE. These problems led the government and the national banks to finance the development of infrastruc-

tures and basic industries, particularly during the 1950s. However, due largely to the inadequacy of the funding, none of the three countries succeeded in equipping itself with a high-performance heavy industry capable of meeting the needs of light industry and promoting increased economic growth. These difficulties, together with the surplus of capital that existed in the western countries, explain the transition of the three countries toward the second, more open, liberal phase of import substitution during the 1960s.

3. State assumption of control over health and education services; creation of various income and purchasing power support programs (retirement, unemployment, social assistance programs, and so on).

4. Durable consumer goods include cars, home electrical appliances, electronic appliances (televisions, transistor radios, video recorders, computers, and so on).

5. The expression 'European Community' (EC) designates the three communities which merged in 1965: the Coal and Steel Community (ECSC), instituted by the Treaty of Paris in 1951; the European Atomic Energy Community (EURATOM) and the European Economic Community (EEC) created by the Treaty of Rome in 1957. The EEC is a common market whose construction began with the Treaty of Rome and was completed on January 1, 1993, by the implementation of the majority of the provisions contained in the Single Europe Act (SEA) adopted in 1986. Since the ratification of the Treaty on European Union (TEU) in 1993, the EEC has entered the construction phase of the European monetary and political union. For the period prior to 1993, we shall thus employ the acronym EEC, whereas for the period following 1993, we shall utilize the expression 'European Union' (EU).

6. Between 1962 and 1973, the percentage of exports from Spain and Portugal to the United States went from 10.7 to 13.8% in the former case, and 9.7 to 6% in the latter, while the percentage of exports into the EC increased from 29.5 to 47.4% and from 37 to 47.9%. During the same period, the percentage of Spanish imports from the United States dropped from 19.8 to 16% and that of imports from the EC increased from 40.3 to 42.5%; the percentage of Portuguese imports from the United States decreased from 8.9 to 8% and that of imports from the EC from 51.6 to 44%. On the transformations in the productive structures and external trade by the countries of the Iberian peninsula during the period 1960–1975, see in particular D. Charles Le Bihan et al. (1986, 79–103). On the Greek situation, see R. Hudson and J. Lewis (1985).

7. The Spain–EC Preferential Trade Agreement of 1970 established a general, mutual system of commercial preferences between the two partners. This system had to be established in two steps, the first of which was to last at least six years and the second remaining conditional on a new agreement between the signatories. In the area of industrial products, Spain had to proceed with a reduction of its customs duties of between 25% and 100%, depending on the category of products. The EEC agreed to progressively reduce its customs duties on Spanish products in order to allow it three years (1970–73) to meet the Common External Tariff (CET) applied to imports from third countries. In the area of agricultural products, the agreement stipulated that Spanish quotas on several products be reduced, and that the rules of the Common Agricultural Policy (CAP) imposed on third countries be extended to Spain. This was not accompanied by an accord with the ECSC such as the Free Trade Agreement signed in 1972 with Portugal (Tamames, 1988, 284–90).

8. This agreement provided for the creation of a customs union, the development of common shares, the harmonization of Greek policies with those of the EC in various domains (economy, agriculture, free circulation of manpower, transportation, taxation, standards of proficiency), extending various forms of assistance to Greece in order to facilitate the adaptation of its economy to the common market, the creation of common institutions and the its eventual membership in the EEC (Tamames 1988, 248).

9. The Portugal–EEC agreement of 1972 imposed the complete and mutual elimination of customs rights on imports and exports of industrial products. A complete dismantling of tariff restrictions was to have been carried out in five steps (1973, 1974, 1975, 1976, 1977) each involving a 20% reduction in customs duties. The Portugal–ECSC agreement applied the same provisions to trade in iron, coal and steel products. Nonetheless, it permitted quotas on imports and exports to be maintained until 1977 (Alvares, 1986, 45–8).

10. I consider the most pertinent explanation of the causes of the democratic transitions in Southern Europe to be the one proposed by G. O'Donnell and P. Schmitter (1986) based on Southern European case studies by P. Schmitter, J.M. Maravall and J. Santamaria, K. Maxwell and P.N. Diamandouros (1986), who maintain that the transitions towards democracy were triggered by the appearance of dissension within the authoritarian regimes; certain actors (the *blandos*) judged that the cost of maintaining the status quo would from then on be higher than that of a transition towards democracy, while others (the *duros*) maintained the opposite. The change in the perceptions by part of the decision makers and supporters was determined by several factors, whose respective influences on the psychology of the actors is impossible to determine: military defeats (in Greece and Portugal); the succession of Franco (in Spain); the development of opposition movements within civil society following the economic, social, and cultural modernization of the sixties; international pressures and economic crisis. The crisis of the authoritarian regimes led to the restoration of democratic rules and institutions, the end of the process being marked by the adoption of democratic constitutions. These transitions took place in accordance with various scenarios. *Greece* (July–December 1974): the ceding of power, by the military, to a right-wing provisional government led by Caramanlis, which was charged with bringing about the return of democratic institutions. *Spain* (November 1975–December 1978): following the death of General Franco, negotiation of the terms of restoring democracy by the major forces of the right, centre and left, under the direction of the reformist elements of Francoism, notably Juan Carlos, Franco's designated successor, and Adolfo Suarez, the interim prime minister named by Juan Carlos. *Portugal* (April 1974–April 1976): overthrow of the authoritarian regime of Caetano by a party of intermediate and high-ranking officers affiliated with the Armed Forces Movement (AFM); gradual re-establishment of democracy under the direction of AFM provisional governments.

11. The association agreement of 1962 provided for Greece to become a member of the EC by 1975. The right-wing forces which led the democratic transition in Greece – Caramanlis and the ND – asked the EC to respect this commitment during the changeover to democracy. Brussels refused this request because of dissention within the council and because of economic problems raised by the integration of Greece in the context of the crisis of the seventies. It was with a great deal of reticence that Athens was obliged to submit a new request for

membership in 1975 and to enter into four years of negotiations (1976–79) with the EC (Verney, 1990). Those in charge of economic policy for the Francoist regime were unsatisfied with the preferential agreement of 1970; they wished to obtain a widening of customs concessions on agricultural products that would compensate for the liberalization of industrial exchanges, which were unfavourable to Spain. The negotiations conducted on this issue between 1973 and 1975 gave rise to the Ullastres–Kergolay agreement of the spring of 1975. The execution of those responsible for the assassination of Carrero Blanco in September 1975 however, led the EC to suspend this agreement. Between 1975 and 1977, the conservative forces responsible for the democratic transition – Suarez and the UCD – informed the EC that they rejected the basis of the 1975 accord and requested the opening of negotiations on the full and complete membership of Spain in the Europe of the Nine. A request to this effect was formally transmitted to Brussels in July 1977, more than a year before the ratification of the new democratic constitution, in December 1978. This position was supported by the other actors in the transition: the socialist party and the communist party (Myro, 1990, 483–4). In Portugal, the new socialist party created by Mario Soares in 1973, the Christian democrats and the social-democrats had, since 1972, wanted the free-trade agreement to be converted into a membership agreement. This explains why, in March 1977, the first constitutional government of the socialist party sent to Brussels Portugal's official request for membership in the EC.

12.   In 1976, the European Communities Commission (ECC) and the Council of Ministers ratified Greece's request for membership submitted in June 1975 (ECC, 1976). The negotiations began in 1976 and were completed in 1979. Greece became a member of the EC on January 1, 1981. Portugal submitted its membership application in March 1977 and Spain in July 1977. These requests received a favourable response from the EC in 1978 (ECC, 1978a, 1978b). Negotiations began officially in October 1978, with Portugal, and in February 1979 with Spain. They ended during the first quarter of 1985. The membership treaties of the two countries were ratified in the same year and came into force on January 1, 1986.

13.   The content – and the constraints – of the EC membership treaties are set out in the presentation of each country's economic policy.

14.   The end of the European Common Market was marked by the adoption, in 1986, of the SEA. This provided for the elimination of physical, technical, legal and tax barriers which still impeded the complete liberalization of the exchange of merchandise, persons, services and capital between the member states. It also included a reform of the CAP and a reinforcement of the economic and social cohesion policies (ESCPs) designed to offset the discrepancies in regional development and social equality within and between the member states. The application of the SEA, between 1986 and 1983, gave rise to a series of reforms, certain of which have yet to be completed. The abolition of physical impediments resulted in the disappearance of border controls between the various member states in 1994. This change involved a harmonization of national legislation with respect to the application of VAT and immigration, the strengthening of customs controls on the community's borders, and the development of intracommunity cooperation with respect to security. The elimination of technical barriers was carried out through the harmonization of non-tariff trade barriers (hygiene,

quality, security, quota standards, preferential treatment, and so on); the opening of public markets to suppliers from the other member states; the establishment of equivalences for diplomas and professional qualifications; complete liberalization of movements of capital and objectives which involved the stabilization of currencies and the convergence of political economies; the development of industrial cooperation between companies (creation of the ESPRIT and BRITE community programs; the elimination of legal barriers demanded a strengthening and an extension of community corporate law: the status and fiscality of companies, public shares offers, protection of intellectual property, and public assistance). The elimination of fiscal frontiers led to the harmonization of the indirect tax systems (VAT) and the specific taxes of the member states. The reform of the CAP resulted in new measures aimed at reducing the surface area of cultivated land and agricultural labour, and modernizing and merging operations. The objectives of these measures were to reduce excess production and to increase the competitiveness of the operations in order to reduce the cost of community subsidies (guaranteed prices, export assistance). The strengthening of ESCPs gave rise, in 1988, to the reform of the structural funds (SFs) the major instruments for applying ESCPs: the European Agricultural Guidance and Guarantee Fund (EAGGF), the European Fund for Regional Development (EFRD), the European Social Fund (ESF). This reform modified the objectives and the operations of the SF, while considerably increasing their financial resources (see below) (De Ruyt, 1987).

15. The Treaty on the European Union (TEU), which was adopted by the EC Council in December 1991, ratified by each of twelve member states in 1992 and 1993 and implemented as of 1991/92, provides for the replacement of the Common or Single Market by an economic monetary and political Union. It establishes European citizenship and introduces a second reform of the SF, aimed at further strengthening the ESCPs. The Economic and Monetary Union (EMU) had to be realized in three steps. (1) Before January 1, 1994 the member states must complete the liberalization of their legislation with respect to inflow and outflow of capital and adapt their economic policies to the convergence criteria fixed by the EC: budget deficit/GDP ratio (3%); public debt/GDP ratio (60%); annual inflation rate (3%); interest rate (9.8%). (2) Between 1994 and 1999, various means, including the creation of the European Monetary Institute (EMI), must be adopted, aimed at reinforcing the coordination of the national central banks and the convergence of the member states' monetary policies. (3) During the third phase, which must begin in 1996 at the earliest and in 1999 at the latest, depending on the degree of progress made in the national economic and monetary policy convergence process, the national currencies and the central banks must be replaced by a common currency – the ecu – and a common central European bank (Dutriaux, 1992, chs 5 and 7).

CHAPTER TWO

1. Membership in the EC entails each candidate ratifying the Treaty of Paris and the Treaty of Rome in order to become a member of the three European communities: ECSC, EEC and EURATOM. In this text, therefore, the plural form (treaties) is used throughout.

2. Negotiations were delayed by, in particular, the problem of the British contribution to the Community budget (resolved in 1980), the drafting of the common fishing policy (passed in 1983) and the cost of assistance programs to Spain and Portugal prior and subsequent to their membership (solved in 1984).

3. Increased percentage ranges fixed by the IFA: 1980: 13–15% (McElrath, 1989, 169).

4. Lowering the retirement age from 69 to 60; limiting overtime to 100 hours per year; 23 paid vacation days for all workers; marriage leave (14 days), maternity leave (14 weeks) and sickness leave; basing promotions on objective criteria (qualifications, merit, years of service, needs of the company) and so on.

5. Conditions justifying layoffs: insufficient qualifications, unadapted to technological changes, disciplinary offences, need to abolish one or several positions.

6. Notably, the *Instituto de Credito official* (ICO), the *Instituto nacional de Industria* (INI), the *Instituto nacional de Hidrocarburos* (INH), and the *Direccion general del Patrimonio Español* (DGPE). The companies controlled by these holdings produced 69% of the added value of the industrial sector.

7. Between 1960 and 1980 the total share of employment provided by agriculture went from half to one-sixth, and the share of agricultural exports in relation to total exports dropped from two-thirds to one-seventh (Balboa and Garcia Delgado, 1990, 122).

8. The liberalization of the monetary policy, combined with an increase in interest rates, promoted a strong upsurge in foreign investments. This phenomenon resulted in a re-evaluation of the peseta, which cancelled out the measures aimed at reducing the value of the currency and renewing exports. Furthermore, the higher interest rates increased the level of indebtedness of the governments (Linde, 1990, 35–59).

9. On the relations between the PSOE's economic reforms, between 1986 and 1989, and the constraints of membership in the EC and the SEA, see, in particular, Trestour (1988) and *Problèmes économiques* (1991).

10. The work of Garcia Delgado (1990) and various official publications including ICEX (1988a) contains a detailed array of SMs and SCMs adopted during the first PSOE mandate. Salmon's book (1991) and the report of Business International (1988) propose a detailed review of the structural reforms applied between 1982 and 1990. The legislative and structural modifications resulting from the membership treaties have been analysed by Alonso (1985), Charles Le Bihan (1986), ESIC (1986), Riera et al. (1986), Tamames (1986) and Ruesga (1989).

11. For details on the structural reforms in industry see in particular Maravall (1987); MIE (1987); Arancegui (1989); Buesa and Molero (1990); Vasquez Barquero and Herbert (1990, 81–119); Salmon (1991); Clyde and Clifford (1992); MICYT (1992).

12. Membership in EURATOM did not impose any restructuring of the Spanish nuclear industry, but it obliged Spain to apply the provisions of the community policy in this sector, provisions primarily concerned with health protection, investments, supplies, and safety controls for nuclear power plants.

13. Before the first reform of the SF resulting from the SEA in 1988, these programs related primarily to the economic (particularly industrial) development of the regions that were lagging behind, and to the restructuring of declining industrial

zones and excess or uncompetitive industries (textiles, shipbuilding, iron and steel, shoes, automobiles, paper and cardboard, synthetic fibres, and so on) (ESIC, 1986, 75).

14. 1986: 10%; 1987: 12.5%; 1988: 15%; 1989: 12.5%; 1990: 12.5%; 1991: 12.5% 1992: 12.5%; 1993: 10%.

15. Spain was authorized to postpone the abolition of its restrictive measures with regard to certain imports originating in the EC: automobiles (1986–89); other products – radios, televisions, firearms, chemical products, tractors, and so on – (1986–88). The EC benefited from a three-year delay to raise its quotas with regard to certain imports, particularly textiles and iron and steel products of Spanish origin.

16. On the transformations in the agricultural sector during the eighties, see: ESIC (1986); Ruesga (1989) and Balboa and Delgado (1990, 119–55).

17. The CAP, which was adopted in 1962, established a common agricultural product market within the EC: free trade of agricultural products between member states; imposition of a CET on imports from third countries, standardization of agricultural policies of the member states. In order to ensure decent revenues and equivalent and constant income to the community's farmers, the CAP established a bottom price for their products. The maintenance of this bottom price is guaranteed by buying up excess production and by subsidies to companies that buy and market the farmers' products. This guaranteed price system is complemented by mechanisms for protecting the internal market. In addition to the CET, the EC levies special customs duties on imports from third countries when the price of these is higher than the suggested or maximum price of community agricultural products. Finally, the EC subsidizes the exports of European farmers in order to guarantee their competitiveness. The EAGGF, whose resources are provided by the CET, import levies and VAT, finances the price guarantee system and export subsidies. The organization's orientation section is responsible for agricultural structure modernization programs. For a more detailed analysis of the CAP, see in particular Tamames (1986, 123–55).

18. The democratic constitution of 1978 accorded statutes of autonomy to 17 nations and regions of Spain. Under the statutes, each region has its own political institutions (parliament, government, courts, and so on) and possesses legislative, executive, and administrative powers. The nature and importance of the legislative powers of the autonomous communities varies from one region to another. The content of the statute of autonomy was negotiated between Madrid and each separate region between 1978 and 1980, and approved by referendum in 1980. Nevertheless, under the constitution, the content of the autonomy statutes is never final. It may be modified constantly through agreements between Madrid and any of the regional governments. This explains the development of the autonomy statutes since 1980.

19. For a detailed explanation of the content of this legislation, see ICEX (1988b). Under the terms of the membership treaties, Spain would have been able to postpone the liberalization of Spanish investments in the EC until 1988–90.

20. The peseta joined the EMS in 1989. The EMS was created in 1979 as a replacement for the existing European monetary tangle. It operates according to following rules: (1) each member state fixes the exchange rate of its currency with each of the currencies of the other member states (bilateral pivots); (2)

each member state undertakes to maintain these exchange rates in force; this supposes that the central bank will intervene on the monetary market by selling or buying the national currency when the value of the latter fluctuates up or down; (3) each currency may fluctuate by + or –2.25% in relation to the bilateral pivots. A member state cannot belong to the EMS if its economic and monetary policies do not sufficiently respect the convergence standards set by the EC: balance of BP, confidence of financial markets toards its national currency, high level of employment, stability of prices (Tamames, 1986, 189).

21.   Lloyds Bank, Crédit Lyonnais, Société générale de Banque, Banca nazionale del Lavoro.

22.   On this aspect of the adjustment process see, in particular, McElrath (1989); Ethier (1992); Sanchez Munoz (1993).

23.   Three years before retirement, an employee may begin to receive pension payments as long as he shares 50% of his working hours with an unemployed worker and accepts a part-time work contract.

24.   The costs of protection against layoffs are high for Spanish employers. In 1985 alone, the unions lodged 200000 complaints before the labour tribunals for illegal firing. On average, employers found guilty had to pay the victims six months' salary plus devote six hours a week to looking for a new job. In the case of collective layoffs, the punishments are even heavier. In the banking sector, they represent an average of 60 paid working days for each year of service.

25.   Although the membership treaties required Spain to apply the clauses of Article 48 of the Treaty of Rome regarding the free circulation of workers as of January 1, 1986, Spain was allowed to postpone, until January 1, 1993, the application of the EC rules guaranteeing workers in each member state free access to employment and conditions of employment equivalent to those enforced in the other member states. The end of this transition period, which coincided with the delay in the application of the SEA provisions – which above all provided for the abolition of the last remaining impediments to the free circulation of workers (see Chapter 1, note 14) – led Spain to modify its legislation in 1992.

26.   In Spain as in all of the countries of the EC, the social security system consists of four regimes: (1) universal social protection programs (health, social aid, family allowances, retirement, and so on); (2) unemployment insurance; (3) professional training; (4) salary insurance. On social security reform, see in particular Serrano Perez (1989), Espina (1990), Andersen (1992, 1993), Sanchez Munoz (1993), Duquette and Ethier (1996). For an exhaustive survey of legislation devoted to retirement and social security plans between 1975 and 1991, see MTSS (1992).

27.   Although the integration of Greece, Spain and Portugal was followed by a top-down harmonization of the social legislation, the standardization of the labour relations and social security plans within the framework of the SEA and the TEU, favoured by Jacques Delors and the partisans of social Europe, never came to pass (see Ethier, 1994a).

28.   In 1993, contributions by businesses, individuals and the state to the various social security plans represented 31.5%, 6.1% and 62.3% of financing respectively (Andersen, 1993, 137). According to Jimenez Fernandez (1991, 56–7), the share of social contributions in funding the social security budget dropped from 89% in 1980 to 69% in 1991, whereas that of transfers from the state and other income

(less than 11% in 1980), reached 31% of the overall budget in 1991. Total social security expenses went from 1.7 billion pesetas in 1980 to 7.1 billion pesetas in 1991 (including 4.2 billion for the retirement plan and 2.2 billion for the sickness, accident and maternity insurance plans).

CHAPTER THREE

1. The primary reference sources used for this section of the text are Rudel (1980–94), The Intelligence Unit (1980–94), OCDE (1980-94), Leonard (1990–95), Maravall (1993).
2. The AFM was formed of a group of 200–300 young officers, primarily from the air force and infantry, who were hostile to the continuance of the colonial wars in Africa. The majority of the members of the AFM supported leftist ideas, unlike most of the army, which remained conservative. It was these leftist elements of AFM that were to organize the *coup d'état* of April 25, 1974, which was to dominate the provisional governments of the period 1974–76 and control the revolutionary council between 1976 and 1982 (Gladdish, 1990, 113).
3. Maravall (1993, 86) stresses that following these nationalizations and those carried out between 1975 and 1980, state control over the property of enterprises rose from 18% to 45%, and the contribution of public corporations to GDP reached 15%. Nevertheless, the relative weight of the public sector in the economy remained comparable to that of the other countries in the EC. By nationalizing the 32 national banks, Portugal nonetheless became the only European state characterized by an entirely public banking sector.
4. In 1975, Portugal received 150 million ecus in emergency aid from the European Investment Bank (EIB).
5. The constitution of 1976 established a semi-presidential regime characterized primarily by: (a) sharing of executive power between the Revolutionary Council – controlled by the military – the president of the republic – elected by universal suffrage – and the Council of Ministers; (b) a monocameral parliament (Gladdish, 1990, 107).
6. This protocol adapted the 1972 agreement to the new conditions created by the entry of Ireland, the United Kingdom and Denmark into the EC in 1973. It delayed the application of tariff reductions planned for certain exchanges between Portugal and these countries (Alvares, 1986, 49–50).
7. The revised constitution of 1982 abolished the Revolutionary Council and reduced the powers of president in favour of the National Assembly. On this topic, see Bruneau (1990) and Gladdish (1990).
8. Unlike Spain, which negotiated its membership in the EC without taking into account previous agreements reached with Brussels, negotiations for Portugal's membership took the form of a widening of the free-trade agreement of 1972. This widening was translated by the conclusion, in 1979, of a complementary protocol to the 1972 agreement; the signing, in 1982, of a transitional protocol modifying the 1972 agreement and the additional protocol of 1976; the conclusion, in 1984, of a free membership protocol and a protocol on the automobile sector (Alvares, 1986, 51–65).

9. In 1984, a survey revealed that 52% of Portuguese citizens were pessimistic about the economic and political future of the country and that 45% wanted to emigrate (Rudel, 1985).

10. In 1983, the socialist agrarian reform had already been largely dismantled. Of the 580 CPUs created by the expropriation of 1.16 million hectares of land belonging to the great landowners who originally employed 70000 labourers, there remained only 530 CPUs, in charge of 470000 hectares and employing 35000 workers. The failure of this reform is attributable both to legislative reprivatization measures and to the inability of the PCP, the primary promoter of socializing the means of production, to increase the productivity of the collective agricultural operations and to offer the labour force incomes higher than, or even equivalent to, those they were getting in the old system.

11. In 1984 the unemployment rate rose by 15%; approximately 93 000 workers saw the payment of their thirteenth month of salary, or of the raises provided for in the collective agreements, delayed. Problems related to famine, malnutrition and certain sicknesses which had practically disappeared, such as tuberculosis, reappeared in the working neighbourhoods of urban centres.

12. Between 1983 and 1984 the cover rate between imports and exports rose from 54.2% to 65%; the increase in exports of textile products alone was 40%. The value of foreign investments of French origin rose from 80 to 110 billion escudos.

13. It is important to point out here that Portugal, unlike Spain, did not have any structural reforms of its industry or its agriculture imposed on it by the EC during the pre-membership period. Due to their smaller size, Portuguese industry and agriculture did not represent as great a threat to European markets as Spanish industry and agriculture. Although the membership negotiations for Spain and Portugal were conducted according to different scenarios, the results were similar. The content of Portugal's membership act does not differ from Spain's except in a few respects. (1) Given that the 1972 agreement had already reduced customs duties on trade in industrial products between Portugal and the EC, the disarmament schedule imposed on Portugal involved slightly lower reduction rates than those applied to Spain (see Chapter 2, note 14). These are 10% (for the 1st, 2nd, 4th and 5th years) and 15% (for the 3rd, 7th and 8th years). (2) Portugal did not benefit from any temporary overriding measures for the automobile sector, as the latter was almost non-existent and had no harmonization imposed on its legislation respecting patents and public monopolies of a commercial nature. (3) The Membership Act authorized Portugal to postpone the introduction of the VAT until January 1, 1991. (4) The treaties granted Spain a period of four years to liberalize its investments in the EC. The time allowed for liberalizing Portuguese investments in the EC was five years. As for Spain, the dismantling of tariff barriers in the agricultural sector extended over seven or ten years, depending on the category of products. Nevertheless, the types of products involved in each transition differ from those of Spain. On the content of the membership treaties for the two countries, see Flaesch-Mougin (1986, 31–77).

14. According to Rudel (1986, 185), who quotes the figures of Portugal's general inspectorate of labour, the percentage of workers employed on a temporary contract basis was 38.4% in 1985–86 in construction, 28.1% in the hotels trade, 26% and 23.1% in the shoe and clothing industries.

15. The EC provided 400 billion escudos for the 1988–93 phase of the PEDIP project and 813 billion escudos for the 1988–93 regional development programs (Rudel, 1989).

16. Under the Membership Act, Portugal had to restructure its fishing industry in order to bring it in line with the requirements of the common fishing policy.

17. Decree law 64-A of February 27, 1989, specifies the nature of the just causes authorizing the cessation of individual work contracts: (a) normal or exceptional end (closing of a company, employee disability) of the working contract: (b) revocation by mutual assent between employer and employee; (c) unilateral revocation by the employee; (d) collective layoff decreed by the company or elimination of posts for objective causes of a structural, technological or social economic nature. Overall, the legislation accords a wide margin of freedom to employees with regard to layoffs. In addition, the decree law widens the list of conditions allowing the issue of temporary or undetermined length work contracts: temporary replacement of an employee, exceptional temporary activity of the company, seasonal activity, launching and developing a project, construction activities, and so on (Alegre and Alegre, 1989).

18. This law allows the government to name administrators in certain privatized enterprises; it authorizes it to intervene whenever it judges that the public or national interests are threatened, and limits, in accordance with terms specific to each transition, the purchase of shares by foreign companies (Rudel, 1989, 185).

19. The numerous previous taxes were replaced by an individual income tax and a company income tax. The marginal rate of taxation was brought down from 60% to 40%, but the number of tax brackets was reduced, which raised the tax burden of the middle classes, whose numbers are the greatest. Half a million low-income families saw their taxes go down by 40%. On this reform and the additions of 1989 and 1990, see Carvalho (1990).

20. Ten months for unemployed workers between the ages of 25 and 55, and 25–30 months for laid-off workers of 55 and over (Campbell, 1990, 4).

21. Reform of school programs; creation of a new type of secondary school designed to facilitate entry into the labour market and respond to the needs of local and regional economic development; launching of the second phase of the program for the development of the Portuguese education system (PRODEP), in particular the MINERVA project, aimed at giving students greater access to new technologies.

22. Laid-off workers from now on had a right to compensation equal to one month of salary per year or fraction of a year of seniority, the amount granted never being less than three years seniority.

23. Prolongation of the motorway network by 300 km; modernization of secondary transborder roads; improvement of transport and the metro system in Lisbon; construction of a new bridge over the Tage and of a new airport in the capital; construction of an underground rail system and waste treatment centres in Porto; installation of a gas pipeline between the port of Setubal and Braga; construction of new hydro-electric dams at Foz da Coa and Algueva, and so on.

CHAPTER FOUR

1. The crisis of the regime of the colonels, who had been in power since 1967, was the result of a combination of factors, the most immediate of which were the repression of the student uprising at the Polytechnic in 1973, and the failure of the July 1974 *coup d'état* against the government of President Makarios in Cyprus, which led to a war between Greece and Turkey. The crisis was resolved by the transfer of power to an interim conservative government led by Caramanlis, who was charged with re-establishing democracy, order and stability. For more on this topic, see Diamandouros (1986).

2. In February 1977 Greece signed a financial protocol with the EC, which provided for a total of 280 mecus in assistance in the form of improved loans (Boutillier and Uzundis, 1991, 96).

3. In 1979, Caramanlis was elected President of the Republic and George Rallis became chief of the ND and Prime Minister.

4. The second Caramanlis government widened access to universities by easing entrance requirements for candidates and attempting to improve the quality of teaching by urging teachers without formal certification to accept voluntary retirement in return for compensation.

5. Greece's Membership Act contained clauses similar to those of the Membership Acts of Spain and Portugal. Nonetheless, this act provided for a four-year rather than a seven-year transition period for the establishment of these provisions: application of the CAP, introduction of VAT, liberalization of trade in goods, capital and services, free circulation of workers. In order to attenuate the cost of this transition, Greece benefited from various EC aid programs. Moreover, the PASOK succeeded in obtaining an increase in this aid by making its support for the entry of Spain and Portugal conditional on the award of new resources aimed at speeding up the adaptation of its agriculture. With this aim in view, the community agreed, in 1984, to create the Integrated Mediterranean Programs (IMPs), which were extended to all the agricultural regions of southern Europe that were likely to be affected by the membership of the Iberian countries. Two IMPs were awarded to Greece: one for Crete (1984–87) and the other for Western Greece and the Peloponnese (1987–90), which received a total of 6312 mecus in grants and loans.

6. According to Stournaras (1990, 414–15), the major cause of the Greek government's higher budget deficit during the eighties was the strong increase in social spending, particularly with regard to retirement plans. Between 1981 and 1988, the cost of retirement plans reportedly increased by 6% per year in real terms as a result of increased benefits and the extension of protection to new categories of recipients, particularly immigrant workers who had returned from Eastern Europe. As a result of these measures, the level of social spending in Greece, which in 1975 stood at 4.8% of GDP (compared with 10% in France, Germany and Italy), reached 10.7% in 1985 (compared with 13.5% in the same countries).

7. The effect of these measures was to reduce the gap between high salaries and the guaranteed minimum wage from 5.5% to 2.6% between 1980 and 1988.

8. Like the measures adopted by the ND, this law was aimed at adapting the Greek university system to the standards of the EC. It restructured the universities on the basis of units and departments; it established a status hierarchy for teaching

personnel: (1) lecturers, (2) assistant professors, (3) associate professors, (4) professors; it prohibited professors from holding any other job; it sub-divided the university year into two semesters, and it replaced the evaluation system based on end-of-year exams with a system based on obtaining points or credits for individual courses. The constitutionality of several of these provisions was nonetheless contested before the Special Superior Court.

9. From now on the indexation of salaries to the cost of living no longer took into account the increased price of imports and was based on the anticipated inflation rate rather than the real inflation rate.

10. On the obligations attached to Membership Treaty, see Chapter 4, note 5. On the constraints inherent in the SEA, see Chapter1, note 14. It must be remembered that the two legal agreements did not formally impose any reforms on the new member states with regard to labour and social security legislation, except for the abolition of the obstacles to the free circulation of labour.

11. The Synapismos or the 'Coalition of the Forces of the Left and of Progress' formed in 1988, was formed by the KKE (Communist party of the pro-Soviet exterior), the small organizations under its control and the EAR (the Communist party of the pro-Albanian interior that had become the party of the Hellenic left in 1987).

12. The parliament was to set up commissions of inquiry into the fraudulent practices (manufacture and use of counterfeit) of Koskotas, President of the Bank of Crete, and the illegal dealings of the Papandreou government, suspicious armament contracts with certain foreign countries, phone tapping, sale of 'Greek' corn imported from Yugoslavia, and the purchase of Mirage 2000 aircraft at an unusually high price. Koskotas avoided these inquiries by fleeing to the United States. The American authorities nonetheless proceeded to arrest and imprison him. Andreas Papandreou and several of his ministers appeared before a special jurisdiction, at the close of these commissions. In 1990, former Minister Athanassopoulos was condemned to a year and a half in prison for his role in the Yugoslavian corn affair. Former Vice-President Agamemnon Koutsogiorgas, who was involved in Koskotas' fraudulent dealings, was jailed the same year. Subsequently freed on bail, he was to die during his trial in April 18, 1991.

13. Thus, before this reform, the mother of a family could receive retirement benefits after 15 years of work.

14. Among these, we should mention Law 1892 of 1990, which guaranteed the rights of part-time workers (minimum wage scale, protection of labour legislation); the various regulations of 1990 which lengthened maternity leave to 15 weeks while extending it to all female employees; Law 1836 of 1989, which extended the scope of the legislation on health and work safety to local government employees and to individuals (ECC, 1990a).

15. Law 2000/1991 of December 1991.

16. The sale, which had been concluded for 124 billion drachmas (approximately US$1 billion), was described as a sidewalk sale by Andreas Papandreou, who estimated the value of the company at 350 billion drachmas.

17. The commercial embargo decreed by the western countries and its allies deprived Greece of its northern outlets to Central Europe.

18. On April 17, 1992 the Minister of Foreign Affairs, Antonis Samaras, was removed from the government as a result of his intransigent attitude towards

the Macedonian question. Following the independence of the former Yugoslavian republic of Macedonia in 1991, Greece asked the EC not to recognize the latter if the new state insisted on adopting the name of Macedonia, which also designated a territory in the North of Greece. After acquiescing to this request, the European Council and the United States asked Athens to soften its position due to support within international public opinion for Skopje's position. The refusal of Minister Samaras to negotiate any compromise on this point with Greece's European partners led to the expulsion of the government. Following its departure, Samaras founded a new party, 'Political Spring' in order to denounce Athens' and the EC's abandonment of their initial position with regard to Skopje. When three ND deputies went over to this party, in September 1993, the Mitsokakis government lost its absolute majority in the House.

19. It will be recalled that it was Simitis who initiated the stabilization measures under the second Papandreou government, but had to resign when the government abandoned this program in 1988. This time he has surrounded himself with a homogeneous team whose members share his modernist, Europeanist and liberal views. The two most important new ministers, long-standing opponents of Papandreou, in the style of Simitis, are: Theodoros Panaglos (Foreign Affairs) and Mme Vasso Papandreou (no relation to the former Prime Minister), who has been put in charge of a super Development Ministry, uniting industry, trade and tourism. The ministers formerly responsible for economy and finance. Iannos Papantoniou and Alexis Papadoulos, have been reassigned to other functions, since they were committed to respecting the objectives and convergence criteria of the EMU. Papandreou's most tenacious supporters, who would still like to see him as head of state in spite of his poor state of health, have been fired; these include: George Lianis (ex-Minister of Sports and cousin of Dimitra, Papandreou's new wife) and Dimitris Krémastinos (ex-minister of health and Papandreou's personal physician). On the other hand, Papandreou's son George, a moderate who has contributed towards speeding up his father's succession, has retained his post as Minister of Education.

CHAPTER FIVE

1. According to the ECC (1990b, 4), 50.4% of DFI in Spain and 14.7% of that in Portugal in 1986 originated in the EC countries.

2. A state's ability to repay is frequently measured by the percentage of overall income from exports represented by the value of the total public debt. In 1992, this percentage was 747.7 in Greece, 318.6 in Spain and 180 in Portugal (Eurostat, 1991).

3. Belgium: 4.8; France: 2.8; Luxembourg: 4.7; Netherlands: 3.2; United Kingdom: 4.6; United States: 4.2; Japan; 5.8. See ECC (1993).

4. Between 1978 and 1988, the contribution to the GDP of ECG industries dropped from 60.2% to 48.5% and those of EIG increased from 12.9% to 21.8% and from 26.9% to 29.7% respectively (Boutillier and Uzundis, 1991, 41).

5. In 1985, companies employing less than ten workers accounted for 93.9% of the current consumer goods factories, 86.5% of factories producing intermediate goods and 95.5% of equipment goods factories (Boutillier and Uzundis, 1991).

6. Between 1980 and 1988 the distribution of the Greek government's investments with regard to the formation of fixed capital, was characterized by: maintaining the share devoted to the primary sector (8.2%); increasing the share allocated to manufacturing industries from 15% to 18%; reducing spending on construction and infrastructures (energy, transportation, telecommunication) from 3% and 22% respectively (Boutillier and Uzundis, 1991).

7. In 1992, the automobile sector was completely controlled by the multinationals Volkswagen, Fasa-Renault, GM, Ford, FIAT, PSA, Nissan, and Daimler–Benz; the agro-food sector was 40% controlled by Feruzzi, Nestlé and BSN; the computer, chemical and electronics sectors were entirely owned by a few groups: Siemens, Dow Chemicals, IBM, Alcatel, Ericsson, Sony (Mattei and Lacharme, 1992).

8. In 1985, labour costs in Spain were equal to 55% of average costs in the OECD; in 1990 they represented 80% of average costs (Mougey, 1991).

9. Objectives of the PEDIP: Program 1 'Basic Infrastructures and Technologies': development and modernization of productive energy installations, highways, railways, ports, industrial parks; increasing the productivity, specialization and quality of the products of the traditional industries through technical and technological modernization. Program 2 'Professional Training': improving the professional training of the work force in industry. Program 3 'Productive Investment Incentives': financial participation in funds lost to various R&D projects, technological innovation, quality management, development of new facilities. Program 4 'Financial Engineering': reform of the system for financing industries. Program 5 'Productivity Missions': improving training of managers of industrial enterprises, promoting cooperation between enterprises, perfecting quality management methods. Program 6 'Industrial Quality and Design Missions': enhancing the quality and design of products. Program 7 'Disclosure, Implementation and Control' (of PEDIP) (Ministerio da Industria e Energia, 1988). For the years 1988 and 1989 alone, the total budget of the PEDIP totalled almost 3 billion ecus (Ministerio da Industria e Energia, 1990).

CHAPTER SIX

1. The widening of the ECs, in conjunction with an acceleration of the integration process, were provided for in the Treaty of Rome. The membership of Greece, Spain and Portugal, which had been delayed for political (the existence of dictatorships) and economic (the constraints of the second enlargement) was accepted within the perspective of the approaching completion of the Common Market. This was perceived as an essential condition of the success of the widened membership and the renewal of economic growth in the Europe of the Twelve. The preliminary discussions on the SEA were furthermore instigated at the beginning of the eighties, concurrently with the continued negotiations with Madrid and Lisbon.

2. As was already stated in Part One, in the social sphere, there was very little Community legislation of a compulsory nature (regulations voted by the Council). These essentially related to the equalization of work conditions offered to national workers and to workers originating in other EC countries,

the harmonization of health and work safety rules and rules related to the equality of hiring conditions and the treatment of male and female workers.

3. This fear was mainly shared by the member states who have the more generous and costly social systems (France, Germany, Benelux, Denmark). Great Britain, which social policies are less developed, did not fear an exodus of its enterprises and jobs towards south. On the other hand, the Thatcher government was very reluctant to increase its contribution to ESCPs after the third enlargement. Therefore, it strongly supported the rise of Southern European social expenditures, hoping that this policy would contribute to reduce the future needs of help of Greece, Spain and Portugal (Duquette and Ethier, 1996).

4. Before their entry into the EC, Greece, Spain and Portugal received various non-conditional aids from Brussels aimed at modernizing the less competitive sectors of their economies: agriculture (Greek IMP from 1986–92 – 470 million ecus), fisheries, iron and steel industry (Spain and Portugal), shipbuilding (Spain). However, these aids were considerably smaller than those obtained under SEA and TEU.

5. In 1995, one ecu was roughly equivalent to US$1.25.

6. In some member states international agreements and/or constitutional amendments must be subjected to a popular referendum. In Greece, Spain and Portugal, the Maastricht Treaty was subject only to the parliaments.

7. Simplifying in the extreme, the major issues separating left and right could be considered to be (a) at the political level: the defence of order, safety, stability and the effectiveness of the political power versus the protection of individual and collective rights and freedoms and the widening of representation of various interests within the political system; (b) at the moral level: the promotion of traditional values particularly those enshrined in Christian doctrines, versus the promotion of humanist, secular values; (c) at the social level: the justification of natural inequalities and hierarchical social structures versus the defence of equality of opportunity, of social mobility and of the more equitable redistribution of wealth.

8. Mitsokakis was replaced by Miltiade Evert as the head of the ND.

9. For an in-depth analysis of the PASOK and its policies during the eighties, see Clogg 1993. On the ideology and structures of the PASOK, see also Spourdalakis (1992b).

10. In 1973 the PCE, the Italian Communist Party and the French Communist Party adopted a new Euro-communist program, which advocated an alliance with the socialist parties, opening up communist parties to the middle classes, taking power by legal, democratic means, and the implementation of reforms (nationalization, extending workers' and social rights, and so on) aimed at strengthening the national, humanistic character of capitalism rather than the establishment of socialism.

11. *Cambio 16*, no. 516, October 19, 1981, p. 30. Figures quoted by Buse (1984, 204).

12. On the recent history of the PSOE, see in particular: Ethier (1986, 258–65); Kedros (1986); Gillespie (1989); Fishman (1990); Maravall (1992); Heywood (1995, 189–217).

13. 1995 was marked by the accession of a new leader, Antonio Guterrez, to the head of the PSP, and by the victory of the PSP in the fall legislative elections. Jorge Sampaïo succeeded Mario Soares as President of the Republic in 1996.

These changes, however, are too recent to permit an analysis of their consequences on the unity and ideological orientation of the PSP, particularly at the economic level. Moreover, such an analysis is outside the framework of this study, which is limited to the period 1975–95.

14. A survey published by the daily *Diario de Noticias*, at the beginning of 1985, revealed that 52% of Portuguese citizens were pessimistic over the political and economic future of their country. This pessimism was confirmed when 45% expressed the wish to emigrate and by the mixed feelings shown towards EC membership (25% for, 26% against and 35% undecided) (Rudel 1985, 199).

15. 'We cannot remain indifferent to the drop in production and investment, the explosion of prices, the loss of buying power and the upsurge in unemployment' (Declaration by Cavaco Silva published in *Le Monde*, June 6, 1985).

CHAPTER SEVEN

1. In conformity with Haggard and Kaufman (1992) and Haggard and Webb (1994) we associate the autonomy of the executive with the margin of manoeuvre or freedom of action that the support of political and social forces procure for it.

2. Bermeo (1994b, 7) notes that in 1977, there were 974 strikes in Spain; in 1978, this figure rose to 1356. During the same period the number of lost working hours rose from 92 000 to 129 000.

3. Evolution of the membership of the major Spanish trade union organizations between 1976, 1978, 1981 and 1985: UGT (socialist): 6000, 1 000 000, 806 000, 663 000; CC.OO (communist): 94 000, 1 600 000, 897 000, 500 000; USO (independent): 18 000, 556 000, 205 000, 50 000; ELA–STV (nationalist): n.a; n.a; 58 000, 110 000 (McElrath, 1989, 104). In 1988, the UGT and the CC.OO shared 75% of the voices in the professional elections. The UGT obtained 40.5% of the votes (70 000 delegate posts) and the CC.OO obtained 34.1% of votes (59 000 delegate posts). These elections gave the UGT control over the majority of company comittees in 14 out of 17 autonomous communities and 46 out of 50 provinces (Moderne 1989).

4. In 1978 and 1980, the UGT controlled 21.6% and 29.2% of delegates' posts; the USO, 3.8% and 8.6%; the CC.OO 34.5% and 33.8%; the ELA–STV 11.8% and 25.6% (McElrath, 1989, 106). After 1982, almost all of the delegates were divided equally among the UGT, the CC.OO and the ELA–STV.

5. For an analysis of the conditions which favoured the PSOE's hegemony, see also Craig (1994) and Boix (1995).

6. The PNV is the main Basque party; it controls the legislative and executive powers of the Basque Autonomous Community. The CiU is the main Catalan party; it dominates political institutions of the Catalan Autonomous Community. The CDS is a new national party created by Adolfo Suarez after the dissolution of the UCD.

7. In 1984, a faction of members of the PCE rejected the Euro-communist doctrine advocated by Santiago Carrillo and his successor to the position of Secretary General, Gerardo Iglesias, and created a new pro-Soviet Marxist-Leninist party, the *Partido comunista de los Pueblos de España* (PCPE), under the leadership of Ignacio Gallego. Carrillo was himself excluded from the PCE in 1986 and

formed the *Mesa para la unidad de los comunistas*, which later became the *Partido de los Trabajadores de España-Unidad*. The same year, the PCE formed a new leftist coalition, *Izquierda Unida* (IU), with the PCPE, the *Partido humanista*, the *Partido carlista*, the *Federacion progressista*, the *Partido de Izquierda republicana*, the *Partido de Accion socialista* and a number of independents.

8.   The study conducted by Maravall (1982, 33) on the development of Spanish unionized workers' attitudes towards social inequality clearly shows that, during the transition towards democracy, these workers abandoned their socialist ideals in favour of a more pragmatic, social-democratic vision. The analysis carried out by Fishman (1984) on the motivations of the unionized workers in relation to the limitations on their economic demands, confirms that the majority of these workers supported the government austerity policy, yet shows that this support was more motivated by the danger of company closings, the need to consolidate democracy and the poor fighting spirit of the working class, than by the goals of fighting inflation and improving productivity. The study by Perez Dias (1993, 236–81) confirms Maravall's and Fishman's conclusions.

9.   The impact of the positive effects of EC membership on the success of adjustment has been analysed, notably, by De la Dehesa (1994).

10.   The ESCPs were implemented in two phases: 1983–93 and 1993–99. The primary evaluative instruments available for the first phase are the annual and pluriannual reports of the European Communities Commission (ECC). These show that the effectiveness of the programming and implementation of the ESCPs had improved significantly, that the credits set aside were allocated within the prescribed time frames, and that the principles of additionality of expenditure and partnership were respected overall. However, in the opinion of Bruce Millan, the former director of the division responsible for regional development within the commission (DG-XVl) (1992), it is at the present time difficult to evaluate the macro-economic impact of the ESCPs, due, on the one hand, to the numerous other factors influencing the evolution of their areas of intervention, and, on the other, of the methodological problems encountered by the national monitoring committees. Nevertheless, the Commission's last report (ECC 1994), provided certain indicative data on the impact of objective 1 (the economic development of backward regions). According to this data, the increase in gross capital generated by the ESCPs alone between 1989 and 1993 was 2.2% in Portugal and Greece, compared with 1.2% in Spain; the annual impact of the ESCPs on the growth rate was 0.7% in Portugal , 0.5% in Greece and 0.2% in Spain. The Commission estimated however, that the sudden interruption in aid was probably responsible for a 3.2% drop in the growth rate in Portugal, 2.4% in Greece and 1% in Spain. The percentage of jobs created between 1989 and 1993 as a result of the ESCPs is estimated at 4% in Portugal, 2% in Greece and 1% in Spain. Overall, the Commission considers that the ESCPs allowed Spain and Portugal to experience growth rates higher than those in the EC between 1989 and 1993, whereas they stabilized growth in Greece. It was not possible to compile any precise figures on the impact of objectives 2 (revitalization of declining industrial zones), 3 and 4 (the fight against long-term unemployment) and 5 (the modernization of agricultural structures).

11.   The new cabinet is primarily made up of liberals. Carlos Solchaga, the leader of the liberal faction, moreover, became president and spokesman for the

socialist group in parliament, replacing *Guerrista* Martin Toval. On the rivalry between liberals and *Guerristas*, see Chapter 6.

12. These measures, that accompanied the Plan for Economic Convergence, have been already expounded in the last section of Chapter 2.

13. Among the numerous conflicts of interest which sullied the records of the Gonzalez governments, the most controversial were the lucrative deals made by Juan Guerra, based on privileged information obtained from his brother, Alfonso Guerra. The GAL scandal relates to the accusations made against the Prime Minister, the Minister of the Interior and several leaders of the PSOE concerning the illegal constitution of para-police commando units – *Grupos anti-terrorista de liberacion* (GAL) – which between 1983 and 1987, purportedly kidnapped and murdered at least 22 Basque separatists in Southwest France. Felipe Gonzalez, Narcis Serra (former Minister of Defence and ex-Vice-President of the government) and José Maria Benegas (a Basque member of parliament) were cleared of these allegations by the Supreme Court in March 1996. At the time of writing, criminal proceedings are still under way in this affair, with the former Minister of the Interior, Jose Barrionuevo, as the principal accused.

14. The new Spanish government had hardly come to power when it announced 200 billion pesetas (US$1.6 billion) in budget cuts and projected cuts in the coming months. José Maria Aznar claimed that he would reduce the public deficit sufficiently in 1997 to allow Spain to take 'the first single currency train' (AFP, 1996). He also announced 'a major clean-up operation' and a reorganization of the state's administrative structures (Bôle Richard, 1996).

15. At the end of 1985 over 105 000 workers in about 750 companies were waiting for their wages to be paid, involving a total of 100 billion escudos (US$140 million).

16. The index of Eurobarometer which calculates the satisfaction rate toward the economic situation is positive when it is above 2.50 and negative when it is below 2.50. In Portugal this index has increased from 2.06, in 1985, to 2.80 in 1986 and it remained positive all along the further period, reaching 3.57 in 1991, despite the beginning of a new recession cycle and the adoption of the Quantum. See *Eurobarometer Trends 1974–93*, table B26.

17. These changes, which were adopted at the party's XXII congress in 1988, proposed that the party become an open forum for discussion and that the leaders be elected by secret ballot. This new procedure did not prevent Alvara Cunhal, 75, being re-elected to the post of Secretary General (Rudel, 1989).

18. For example, *the Pacto laboral* of 1987, which was signed only by the UGT, related exclusively to the provisions with respect to control over the growth of salaries. Both the UGT and the CGTP-IN refused to ratify the measures aimed at softening hiring conditions in companies (Rudel, 1988).

19. For example: (1) the 'defence days' of June 28–29, 1988, organized by the CGTP-IN aimed at protesting against the agrarian reform which increased the reserve of lands intended for former expropriated property owners and their heirs, which led, in practice, to the disappearance of the collective production units (CPU) created by the PCP after the Revolution of the Carnations; (2) March 17, May 12, July 5 and December 29, 1988: Lisbon Metro employees strike for pay increases; (3) October 1988: student work stoppages at the University of Lisbon; (4) December 4, 12 and 13, 1988: magistrates' work stoppage; (5)

December 16 and 30, 1988: strike by Air Portugal employees; (6) 1988–89: work stoppages in the public services, the municipal civil service, naval shipyards.

20. Except in regard to certain provisions that were judged to be unconstitutional by the labour court (see Chapter 3).

21. On the PASOK's institutional reforms, see also Alivizatos (1993).

22. The reform aimed at submitting the army to civil power was instituted by the ND in 1977. Act 60 of August 1977 gave the government sole responsibility for the national defence policy, after abolishing the extraordinary powers granted to army chiefs-of-staff under the dictatorship of the colonels (Veremis 1987).

23. Law 1257 (1982) modifying the operation of IGs; law 1264 (1982) regulating the functioning of worker's trade unions; law 131 (1983) regulating farmers' associations; law 1712 and 1746 (1987) governing merchants', retailers' and craftsmen's associations. Law 1257, for example, reduced the power of the large farmers' cooperatives, which were more favourable to the ND, in relation to that of the smaller cooperatives, which were closer to the PASOK or the KKE. By instituting the rule of one man, one vote and by increasing the membership of PASEGES by 130000 new members, law 1257 increased the PASOK's majority to 55% and granted the KKE a 14% over-representation. Law 1264 applied a similar logic by authorizing an increase in the number of individual and collective members in the GSEE. It also favoured increasing the influence of Papandreou's supporters within ADEDY. By imposing the rule of one man, one vote and by authorizing the increased membership, law 1712 strengthened the influence of the PASOK within the EESE. It was above all law 1746, however, which obliged chambers of commerce and industry to merge with artisans' and small retailers' associations, that the PASOK succeeded in weakening the influence of the ND over the owners' organizations and 'the oligarchy of industrial and shopkeeper elites' (Mavrogordatos, 1993, 53).

24. For a more detailed analysis of Greek IGs and their relations with European IGs, see Aligisakis and Papadopoulos (1990).

25. The KKE, which was a pro-Soviet communist party along the lines of the PCP, however, changed more on the ideological level than its Portuguese counterpart during the eighties, in particular since it had more closely supported the policy of Mikhail Gorbachev than the PCP. Thus, after being fiercely opposed to Greece's membership in NATO (1980) and the EC (1981), it accepted these changes while continuing to denounce the country's dependence on American imperialism and the presence of American military bases on national soil (Verney 1990). At the end of the eighties, under the influence of *glasnost* and *perestroika*, it became reconciled with the pro-Albanian communist party of the interior, which in 1987 became the Hellenic party of the left (EAR). During the elections of 1989, the KKE and the EAR formed an alliance, the 'Forces of the Left and the Progress', which defended the role of private initiative and agreed to form a coalition government with the ND (Catsiapis 1988–90 – Table 34). However the KKE was constantly opposed to the liberal reforms of the PASOK and the ND due to its very close links with the working class and small family enterprises of the rural regions, two groups that were particularly threatened by these reforms.

26. As Fakiolas (1987) points out '[in Greece] the trade unions have been the most prominent set of interest groups ... the majority is wielded by active party members, so that party and union politics mingle together and the unions are but pure extensions of the political parties'.

References

Adelman, Irma and Taft Morris, C. (1973), *Economic Growth and Social Equity in Developing Countries,* Stanford, Stanford University Press.

Agence France Presse (AFP) (1996), 'L'Union européenne au régime de la rigueur budgétaire', *Le Devoir,* May 14 1996, B3.

Aguilar, M., Gaviria, M. and Laparra, M. (1992), 'Les limites de l'Espagne sociale', *Revue française des Affaires sociales.*

Alegre, Carlos and Alegre, Teresa (1989), *Lei dos despedimentos e contratos a termo,* Coimbra, Livraria Aledina.

Aligisakis, Maximos and Papadopoulos, Joannis (1990), 'L'insertion des groupes d'intérêt grecs dans la Communauté européenne' in D. Sidjanski and U. Ayberk (eds), *op.cit.,* 85–115.

Alivizatos, Nicos C. (1993), 'The Presidency, Parliament and the Courts in the 1980s' in R. Clogg (ed.), *op.cit.,* 65–78.

Alonso, Antonio (1985), *España en el Mercado Comun. Del acuerdo del 70 a la Comunidad de Doce,* Madrid, Espasa calpe.

Alonzo Olea, Manuel et al. (1992), *España y la Union Europea. Las consecuencias del Tratado de Maastricht,* Madrid, Plaza y Jaurès.

Alvares, Pedro (1986), *Portugal na CEE,* Lisbon, Publicaçôes Europa-América.

Andersen, Arthur (1992, 1993), *A Guide to Business in Spain,* Madrid, ICEX.

Arancegui, Mikel Navarro (1989), 'La politica de reconversion industrial en España', *Informacion comercial española,* Ministerio de Economia y Hacienda, February, 45–68.

Argandoña, Antonio et al. (1991), *La politica economica española en la Union Economica y Monetaria Europea,* Madrid, Circulo de Empresarios.

Ariztegui, Francisco Javier (1990), 'La politica monetaria: un periodo crucial' in J.L. Garcia Delgado (ed.), *op.cit.,* 307–43.

Armijo, Leslie E. (ed.) (1995), *Conversations on Democratization and Economic Reform,* Working Papers of the Southern California Seminar, Center for International Studies, University of Southern California, Los Angeles.

Armijo, Leslie E., Biersteker, Thomas J. and Lowenthal, Abraham F. (1995), 'The Problems of Simultaneous Transitions' in L. Diamond and M.F. Plattner (eds), *op.cit.,* 226–41.

Aslund, Anders (1995), 'The Case for Radical Reform' in L. Diamond and M.F. Plattner (eds), *op.cit.,* 74–86.

Baeza, Emilio Ontiveros (1990), 'La apertura financiera al exterior' in J.Garcia Delgado (ed.), *op.cit.,* 361–95.

Balboa, Carlos A. and Delgado, Luis Garcia (1990), 'La agricultura y la alimentacion: una nueva etapa de cambio estructural' in J.Garcia Delgado (ed.), *op.cit.,* 119–69.

Balcerowicz, Leszek (1995), 'Understanding Postcommunist Transitions' in L. Diamond and M.F. Plattner (eds), *op.cit.,* 86–101.

Baloyra, Enrique (1987), *Comparing New Democracies,* Boulder, Westview Press.

Bermeo, Nancy (1994a), 'Sacrifice, Sequence and Strength in Successful Dual Transitions: Lessons from Spain', *Journal of Politics,* vol. 56, no. 3, August, 601–27.

Bermeo, Nancy (1994b), *Economic and Political Liberalization in Spain: False Leads and Real Lessons for other States*, Draft Paper, Department of Political Science, Princeton University.

Boix C. (1995) 'Building a Social Democratic Strategy in Southern Europe: Economic Policy Under the Gonzalez Government (1982–93)', *Instituto Juan March* (IJM) *Working Papers* no. 1995/69, Madrid, IJM.

Bole Richard, Michel (1996), 'José Maria Aznar a formé un cabinet "centriste" et réduit', *Le Monde*, May 7.

Bon, Pierre (1990–95), 'L'Espagne en...' in A. Grosser (ed.), *op.cit.*

Boutillier, Sophie and Uzundis, Dimitri (1991), *La Grèce face à l'Europe*, Paris, L'Harmattan.

Bresser Pereira, Luis Carlos, Maravall, José Maria, Przeworski, Adam (1993), *Economic Reforms in New Democracies. A Social-Democratic Approach.* Cambridge, Cambridge University Press.

Bruce, Peter (1991), 'Climate Control in Corporate Spain', *Financial Times*, July 16, reproduced in *Problèmes économiques*, no. 2, 244, October 9, 30–2.

Bruneau, Thomas (1990), 'Constitutions and Democratic Consolidation: Brazil in Comparative Perspective' in D. Ethier (ed.), *op.cit.*, 173–97.

Bruneau, Thomas (1991–92), 'Defense, Modernization and the Armed Forces in Portugal', *Portuguese Studies Review*, vol. 1, no. 2, 28–44.

Buesa, Mikel and Molero, José (1990), 'Crisis y transformacion de la industria española: base productiva y comportamiento technologico', *Pensamiento iberamericano*, no. 17, 119–54.

Buse, Michael (1984), *La nueva democracia espanola. Sistema de partidos y orientacion del voto (1976–1983)*, Madrid, Union Editorial.

Business International (1988) *Spain to the Year 2000*, Geneva, Business International, 123.

Camacho, Marcelino (1979), *Espagne: une Conquête de la Démocratie*, Paris, Flammarion.

Campbell, G. Ricardo (1990), 'Social Security in Portugal: Harmonizing for Europe 1992', *Social Security Bulletin*, vol. 53, no. 8, August, 2–8.

Carvalho, Antonio Joaquim (1990), 'Taxes in Portugal', Portuguese *Industrial Association Newsletter*, no. 3, July–September.

Catsiapis, Jean (1984–95), 'La Grèce en ... 'in A. Grosser (ed.), *op. cit.*

Charles Le-Bihan, Danielle et al. (1986), 'L'Espagne et le Portugal dans la CEE. Interrogations et enjeux', *Notes et Etudes documentaires*, no. 4819.

Clogg, Richard (1984), 'The PASOK Phenomenon', Center for Greek Studies, *University of Florida staff paper*, 4 November.

Clogg, Richard (ed.) (1993), *Greece 1981–89. The Populist Decade*, New York, St Martin's Press.

Clyde, Mitchell and Clifford, J. Hendel (1992), 'Tendencias españolas en la privatizacion', *Economia española*, no. 2327, 1–7 juin, 1745–47.

Craig, Patricia (1994), 'The PSOE: Slouching Toward Hegemony of the Party's Over?', paper delivered to the American Political Science Association Annual Meeting, New York, 1994.

Dahl, R. (1971), *Polyarchy: Participation and Opposition*, New Haven/London, Yale University Press.

D' Aubert, François (1994), *Main basse sur L'Europe, Enqûete sur le derines de Bruxelles*, Paris, Plau, chapters 6 and 7.

De la Dehesa, Guillermo (1994), 'The European Periphery – Spain' in J. Williamson (ed.), *op.cit.*, 123–41.

De Ruyt, Jean (1987), *L'Acte Unique Européen. Commentaire*, Bruxelles, Presses de l'Université libre de Bruxelles.

Desai, Padma (1995), 'Beyond Shock Therapy' in: L. Diamond and M.F. Plattner (eds.), *op.cit.*, 101–12.

Diamandouros, P. Nikifouros (1986), 'Regime Change and the Prospects for Democracy in Greece: 1974–1983', in G. O'Donnell, P. Schmitter and L. Whitehead (eds), *op.cit.*, vol. I: Southern Europe, 138–65.

Diamandouros, P. Nikifouros (1993), 'Politics and Culture in Greece, 1974–91: an Interpretation' in R. Clogg (ed.), *op.cit.*, 1–26.

Diamond, Larry, Linz, Juan J.C. and Lipset, Seymour Martin (eds) (1989), *Democracy in Developing Countries*, 3 volumes, Boulder, Lynne Rienner.

Diamond, Larry and Plattner, Marc F. (eds) (1995a), *Economic Reform and Democracy*, Baltimore/London, The Johns Hopkins University Press. The texts of this book were previously published in *Journal of Democracy*, October 1994, vol. 5, no. 4.

Diamond, Larry and Plattner, Marc F. (1995b), 'Introduction' in L. Diamond and M.F. Plattner (eds), *op.cit.*, ix–xxii.

Dimitras, Panayote (1985), *Greek Opinions: Special Report on Greek Politics*, Athène.

Dimitras, Panayote (1987), 'Changes in Public Attitudes' in K. Featherstone and D. Katsoudas (eds), *op.cit.*, 64–85.

Doutriaux, Yves (1992), *Le Traité sur l'Union Européenne*, Paris, Armand Colin.

Duquette, Michel and Ethier, Diane (1996) *Is Economic Adjustment Compatible with Redistributive Policies? Chile and Spain in Comparative Perspective*, Paper presented to the annual American Politial Science Association (APSA) Conference, San Francisco, August 28–September 3.

Escuela Superior de Gestion Comercial y Marketing (ESIC) (1986), *Consecuencias para la economia española de la integracion de España en la CEE*, Madrid, ESIC.

Espina, Alvaro (1990), *Empleo, democracia y relaciones industriales en España: de la industrializacion al Mercado Unico*, Madrid, Ministerio del Trabajo y de la Seguridad social.

Espina, Alvaro (1993), *Diez años de politica industrial*, Madrid, Ministerio de Industria, Comercio y Turismo, Secretaria de Estado de Industria. Reproduction of a paper published in *Leviathan*, no. 50.

Ethier, Diane (1986), *La crise et la démocratisation des régimes autoritaires dans les pays semi-industriels: étude comparée des cas espagnol et brésilien*, PhD thesis, Department of Political Economy, Université Paris VIII.

Ethier, Diane (ed.) (1990), *Democratic Transition and Consolidation in Southern Europe, Latin America and Southeast Asia*, London, Macmillan.

Ethier, Diane (1991), 'Les impacts de l'adhésion à la Communauté européenne sur la balance commerciale de l'Espagne et du Portugal', *Etudes internationales*, vol. XXII, no. 1, March, 25–46.

Ethier, Diane (1992), 'Labour Market Changes in Spain and Portugal within the Context of their Integration into the European Community', *Social Development Issues*, vol. 14, no. 2–3.

Ethier, D. (1993) 'The Reform of the European Community's Structural Funds: from the Single Act to Maastricht and After', *International Review of Administrative Sciences*, vol. 59, no. 2, June 1993, 195–213.

Ethier, Diane (1994a), 'L'Espace social européen: un projet sans lendemain?' in C. Deblock and D. Brunelle (eds), *L'Amérique du nord et l'Europe communautaire: intégration économique, intégration sociale?*, Québec, Presses de l'Université du Québec.

Ethier, Diane (1994b), *L'adhésion à la Communauté européenne et la consolidation des démocraties sud-européennes*, paper presented at the International Political Science Association (IPSA) XVIth World Congress, Berlin, August, 21–25.

Ethier, Diane (1995), 'La politique des gouvernements socialistes de l'Europe méridionale' in Jean-Pierre Beaud and Jean-Guy Prévost (eds), *La social-démocratie en cette fin de siècle/Late Twentieth-Century Social Democracy*, Quebec, Université du Québec Press, 91–115.

Europe (European Commission's Press Agency) (1994), 6 January, 19 January, 4 June and 5 December bulletins.

European Communities Commission (ECC) (1976), 'Avis sur la demande d'adhésion de la Grèce. Communication de la Commission au Conseil le 29 janvier 1976', *Bulletin des Communautés européennes*, Supplement 2/76.

ECC (1978a), 'Réflexions d'ensemble relatives aux problèmes de l'élagissement. Communication de la Commission au Conseil transmise le 20 avril 1978', *Bulletin des Communautés européennes*, Supplement 1/78.

ECC (1978b), 'Avis sur la demande d'adhésion de l'Espagne', *Bulletin des Communautés européennes*, Supplement 9/78.

ECC (1989a) *Community Support Framework (CSF) 1989–1993 (Objective l) Spain*, Brussels/Luxemburg, Office of the Official Publications of the European Communities (OOPEC).

ECC (1989b), *CSF 1989-1993 (Objective 1) Portugal*, Brussels/Luxemburg, OOPEC.

ECC(1990a), *L'Europe sociale*, Brussels, OOPEC.

ECC (1990b), 'Tendances conjoncturelles', *Economie européenne, Supplément A* no. 4–5, April–May.

ECC (1990c), *CSF 1989–1993 (Objective 2) Spain*, Brussels/Luxemburg, OOPEC.

ECC (1990d), *CSF 1989–1993 (Objective 1) Greece*, Brussels/Luxemburg, OOPEC.

ECC (1990e), 'La nouvelle politique structurelle de la Commission européenne', *Le Dossier Europe*, June–July.

ECC (1991), *CSF 1989–1993 (Objective 5b) Spain*, Brussels/Luxemburg, OOPEC.

ECC (1992), *European Social Fund, CSF 1989–1993 (Objectives 3 and 4) Spain*, Brussels/Luxemburg, OOPEC.

ECC (1993), *Economie européenne, Supplément A*, no. 5, May 1993.

ECC (1994), *Cinquième rapport périodique sur la situation et l'évolution socio-économique des régions de la Communauté*, COM (94) 322 final, Brussels, July 19.

European Industrial Relations Review (1992), 'Spain: Radical Labour Market Reform', no. 220, May, 12–15.

Eurostat (1990), 'Actions ayant un impact sur la situation du marché de l'emploi dans les pays membres des Communautés européennes – Espagne', *Thème 3 – Populations et conditions sociales, Série D – Etudes et analyses*, Brussels, OOPEC, 136–69.

Eurostat (1991), *Basic Statistics of the Community*, Brussels, OOPEC.

Fakiolas, Rossetos (1987), 'Interest Groups – an Overview' in K. Featherstone and D. Katsoudas (eds), *op.cit.*, 174–214.

Featherstone, Kevin and Katsoudas, Dimitrios (eds) (1987), *Political Change in Greece. Before and After the Colonels*, New York, St Martin's Press.

Featherstone, Kevin (1987a), 'PASOK and the Left' in K. Featherstone and D. Katsoudas (eds), *op.cit.*, 112–35.

Featherstone, Kevin (1987b), 'Elections and Voting Behavior' in K. Featherstone and D. Katsoudas (eds), *op.cit.*, 34–64.

Featherstone, Kevin (1990), 'The Party-System in Greece and the Fall of Papandreou', *West European Politics*, vol. 13, no. 1, January, 101–15.

Featherstone, Kevin (1994), 'The Greek Election of 1993: Backwards or Forwards', *West European Politics*, vol. 17, no. 2, April, 204–11.

Fishman, Robert M. (1984), 'El movimiento obrero en la transicion: objectivos politicos y organizativos', *Revista espanola de Investigaciones sociologicas*, no. 26, April–June, 61–113.

Fishman, Robert M. (1990), *Working-Class Organization and the Return to Democracy in Spain*, Ithaca, Cornell University Press.

Flaesch-Mougin, Catherine (1986), 'Une intégration effective différée' in Charles Le Bihan et al., *op.cit.*, 31–77.

Fuentes Quintana, Enrique (1990), 'De los Pactos de la Moncloa a la constitucion (julio 1977–diciembre 1978)' in J.L. Garcia Delgado (ed.), *op.cit.*, 23–35.

Gallagher, T. and Williams, A.M. (eds) (1989), *Southern European Socialism*, Manchester/New York, Manchester University Press.

Gallagher, T. (1989), 'The Portuguese Socialist Party: the Pitfalls of Being First' in T. Gallagher and A.M. Williams (eds), *op.cit.*, 12–34.

Garcia Delgado, José Luis (ed.) (1990), *Economia española de la transicion y la democracia*, Madrid, Centro de Investigaciones Sociologicas, 1990.

Gillespie, R.(1989), 'Spanish Socialism in the 1980s' in T. Gallagher and A.M. Williams (eds), *op.cit.*, 59–86.

Gillespie R. (1990a), 'The Break-Up of the 'Socialist Family': Party Union Relations in Spain 1982–89', *West European Politics*, vol. 13, no. 1, January, 47–62.

Gillespie, R. (1990b), 'Regime Consolidation in Spain: Party, State and Society' in: G. Pridham (ed.), *op.cit.*, 126–47.

Gladdish, Ken (1990), 'Portugal: an Open Verdict' in G. Pridham (ed.), *op.cit.*, 104–26.

Gonzalez, B.R. and Fernandez, A.G. (1993), 'Health and Social Welfare Policies' in A.A. Barbado (ed.), *Spain and EC Membership Evaluated*, London/New York, Pinter Publishers/St Martin's Press, ch. 16.

Graham, Carol (1995), 'The Politics of Safety Nets' in L. Diamond and M.F. Plattner (eds.), *op.cit.*, 211–26.

Graham, Lawrence (1992) 'Redifining the Portugese Transition to Democracy' in J. Higley and R. Gunther (eds), *op. cit.*, 282–300.

Grosser, Alfred (ed.) (1984–95), 'Les pays de l'Europe occidentale', annual issue of *Notes et Etudes documentaires*, articles devoted to Portugal, Spain and Greece.

Gunther, Richard (1992), 'Spain, the Very Model of the Modern Elite Settlement' in J. Higley and R. Gunther (eds), *op.cit.*, 38–81.

Gunther, Richard, Diamandouros, P. Nikiforos and Puhle, Hans-Jürgen (eds) (1995), *The Politics of Democratic Consolidation. Southern Europe in Comparative Perspective*, Baltimore, The Johns Hopkins University Press.

Haggard, Stephen and Kaufman, Robert K. (eds) (1992), *The Politics and Economic Adjustment: International Constraints, Distributive Conflicts and the State*, Princeton, Princeton University Press.

Haggard, Stephen and Kaufman, Robert R. (1995), 'The Challenges of Consolidation' in L. Diamond and M.F. Plattner (eds), *op.cit.*, 1–13.

Haggard, Stephen, and Webb, Steven B. (eds) (1994a), *Voting for Reform. Democracy, Political Liberalization and Economic Adjustment*, Oxford/New York, Oxford University Press/The World Bank.

Haggard, Stephen and Webb, Steven B. (1994b), 'Introduction -International Influences on the Adjustment Process' in S. Haggard and S. Webb (eds), *op.cit.*, 25–9.

Heinz-Jürgen, Axt (1991), 'Southern Europe Facing the Single Market's Completion', *Intereconomics*, July–August, 192–202.

Hermet, Guy (1991), 'Présentation: le temps de la démocratie?', *Revue internationale des sciences sociales*, May, 265–75.

Hermet, Guy (ed.) (1984), 'L'Espagne démocratique', *Pouvoirs* special issue, no. 8.

Herzlich, Guy (1995), 'Les Grecs s'opposent à la réforme fiscale', *Le Monde*, March 30, 1995.

Heywood, Paul (1995), *The Government and Politics of Spain*, London, Macmillan.

Higley, John and Gunther, Richard (eds) (1992), *Elites and Democratic Consolidation in Latin America and Southern Europe*, Cambridge, Cambridge University Press.

Holman, Otto (1993), 'Transationalism in Spain: The Paradoxes of Socialist Rule in the 1990's' in H. Overbeek (ed.), *Restructuring Hegemony in the Global Political Economy. The Rise of Transnational Neo-Liberalism in the 1980s*, London, Routledge, 134–62.

Hudson, Ray and Lewis, Jim (eds) (1985), *Uneven Development in Southern Europe: Studies of Accumulation, Class, Migration and the State*, London, Methuen.

Huntington, Samuel (1991), *The Third Wave. Democratization in the Late Twentieth Century*, Norman, University of Oklahoma Press.

Instituto de Comercio Exterior (ICEX) (1988a), *Guide des affaires en Espagne. Panorama économique*, Madrid, ICEX.

ICEX (1988b), *Guids des affaires en Espagne. Investissements étrangers en Espagne et espagnols à l'étranger*, Madrid, ICEX.

ICEX (1992), 'Programa de convergencia con la Comunidad europea', *Boletin ICEX economico Economia española*, no. 2323, May 4–10, 1415–29.

Jacquemot, Pierre and Raffinot, Marc (1985), *Accumulation et développement. Dix études sur les économies du Tiers-Monde*, Paris, L'Harmattan.

Jimenez Fernandez, M.A. (1991), 'Intervention finale du secrétaire général pour la Sécurité sociale, Espagne' in *La convergence des objectifs et politiques de protection sociale*, Proceedings of a Conference held by the Commission of the European Communities.

Julia, Santos (1990), 'The Ideological Conversion of the Leaders of the PSOE: 1976–1979' in F. Lannon and P. Preston (eds), *Elites and Power in Twentieth Century Spain. Essays in Honour of Sir Raymond Carr*, Oxford, Clarendon Press.

Kahler, Miles (1990), 'International Political Economy', *Foreign Affairs*, vol. 69, Fall, 139–51.

Kahler, Miles (1992), 'External Influence, Conditionality and the Politics of Adjustment' in S. Haggard and R. Kaufman (eds), *op.cit.*

Kapetanyannis, Vasilis (1993), 'The Left in the l980s: Too Little, Too Late' in R. Clogg (ed.), *op.cit.*, 78–94.

Katseli, Louka T., 'Macroeconomic Adjustment and Exchange-rate Policy in Middle-income Countries: Greece, Portugal and Spain in the 1970s' in Marcello de Cecco (ed.), *International Economic Adjustment. Small Countries and the European Monetary System*, New York, St Martin's Press, 189–211.

Katsoudas, Dimitrios K. (1987) 'The Conservative Movement and New Democracy: From Past to Present' in K. Featherstone and D.K. Katsoudas (eds), *op.cit.*, 85–112.

Kedros, André (1986), *Les socialistes au pouvoir. Europe 1981–85*, Paris, Plon.

Kourtevaris, George A. (1989), 'Political Elites and Party Organisation in Greece: an Entrepreneurial Model', *Journal of Social, Political and Economic Studies*, vol. 14, no. 2, Summer, 190–213.

Köves, Andras and Marer, Paul (eds) (1991), *Foreign Economic Liberalization. Transformations in Socialist Countries*, Boulder, Westview Press.

Lefeber, Louis (1989–90), 'The Socialist Experience in Greece', *International Journal of Political Economy*, vol. 19, no. 4, Winter, 32–55.

Leonard, Yves (1990–95), 'Le Portugal en...' in A. Grosser (ed.), *op.cit.*

Linde, Luis M. (1990), 'La profundizacion de la crisis economica: 1979–1982' in J. Garcia Delgado (ed.), *op.cit.*, 35–59.

Lipset, Seymour Martin (1959), 'Some Social Requisites of Democracy: Economic Development and Politicla Legitimacy', *American Political Science Review*, vol. 53, no. 1, March 69–105.

Liryntsis, C. (1989), 'PASOK in Power: the Loss of the Third Road to Socialism' in T. Gallagher and A.M. Williams (eds), *op.cit.*

Mainwaring, Scott, O'Donnell, Guillermo and Valenzuela, Samuel (eds) (1992), *Issues in Democratic Consolidation. The New South American Democracies in Comparative Perspective*, Notre Dame, University of Notre Dame Press.

Makler, H.M. (1979), 'The Portuguse Industrial Elite and its Corporative Relations: a Study of Compartmentalization in an Authoritarian Regime' in L.A. Graham and H.M. Makler (eds), *Contemporary Portugal: the Revolution and its Antecedents*, Austin, University of Texas Press.

Makler, H.M., (1979) 'The Consequences of the Survival and Revival of the Industrial Bourgeoisie' in L.S. Graham and D.L. Wheeler (eds) *In Search of Modern Portugal: the Revolution and its Consequences,* Madison, University of Wisconsin Press.

Maravall, Fernando (1987), *Economia y politica industrial en España*, Madrid, Piramides.

Maravall, José Maria (1982), *La political de la transicion 1975–1980*, Madrid, Taurus.

Maravall, José Maria and Santamaria, Julian (1986), 'Political change in Spain and the Prospects for Democracy' in G. O'Donnell, P. Schmitter and L. Whitehead (eds), *op.cit.*, vol. I: Southern Europe, 71–109.

Maravall, José Maria (1992), *Socialist Parties in Europe*, Barcelona, ICPS.

Maravall, José Maria (1993), 'Politics and Policy: Economic Reforms in Southern Europe' in L.C. Bresser Pereira, J.M. Maravall and A. Przeworski, *op.cit.*, 77–132.

Maravall, José Maria (1995), 'The Myth of the Authoritarian Advantage' in L. Diamond and M.F. Plattner (eds), *op.cit.*, 13–28.

Marques, Guilhermina (1990), 'L'intégration des groupes d'intérêt portugais au niveau européen' in D. Sidjanski and U. Ayberk, *op.cit.*, 185–203.

Mattei, Jacqueline and Lacharme, Mireille (1992), 'L'Espagne, paradis des firmes multinationales', *L'Usine nouvelle*, April 23, reproduced in *Problèmes économiques*, no. 2,282, July, 22–27.

Mavrogordatos, George Th. (1993), 'Civil Society under Populism' in R. Clogg (ed.), *op.cit.*, 47–65.

Maxwell, Kenneth (1986), 'Regime Overthrow and the Prospects for Democratic Transition in Portugal' in G. O'Donnell, P. Schmitter and L. Whitehead (eds) *op.cit.*, Vol. I: Southern Europe, 109–38.

McElrath, Roger (1989), 'Trade Unions and the Industrial Relations Climate in Spain', *European Studies*, no. 10, Industrial Research Unit, The Wharton School, University of Pennsylvania, ch. 3, 48–104.

McLeod, Alex (1990), 'The Parties and the Consolidation of Democracy in Portugal: The Emergence of a Dominant Two-Party System' in D. Ethier (ed.), *op.cit.*, 155–73.

Millan, Bruce (1992), *The Management and Future Impact of European Structural Funds.* Audit Commission. Fourth Management Lecture, London, 8 October 1992.

Ministerio de Industria e Energia (MIE) (1987), *España en Europa. Un futuro industrial : la politica industrial en el horizonte 1992*, Madrid, MIE.

Ministerio da Industria e Energia (1988), *PEDIP, Programa especifico de desenvolvimento da industria portuguesa*, Programas operacionais. Sintese. Lisbon, November.

Ministerio da Industria e Energia, Gabinete do Gestor do PEDIP (1990), *Relatorio de execuçâo PEDIP 1989*, Lisbon. April.

Ministerio de Industria, Comercio y Turismo (MICYT) (1992), *Plan de apoyo a la internacionalizacion de la empresa española*, Madrid, Centro de Publicaciones del MICYT.

Ministerio de Trabajo y Seguridad Social (MTSS) (1992), *Guia laboral 1992*, Madrid, MTSS.

Mocoroa, Isabel Vega (1991), 'Principaux problèmes liés à l'abolition des frontières fiscales: le système du 'clearing house' et les coûts économiques pour l'Espagne', *Reflets et perspectives de la vie économique*, vol. XXX, no. 2, 113–27.

Moderne, Frank (1984–89), 'L'Espagne en...' in A. Grosser (ed.), *op.cit.*

Morlino L. and Montero, José R. (1991), 'Legitimacy and Democracy in Southern Europe', paper presented to the XVth Latin American Studies Association (LASA) Annual Conference, Washington D.C., April 4–6.

Morlino, Leonardo (1992), 'Consolidaçôes democraticas na Europa meridional. Indicaçôes teoricas para analise empirica', *Sistema*, no. 99, 39–74.

Morlino, Leonardo (1995), 'Political Parties and Democratic Consolidation in Southern Europe' in R. Gunther, P.N. Diamandouros and H.J. Puhle (eds), *op.cit.*, 315–89.

Mosley, Paul, Harrigan, Jane and Toye, John (eds) (1991), *Aid and Power: The World Bank and Policy-Based Lending*, 2 vols, London, Routledge.

Mougey, Yves (1991), 'Espagne: enjeux et limites d'une politique de compétitivité', *Banque française du Commerce extérieur Actualités*, October 1991.

Mouzelis, Nicos (1976), 'Capitalism and Dictatorship in Post-War Greece', *New Left Review*, no. 96, March–April, 58.

Myro Sanchez, Rafael (1990), 'La evolucion de las principales magnitudes: una presentacion de conjunto', in J.Garcia Delgado (ed.), *op.cit.*, 527–59.

Nelson, Joan (ed.) (1990a), *Economic Crisis and Policy Choice. The Politics of Adjustment in the Third World*, Princeton, Princeton University Press.

Nelson, Joan (1990b), 'Introduction: The Politics of Economic Adjustment in Developing Nations' in J. Nelson (ed.), *op.cit.*

Nelson, Joan (1990c), 'Conclusions' in J. Nelson (ed.), *op. cit.*, 321–63.

Nelson, Joan (1992), *Encouraging Democracy: What Role for Conditional Aid?* Policy Essay No. 4, Washington D.C, Overseas Development Council.

Nelson, Joan (ed.) (1994a), *A Precarious Balance. Democracy and Economic Reforms in Eastern Europe and Latin America*, Washington D.C., International Center for Economic Growth and Overseas Development Council.

Nelson, Joan (ed.) (1994b), *Intricate Links: Democratization and Market Reforms in Latin America and Eastern Europe*, Washington D.C., Transaction Publishers/Overseas Development Council.

Nelson, Joan (1995), 'Linkages Between Politics and Economics' in: L. Diamond and M.F. Plattner (eds.), *op.cit*, 45–59.

O'Donnell, Guillermo, Schmitter, Philippe and Whitehead, Lawrence (eds) (1986), *Transitions from Authoritarian Rule. Prospects for Democracy*, 4 volumes, Baltimore, Johns Hopkins University Press, 1986.

O'Donnell, Guillermo and Schmitter, Philippe (1986), *Tentative Conclusions about Uncertain Democracies,* in G.O'Donnell, P. Schmitter and L. Whitehead (eds), *op.cit* vol. IV.

Organisation de Cooperation et de Developpement Econnomique (OCDE) (1988), *Les nouveaux pays industriels. Défi et opportunités pour les industries des pays de l'OCDE*, Paris, OCDE.

OCDE (1980–94), *Etudes économiques. Portugal*, annual publication, OCDE, Paris.

Oxhorne, Phillip and Ducatenzeiler, Graciela (1995), *The Problematic Relationship Between Economic and Political Liberalization. Some Theoretical Considerations*, Paper presented to the Annual APSA Conference, Chicago, August 31–September 3.

Papadopoulos, Yannis (1989), 'Parties, the State and Society in Greece: Continuity within Change', *West European Politics*, vol. 12, no. 2, April, 54–71.

Papageorgiou, F. and Verney, Susannah (1992), 'Regional Planning and the Integrated Mediterranean Programmes in Greece', *Regional Politics and Policy*, vol. 2, nos 1–2, Spring–Summer, 139–61.

Pechoux, Pierre-Yves (1994), 'La Méditerranéée orientale', *L'Etat du monde 1994*, Paris/Montréal, La Découverte/Borréal, 470–4.

Pepelasis, Adamastios (1990), 'Trends and Prospects of the Greek Economy', *European Affairs*, 85–9.

Perez Amoros, Francisco (1989), *Les relations industrielles en Espagne*, document of the ECC.

Perez-Diaz, Victor (1987), 'Neo-Corporatist Experiments in a New and Precariously Stable State' in Ilja Scholten (ed.), *Political Stability and Neo-Corporatism*, London, Sage.

Perez-Diaz, Victor (1993), *The Return of Civil Society. The Emergence of Democratic Spain,* Cambridge (MA), Harvard University Press.

Petras, James (1990), 'Spanish Socialism: on the Road to Marbella', *Contemporary Crisis*, vol. 14, no. 3, September, 189–217.

Pitta e Cunha, Paulo (1991), 'Tax Reform in Portugal in the Context of Accession to the European Communities', *Bulletin for International Fiscal Documentation*, vol. 35, no. 2, February, 75–8.

Pridham, Geoffrey (ed.) (1984), *The New Mediterranean Democracies: Regime Transition in Spain, Greece and Portugal*, London, Frank Cass.

Pridham, Geoffrey (ed.) (1990a), *Securing Democracy: Political Parties and Democratic Consolidation in Southern Europe*, London/New York, Routledge.

Pridham, Geoffrey (1990b), 'Southern European Democracies on the Road to Consolidation: A Comparative Assessment of the Role of Political Parties' in G. Pridham (ed.), *op.cit.*, 1–42.

Problèmes économiques (1991), 'L'incidence sur l'économie espagnole de sa participation à la Communauté européenne', no. 2, 222, 24 April.

Przeworski, Adam (1990), *Democracy and the Market*, Cambridge, Cambridge University Press.

Przeworski, Adam (1995), *Sustaining Democracy*, Cambridge, Cambridge University Press.

Remmer, Karen (1986), 'The Politics of Economic Stabilization: IMF Standby Programs in Latin America 1954–1984', *Comparative Politics*, vol. 19, 1–24.

Remmer, Karen (1990), 'Democracy and Economic Crisis, *World Politics*, vol. XLII, no. 3, April, 315–35.

Riera, L.L., Guardiola, E., Tornabell, R. et al. (1986), *La empresa española en las Comunidades europeas*, Barcelona, Editorial Hispano Europea.

Rodrik, Dani (1994), 'The Rush to Free Trade in the Developing World: Why so Late? Why Now? Will it Last?' in S.Haggard and S. Webb (eds), *op.cit.*, 61–89.

Rostow, Walter W. (1971), *Politics and the Stages of Growth*, Cambridge, Cambridge University Press.

Rudel, Christian (1984–89), 'Le Portugal en...' in A. Grosser (ed.), *op.cit.*

Ruesga, Santos M. (1989), *1993. España ante el Mercado Unico*, Madrid, Piramide.

Rustow, Dankart (1970), 'Transitions to Democracy: Toward a Dynamic Model', *Comparative Politics*, vol.2, no. 3, April, 337–63.

Sachs, Jeffrey (1994), 'Life in the Economic Emergency Room' in J. Williamson (ed.), *op.cit.*, 501–25.

Salmon, Keith G. (1991), *The Modern Spanish Economy: Transformation and Integration into Europe*, London/New York, Pinter.

Sanchez Munoz, Maria Paloma (1993), *Los grandes retos de la economia española en los noventa*, Madrid, Piramide.

Schmitter, Philippe (1986), 'An Introduction to Southern European Transitions from Autoritarian Rule: Italy, Greece, Portugal, Spain and Turkey' in G. O'Donnell, P. Schmitter and L. Whitehead (eds), *op.cit.*, vol. I: Southern Europe, 3–11.

Schmitter, Philippe and Karl, Terry Lynn (1991), 'Les modes de transition en Amérique latine, en Europe du sud et de l'Est' in G. Hermet (1991), *op.cit.*, 285–303.

Segura, Julio. et al. (1989), *La industria española en la crisis*, Madrid, Alianza Editorial.

Segura, Julio (1990), 'Del primer gobierno socialista a la integracion en la CEE: 1983–85' in J.L. Garcia Delgado (ed.), *op.cit.*, 59–81.

Serrano Perez, F. (1989), 'Las desregulaciones en la crisis: el caso de la seguridad espanola', *Economies et Sociétés*, Hors Série, no. 31, February, 101–28.

Sidjanski, Dusan and Ayberk, Ural (eds) (1990), *L'Europe du sud dans la Communauté européenne*, Paris, Presses universitaires de France.

Smith, William C., Acuna, Carlos H. and Gamarra, Eduardo A. (eds) (1994), *Latin American Political Economy in the Age of Neoliberal Reform*, New Brunswick/London, Transaction Publishers.

Solbes Mira, Pedro (1990), 'La economia española ante la CEE: el proceso de negociacion' in J.G. Delgado (ed.), *op.cit.*, 481–505.

Spourdalakis, Michalis (1992a), 'Social Democracy and European Unification. The Greek Piece in the Puzzle', Paper presented to the III Workshop on 'European Socialist Parties' organized by the Institute de Ciencies Politiques y Socials, Barcelona, December 18–19.

Spourdalakis, Michalis (1992b), 'A Petit Bourgeois Party with a Populist Ideology and Catch-All Party Structure: PASOK' in W. Merkel et al., *Socialist Parties in Europe II: of Class, Populars, Catch-All?*, Institut de Ciencies Politiques i Socials, Barcelona, 97–123.

Stalling, Barbara (1992), 'External Influence on Economic Policy: Debt, Stabilization and Structural Reforms' in S. Haggard and R. Kaufman (eds), *op.cit.*, 41–89.

Stoleroff, Alan D. (1992), 'Between Corporatism and Class Struggle: the Portuguese Labour Movement and the Cavaco Silva Government', *West European Politics*, vol. 15, no. 4, October, 118–50.

Stournaras, Yannis A. (1990), 'Public Sector Debt and Deficits in Greece: the Experience of the 1980s and the Future Prospects', 405–40.

Tamames, Ramon (1986), *Guia del Mercado Comun europea. España en la Europa de los Doce*, Madrid, Alianza Editorial.

The Intelligence Unit (1980–94), *Country Report, Portugal*, quarterly and annual publications by the magazine *The Economist*.

Torres, Francisco (1994), 'The European Periphery – Portugal' in J. Williamson (ed.), *op.cit*, 141–53.

Trestour, Monique (1988), 'L'économie espagnole depuis 1985: un vaste effort d'intégration au sein du marché commun', *Affaires internationales*.

Tzakalatos, Euclid (1991), 'Structural Change and Macroeconomic Policy: the Case of Greece (1981–85)', *International Review of Applied Economics*, vol. 5, September, 253–76.

Tzannatos, Zafiris (1987), 'The Greek Labour Market: Current Perspectives and Future Prospects', *Greek Economic Review*, vol. 9, no. 2, 224–38.

Vasquez Barquero, Antonio and Herbert, Michael (1985), 'Spain: Economy and State in Transition' in R. Hudson and J. Lewis (eds), *op.cit.*, 284–309.

Veremis, Thanos (1987), 'The Military' in K. Featherstone and D. Katsoudas (eds), *op.cit.*, 214–30.

Verney, Suzannah (1990), 'To Be or not to Be within the European Community: the Party Debate and Democratic Consolidation in Greece' in G. Pridham (ed.), *op.cit.*, 203–24.

Vinals, José (ed.) (1992), *La economia española ante el Mercado Unico europeo. Las claves del processo de integracion*, Madrid, Alianza Editorial.

Whitehead, Laurence (1986), 'International Aspects of Democratization' in G. O'Donnell, P. Schmitter and L. Whitehead (eds), *op.cit.*, vol. III: Comparative Perspectives, 3–47.

Whitehead, Laurence (ed.) (1993), 'Economic Liberalization and Democratization Explorations of the Linkages', special issue, *World Development*, vol. 21. no. 8, August.

Williamson, John (1993), 'Democracy and the "Washington Consensus"' in L. Whitehead (ed.), *op.cit.*, 1329–37.

Williamson, John (ed.) (1994), *The Political Economy of Policy Reform*, Washington D.C., Institute for International Economics.

Williamson, John and Haggard, Stephen (1994), 'The Political Conditions for Economic Reform' in J. Williamson (ed.), *op.cit.*, 525–97.

Index